THE UNITED STATES AND THE WASHINGTON CONFERENCE, 1921–1922

THE UNITED STATES

AND THE WASHINGTON

CONFERENCE. 1921-1922

BY THOMAS H. BUCKLEY

THE UNIVERSITY OF TENNESSEE PRESS : KNOXVILLE

LIBRARY OF CONGRESS CATALOG CARD NO. 79–100409
STANDARD BOOK NO. 87049–108–3

Copyright © 1970
The University of Tennessee Press
All Rights Reserved
Manufactured in the U.S.A.

FOR MY WIFE AND CHILDREN

PREFACE

THE WASHINGTON CONFERENCE on the Limitation of Armaments, which met in 1921–1922, seemed at the time to be one of the most important diplomatic assemblages in all history, and yet today its significance has slipped into oblivion. Most Americans of the 1970's probably are unaware that the conference ever met, and many of those who do remember it recall a meeting in which the government of the United States foolishly, so they believe, undertook to limit its weapons at a time when if anything there should have been more weapons. This conference, however, deserves remembrance because it was the only successful arms limitation conference in modern history. Therefore, a study of the conception and implementation of the conference is still relevant to historians of American diplomacy and to contemporary politicians.

This book is an effort to delineate the issues and events of the Washington Conference and to describe what that gathering meant for American diplomacy. I believe that the Washington Conference's hopes and failures were those of a generation of distinguished statesmen and diplomats and that the conference was more than a worthy effort to solve a large problem; its method of solution holds much promise for disarmament negotiations today. The course of the conference of 1921–1922 suggests that nations will disarm only when such an act is to their diplomatic advantage, that is, when they can gain political ends. In the chapters that follow, then, is a subject with a past, present, and (one hopes) a future.

I also believe that the Washington Conference advanced the

national interests of the United States. By entering into an arms limitation agreement, Americans attained a better international position. The delegation, led by Charles Evans Hughes, began with the dubious asset of an unfinished fleet and gained approximate naval parity with Great Britain and superiority over Japan. Little, if any, idealism marked that particular quest. The naval agreement made it possible for the Japanese and British to end their twenty-year-old alliance which threatened American interests in both the Pacific and China. The Japanese also proved willing to pull troops out of Shantung and Siberia. And there can be little doubt that for some years after the conference, talk of war between the United States and Japan lessened.

If these were the successes of the conference, there admittedly were failures: the Open Door policy was reduced to a mere formality, encrusted in the Nine-Power Treaty; and after 1922, so many people thought that disarmament had been accomplished that statesmen failed to follow up the Washington achievements with more measures to slow the international arms race.

ACKNOWLEDGMENTS

There are many debts and much assistance that the author wishes to acknowledge. To Indiana University professors—Charles Leonard Lundin, whose enthusiasms, dedication, and interest influenced my decision to pursue the historical profession, S. Y. Teng, who greatly assisted and encouraged my study of East Asia, and Maurice G. Baxter, whose support has been as constant as his wise advice—I owe much more than just this acknowledgment. Financial support is gratefully acknowledged from the Indiana University Graduate School, the Social Science Research Foundation and School of International Relations at the University of Denver, and the Graduate School of the University of South Dakota. Research assistance from the librarians and archivists of Indiana University, the Library of Congress, the National Archives, Stanford University, Ohio Historical Society, Massachusetts Historical Society, Alabama State Archives, Public Archives of Canada, and the Public Record Office (London) was much appreciated. I am also grateful for the permission given by the legal guardians to use the manuscript collections cited in the bibliography. R. Alton Lee and Donald R. Habbe of the University of South Dakota offered valuable comments and suggestions on the manuscript. The largest contribution, however, came from Robert H. Ferrell of Indiana University. His encouragement, kindness, and friendship have been of immeasurable proportions in the evolution of this book and my professional career. My wife has contributed valuable comments and invaluable encouragement.

Bloomington, Indiana, 1970

CONTENTS

I. THE POLITICS OF THE LIMITATION OF ARMS   3

II. THE ATLANTIC CONTEST   20

III. MAKING STRAIGHT THE WAY   35

IV. THE AMERICAN PLAN   48

V. THE SPEECH   63

VI. THE PACIFIC CONTEST   75

VII. PACIFIC FORTIFICATIONS   90

VIII. ARMS LIMITATION   104

IX. THE FOUR-POWER TREATY   127

X. CHINA: NINE-POWER TREATY   145

XI. CHINA: SHANTUNG AND SOVEREIGNTY   157

XII. THE SENATE AND THE TREATIES   172

XIII. IN CONCLUSION   185

BIBLIOGRAPHICAL ESSAY   191

INDEX   207

ILLUSTRATIONS

✿ ✿

MAP OF THE NORTH PACIFIC *page* 93

PHOTOGRAPHS

The official United States delegation *facing page* 98

The after deck of the *USS Michigan* dismantled for sale 99

The dismantling of the *USS Delaware* 114

The Disarmament Conference in progress on November
21, 1921 115

THE UNITED STATES AND THE WASHINGTON CONFERENCE, 1921–1922

🏵🏵🏵🏵🏵🏵🏵🏵🏵🏵🏵🏵🏵🏵🏵🏵🏵🏵🏵🏵🏵🏵🏵🏵🏵🏵🏵🏵🏵🏵🏵🏵🏵🏵

AT THE TIME of the 1921–1922 Washington Conference on the Limitation of Armaments, most observers, with the exception of naval officers, admired the achievements of the treaties negotiated during the meeting. For example, Prime Minister Jan Christiaan Smuts of the Union of South Africa said a few years after the conference, "I have always looked upon the Washington Treaties as probably the greatest step toward peace yet taken on the road to a stable future world order." [1] But the favorable judgments on the conference, especially on the wisdom of American decisions there, gave way to criticism. After the Japanese attack on Pearl Harbor in December 1941, many writers searching for an explanation of the rapid Japanese advance in the Pacific attacked the conference treaties, concluding that the Japanese had strengthened their position at the expense of the United States. As one author put it, the conference "was in reality one of the costliest bits of diplomatic blundering that ever befell the United States. . . . In a comic script, the United States was cast as the *première stripteuse*, a peace-loving but weak-minded creature who could always draw enthusiastic applause by wantonly denuding herself in the presence of her enemies." [2] After World War II, the conference departed from the public consciousness.

To analyze the Washington Conference and assign it proper significance in American history, one must realize that strong support for disarmament has existed among Americans since the

[1] Speech by Smuts as quoted in the *Congressional Record*, Nov. 12, 1934, p. 1531.
[2] Henry Morton Robinson, *Fantastic Interim* (New York, 1943), 55.

colonial era, when standing armies were considered a threat to liberty and republican government. Following the Revolution and every other American war, military forces were promptly dispersed, the nation relying in the interim on citizens' militia. By the turn of the twentieth century many also believed that the very existence of a large body of men and arms not only threatened republican institutions but also actually caused wars. The World War of 1914–1918, precipitated in part by maneuverings of the military establishments of European powers, seemed to confirm this belief: if arsenals had not bulged with arms, governments would have sought arbitration or other methods of peaceful settlement. Yet, American history before the World War shows only one modest success in arms limitation, the demilitarization of the American-Canadian border, and that, accomplished over the years 1817–1872, developed as much by chance as by deliberate design.[3] It was a small victory indeed. Two other attempts, the Hague Peace Conferences of 1899 and 1907, despite noble aims, did not reduce armaments in any notable way.

One reason for lack of success with disarmament before the Great War was, as the historian Calvin Davis has shown, the "strange duality" of the hope for world peace, at least in the United States.[4] While statesmen, lawyers, and pacifists of the nineteenth century had talked of the limitation of armaments, the American government had not hesitated to use force to expand the national territory from the Mississippi to the Pacific and beyond. The search for peaceful ways to settle problems in foreign relations seldom interfered with fulfillment of the national interest. Realism dictated occasional use of force in an international community full of military power. Disarmament seemed more obtainable in the future. American statesmen of the nineteenth

[3] C. P. Stacey, "The Myth of the Unguarded Frontier, 1815–1871," *The American Historical Review*, LVI (Oct. 1950), 1–18.

[4] Calvin D. Davis, *The United States and the First Hague Peace Conference* (Ithaca, N.Y., 1962), 1. Technically, "disarmament" denotes a complete disarming whereas "limitation of arms" denotes that some arms still exist, as does the term "arms control," but all three terms are used as one in this book.

century longed for the future but lived with experience. It was not uncommon for an American political leader to call for disarmament, which spoke well of his ideals, and simultaneously to support an increase in arms, which bespoke knowledge of his times.

Gradually, however, popular interest in limitation of armaments increased, and at the turn of the twentieth century when the United States began to emerge as a naval power by enlarging its navy—indeed, beginning in the 1880's to build an entirely new navy of steam and steel—disarmament for the first time gathered serious public support. If over the years the small American army had never proved an embarrassment to calls for the limitation of arms, the growth of the United States Navy during the period 1881–1920 did raise difficulties, for the Navy increased to a size second only to the fleet of Great Britain. This growth was in part due to the acquisition of an island empire in the Pacific during the Spanish-American War and the increased participation in world affairs which protection of those new lands seemed to demand. A chain of naval vessels linked the new empire and foiled the potentially evil designs of other nations. The Navy gained the support of such men as Senator Henry Cabot Lodge and Theodore Roosevelt, who subscribed to the doctrine of Captain Alfred Thayer Mahan that the United States must achieve greatness on the sea. The Navy League was formed in 1903 for the sole purpose of advancing navalism.[5] Opponents of the Navy began to gather their forces for a battle against the new American militarists.

Supporters of a reduction in naval arms took heart in late 1912 when Woodrow Wilson became President, for Wilson was a former member of the American Peace Society. A well-intentioned congressman, Walter L. Hensley (D., Mo.), proposed in 1913 a resolution calling upon Europe and America to observe a one-year naval holiday, and the resolution passed the House

---

[5] Armin Rappaport, *The Navy League of the United States* (Detroit, 1962), 4.

by an overwhelming vote, 317 to 11.[6] The Wilson administration did nothing to carry it out. By this time Wilson and Secretary of State William Jennings Bryan were more interested in the Bryan "cooling-off" treaties of conciliation. By late summer of 1914 the World War began. The Hensley resolution did inspire Wilson's Secretary of the Navy, Josephus Daniels, to recommend in his first annual report that the United States convene the powers to secure a naval holiday; Daniels repeated the plea in all eight of his annual reports, but, of course, he spent most of his working days seeking to increase naval tonnage.[7]

The movement in support of a reduction in armaments received what seemed to be a mortal blow in 1916 when Wilson called upon Congress for a huge construction program because American entrance into the war was an increasing possibility. The Naval Act of 1916 authorized 156 vessels. Sixteen were to be capital ships—that is, battleships and battle cruisers. Daniels boasted of "the largest number ever provided for at one time by any nation." [8] The act sought to place the United States at the front of the world's naval powers. Senator William E. Borah of Idaho asked a typical question: "If we are going to play that part which we should play and which we are entitled to play, shall we hope to do so without the ability and the means to protect our own and without that preparation which shall insure respect to the flag and a due regard for our rights?" [9] In accord with American tradition, Congress continued to show interest in limitation of arms, and in debate over the 1916 bill the former president of the American Peace Society, James L. Hayden, prepared a resolution, offered by Representative Hensley, authorizing the President to invite the powers to a conference within a year after the war ended in Europe. By amendment the Senate dropped the proposal that the conference submit a plan for disarmament but stip-

[6] *Congressional Record,* Dec. 8, 1913, p. 480.

[7] Department of the Navy, *Annual Report of the Secretary of the Navy: 1913* (Washington, D. C., 1914), 9–10. Hereinafter cited as *Annual Report.*

[8] Department of the Navy, *Navy Yearbook: 1920–1921* (Washington, D. C., 1922), 490; Department of the Navy, *Annual Report: 1920,* p. 1.

[9] *Congressional Record,* May 27, 1916, p. 11171.

ulated that if any international tribunal, unnamed, should make competitive armament unnecessary, the President could suspend the construction authorized in the Act of 1916.[10]

At the time a reduction of armaments seemed a slight possibility; the United States entered the war in April 1917. The war nonetheless affected the Act of 1916 in ways its proponents had not anticipated. The Allies demanded destroyers for convoy and antisubmarine action, instead of capital ships, and the Wilson administration oversaw the construction of 267 destroyers. The Navy laid the keel of only one of the sixteen capital vessels authorized by the 1916 legislation. Bills of 1917 and 1918 instructed the Secretary of the Navy to begin the ships of 1916 as soon as possible, but by 1918 it was clear that the unfinished program would face difficulties when Congress cut military expenditures to peacetime levels.[11]

At the end of the war, in November 1918, the fate of the great fleet drawn on paper just before American entrance into the war was almost anyone's guess. Big-navy enthusiasts in the administration stepped up their campaign and not only called for the 1916 program, but also called for more vessels. Secretary Daniels submitted a new three-year program for 156 more, including sixteen capital ships. President Wilson, it appeared, favored the additional program; the United States by 1925 could have a more powerful navy than all the great nations combined.[12] Meanwhile the President, attending the Paris Peace Conference, was championing the League of Nations, and worldwide reduction in armaments was an important aspect of his program. At Paris there was little opposition to disarming Germany, but reduction of Allied arms proved more difficult. Wilson preferred an international police force, but his advisers wanted an American navy equal to

[10] Charles L. Hoag, *Preface to Preparedness: The Washington Conference and Public Opinion* (Washington, D. C., 1941), 17; *Congressional Record*, May 27, 1916, p. 8813; Department of the Navy, *Annual Report: 1920*, pp. 3-4.

[11] George T. Davis, *A Navy Second to None* (New York, 1940), 236-37n. See also Department of the Navy, *Navy Yearbook: 1920-1921*, pp. 521, 575, 623.

[12] Department of the Navy, *Annual Report: 1918*, pp. 32-33; *Congressional Record*, Feb. 4, 1919, p. 2682.

that of Great Britain before taking any steps that might limit American naval power.[13]

The President realized that continuation of the 1916 program and the addition of a similar program seemed to run against his plans for world peace, but Wilson apparently decided that a large fleet might provide a diplomatic counter. Publicly he supported a reduction of armaments; privately he gave the British a choice—support the League or lose command of the seas.[14] It was a clever tactic, if not altogether in accord with what most people today would think was a Wilsonian policy. His arch critic, Senator Lodge, thought Wilson's conduct unbelievable.[15] On April 10, 1919, Wilson quietly won the naval battle of Paris. A confidential memorandum passed between Colonel Edward M. House and Lord Robert Cecil in which the British promised to support a League of Nations and agreed not to object to an article in the proposed covenant affirming the Monroe Doctrine. Wilson in return refused to promise to discontinue the ships of the 1916 program already under construction but did agree to postpone vessels not laid down and to withdraw his support from the huge naval program then before Congress. In May 1919 the Wilson administration reversed itself on the additional program.[16] The President then had to make a *volte-face*. When it became obvious that the chances of American entrance into the League were poor, the administration began to press for a large navy; Secretary Daniels in December 1920 announced that he would resubmit the proposal for a second three-year program.[17]

There followed an abortive effort by the new League of Nations, just getting started in Geneva, to interest the Wilson ad-

[13] Ray Stannard Baker, *Woodrow Wilson and World Settlement* (3 vols.; New York, 1922), III, 197–224.

[14] Harold and Margaret Sprout, *Toward A New Order of Sea Power: American Naval Policy and the World Scene, 1918–1922* (Princeton, N.J., 1943), 62–72.

[15] *Congressional Record*, Dec. 21, 1918, p. 727.

[16] Sprout and Sprout, *Toward A New Order*, 71–74; Stephen Roskill, *Naval Policy Between the Wars: The Period of Anglo-American Antagonism, 1919–1929* (London, 1968), 54, 91, 100, argues, "British supremacy at sea was not seriously impaired by the agreements of 1919."

[17] Department of the Navy, *Annual Report: 1920*, p. 2.

ministration in disarmament. The Council in December 1920 sent a careful invitation to the Department of State asking the President to appoint a representative to a League military commission which was soon to discuss disarmament. A resolution in Congress would have authorized the President to accept the invitation. Wilson, through Acting Secretary of State Norman Davis, declined. With what now seems a too-careful logic, Davis wrote to League officials at Geneva that although the United States was interested in any attempt to achieve a lasting peace, it was not a member of the League and for that reason could not participate in discussions of disarmament.[18]

Throughout American history, up to and after World War I, only a great deal of talk, not action, kept alive the issue of disarmament, and supporters of disarmament were saddened to see it now enter the presidential election of 1920 where presumably there would only be more talk. Because the Wilson administration had blown hot and cold on the subject, the issue was somewhat confused: disarmament was an intricate problem, and even though the Senate by rejecting the Treaty of Versailles had disavowed the administration's arms limitation "deal" with the British, it was not easy, and perhaps impossible, for the administration to explain its own actions to the American people. Here, then, was the sort of issue to keep out of a presidential election.

The great danger, of course, was that disarmament would get tangled up with the League of Nations. Governor James M. Cox of Ohio carried the Democratic standard, but Cox's load noticeably increased when he announced support of Wilson's policies in general and the League in particular.[19] The President had failed

---

[18] *Congressional Record*, Dec. 11, 1920, pp. 205–206. It was reported soon after that Wilson intended to call a disarmament conference under the provisions of the Hensley resolution (New York *Times*, Jan. 1, 1921). There is no official record that such an attempt was made.

[19] Cox also began to hedge in the late stages of the campaign when he suggested that he would accept the League but with American interpretative reservations. "Cox Champions Covenant," *Independent*, CIII (Aug. 21, 1920), 216–17. See also Wesley M. Bagby, *The Road to Normalcy: The Presidential Campaign and Election of 1920* (Baltimore, 1962), 134–47.

to calculate that the Republicans might obscure the League issue. On a front porch in Marion, Ohio, shadowed by the very flag which had waved over William McKinley's house in Canton in 1896, the Republican nominee, Warren Gamaliel Harding, avoided commitment. The Republican presidential platform of 1920 contained a compromise foreign policy plank, fashioned by former Secretary of State Elihu Root, to appeal to all groups. The entire naval armaments issue—to build or not to build—soon was lost from sight. The plank criticized the proposed League of Nations and offered instead an international association which would summon immediate conferences when an aggressor threatened peace.[20] Harding's campaign pronouncements—he liked to call them "bloviations"—closely duplicated the platform position. To anti-League supporters he unveiled the dangers of Wilson's proposed League of Nations. To the pro-League group he exhibited what appeared to be a purified League, perhaps a new and separate association of nations.[21] The implication that he would support American participation in some form of international cooperation gave pro-League Republicans a chance to combine party devotion with high principle.[22] Harding won by an unprecedented majority, but even after victory his "gamalielese" continued to obscure his position, and for a time it looked as if everything—League, association of nations, arms control—would disappear in the equivocal and ornate oratory of the new leader.

But as events were to turn out, the electoral confusions over the League—*mirabile dictu*—produced a disarmament proposal. It must have seemed a sort of miracle. During the campaign Hard-

[20] Journalist William Allen White, a member of the Republican platform committee, later wrote, " 'It was fearfully and wonderfully made. It meant nothing except that it frankly did mean nothing' "; quoted in Walter Johnson, *William Allen White's America* (New York, 1947), 326; Republican National Committee, *Republican Campaign Text-Book: 1920* (Chicago, 1920), pp. 117–18.

[21] For examples see New York *Times*, Aug. 29 and Oct. 8, 1920.

[22] In the Senate, Harding had been a strong reservationist and had voted against Wilson's proposed League. *Congressional Record*, Nov. 19, 1919, pp. 8786, 8803. On the final vote of March 19, 1920, Harding did not cast a ballot. *Ibid.*, March 19, 1920, p. 4599.

ing, who had been a big-navy supporter in the Senate, had shown some interest in the reduction of armaments. Officially conveying the nomination to Harding, his colleague Senator Lodge had said that "we have been and are quite ready to join in agreement . . . to bring about a general reduction of armaments." Harding then had replied that he could "hear in the call of conscience an insistent voice for . . . reduced armaments throughout the world. . . . we must give of American leadership to that invaluable accomplishment." [23] True to form, the nominee then qualified his support, announcing belief in "partial, but not permanent" disarmament. Until other nations laid down their arms he would support a navy "equal to the aspirations of this country." [24] He favored a reduction in arms only after the American government had completed its naval program and could lead from strength in an international conference. So he said.

Perceptibly, though, a naval disarmament program began to appear. After the election, leadership in the reduction of armaments movement slipped from the hands of Harding, if it had ever been there, into the more tenacious grip of Senator Borah, who on December 14, 1920, submitted a resolution that the President work toward an understanding with Great Britain and Japan to reduce the naval building programs, as distinguished from existing strength, of the three powers, "annually during the next five years to 50 per cent of the present estimates or figures." As one reason for his resolution he offered the statement of the Japanese delegate to the League of Nations, Viscount Ishii Kikujiro, that the Japanese would reduce their naval program if the Americans would follow suit.[25] Here was a milestone, to use the tired idiom of disarmament writers of the time: a mark toward achievement of the cherished goal. Students since have agreed that Bor-

[23] New York *Times,* July 23, 1920.

[24] *Ibid.,* Dec. 5, 1920.

[25] *Congressional Record,* Dec. 14, 1920, p. 310, and Feb. 28, 1921, p. 4046. Borah's biographer claims that his chief reason was a desire for economy and peace. Claudius O. Johnson, *Borah of Idaho* (New York, 1936), 264. For Ishii's statement see the New York *Times,* Dec. 12, 1920.

ah's resolution marked a modest advance for arms control, both as a popular policy within the United States and a practical matter in world politics.

What happened, roughly, was that when support for the League fell, support for disarmament rose. It was an odd but thoroughly understandable result. From the beginning Borah received large support for his limitation proposal. He rather than Harding had roused discussion.[26] Committees of the lame-duck Congress in January 1921 held three separate hearings which touched disarmament and helped keep up public interest. The women of America, recently enfranchised, received a chance to voice their opinions before the House Committee on Military Affairs and the Committee on Foreign Affairs. The ladies, feeling their new political powers, believed that their influence would purge the country, perhaps the world, of its military vices. They had worked against "Demon Rum," and now they turned their efforts toward the grand problem of war. Money spent on armaments should go to education and science, they contended. One advocate pointed out that Americans need not fear war with the Japanese since a "few sharpshooters could keep Japan out of the Golden Gate." Another suggested that the United States government disarm and set an example for the rest of the world: "Disarmament like charity begins at home." [27] Meanwhile, prominent public figures spoke out in support of a reduction in armaments. Representative Thomas S. Butler remarked before the Committee on Naval Affairs, "Our purpose here really is to keep this subject before the American people; keep it up to fever heat." [28] Acting Secretary of State Davis, Secretary Daniels, General John J. Pershing, General Tasker H. Bliss, Republican House majority leader Frank W. Mondell, and the former diplomat Henry White appeared before

---

[26] Hoag, *Preface to Preparedness*, 41–49. Hoag presents a good survey of newspaper and magazine reaction.

[27] House Committee on Military Affairs, *World Disarmament Hearings* (Jan. 11, 1921), 66 Cong., 3 Sess., 36, 46; House Committee on Foreign Affairs, *Disarmament Hearings on House Joint Resolution 424* (Jan. 1921), 66 Cong., 3 Sess. See also *Congressional Record*, Dec. 12, 1920, p. 616.

[28] Hoag, *Preface to Preparedness*, 52.

the committee. Bliss, Pershing, and Daniels agreed that some disarmament move was desirable but thought that the administration should continue the 1916 naval program until an international conference met.[29]

Borah's naval limitation resolution, amended in the Foreign Relations Committee, now came up for discussion. Elihu Root, the elder statesman of the Republican party, published an open letter in which he argued that action by Congress would only embarrass the President-elect (the date of the letter was January 21, 1921) and might "prove to be just the wrong thing." [30] It is not known if Harding inspired the Root letter, but its effect was to cause Republican congressmen to question a resolution opposed by Root and perhaps by Harding. The wily Borah began to maneuver. He suggested to his Senate colleagues that he had never noticed any reluctance on their part to instruct President Wilson.[31] Borah submitted, albeit unsuccessfully, a second resolution which asked the Senate's Committee on Naval Affairs to decide whether it was feasible to suspend the naval building program for six months while the committee investigated "what constitutes a modern navy." His move was in support of the charge by some military expert opinion that technical advances in submarines, planes, and other armament had diminished the value of battleships. The British, Borah pointed out, had suspended their building program in order to hold an inquiry.[32] By introducing this resolution, Borah kept the attention of the public, of course,

[29] House Committee on Naval Affairs, *Hearings on Disarmament in its Relation to the Naval Policy and the Naval Building Program of the United States* (Jan. 1921), 66 Cong., 3 Sess., 547, 563, 594.
[30] Root to Thomas A. Butler, Jan. 21, 1921, as reprinted in the New York *Times*, Jan. 23, 1921.
[31] *Congressional Record*, Feb. 17, 1920, pp. 3320–21.
[32] *Ibid.*, Jan. 25, 1921, p. 1996. The British cast their vote for the capital ship as the main element of the fleet. Report on the Capital Ship, March 2, 1921, Cabinet Office Index 16, Group 37/1, Public Record Office (London); *Congressional Record*, Jan. 27, 1921, p. 2113. The Committee voted against a suspension and cited a General Board of the Navy report in support of a continuation. A minority report by Senator William H. King of Utah dryly commented that the General Board was hardly an impartial body. *Ibid.*, Feb. 9, 1921, pp. 2825–28, and March 2, 1921, pp. 4273–80.

on the limitation of arms. Consideration of the original Borah resolution came on February 24, 1921, but the resolution was pushed aside in favor of a similar proposal offered as an amendment to the Naval Appropriation Bill by Senator Walter E. Edge of New Jersey, who wished to include the French and Italians as well as the British and Japanese. After objections by Borah and Lodge, who professed to believe that militarism was running amok in France, the names of the additional countries were withdrawn.[33] On March 1, shortly before the lame-duck session ended, the revised Edge amendment passed the Senate, 58 to 0.[34]

It then became apparent that, in truth, there had been a maneuver within a maneuver. The success of the Edge amendment was almost meaningless because the Naval Appropriation Bill—of which the amendment was part—did not pass in that session. Borah successfully had scuttled the naval bill.

Inauguration day, March 4, 1921, offered Harding an opportunity to explore and expand his views on foreign affairs. The ultimate result of this evolvement, but in a way so slow that many contemporary observers failed to realize what was happening, was that the United States government would lead the major naval nations of the world to the grand conference at Washington. In his inaugural speech the President said that his administration would not enter any permanent political or economic alliance: "the League Covenant can have no sanction by us." He qualified his support of isolationism by adding that the American government would associate with other nations "for conference, for counsel . . . to recommend a way to approximate disarmament and relieve the crushing burdens of military and naval establishments." Such limited cooperation would not violate a policy of isolation, for the association would be regulated so that American sovereignty would not be impaired. He stressed that "this is not selfishness; it is sanctity. It is not aloofness. It is not

---

[33] *Congressional Record*, Feb. 24, 1921, pp. 2753–55.
[34] *Ibid.*, March 1, 1921, p. 4172.

suspicion of others; it is patriotic adherence to the things which made us what we are." [35]

The President's position gradually became clearer. A few weeks later he again spoke to Congress. "In the existing League of Nations, world governing with its super powers, this Republic will have no part" because the "deliberate expression of the American electorate" had manifested itself against such a course of action. Harding reiterated his desire for an association of nations, a campaign promise he said he intended to keep. It appeared that he was willing to see his country enter into international cooperation in a limited manner, but only to find a solution to a specific American problem and only by the conference method.[36] Disarmament was one problem a so-called association of nations could deal with. Harding wrote privately to Lodge, "I am quite as convinced as the most bitter irreconcilable that the country does not want the Versailles League. I am equally convinced that the country does wish us to do some proper and helpful thing to bring nations more closely together for counsel and advice." [37] He would not take the United States into the League, but he believed that an alternative would be to have a "free association and frank and honest conference." [38] He argued that when men "sit about the conference table and look each other in the face and look upon the problems deliberately without passions, they find the way to come to an agreement." A conference provided the means by which "just, thoughtful, righteous peoples, who are not seeking to seize something which does not belong to them can live peaceably together, and eliminate causes of conflict." [39]

Harding has long been considered a conservative, but the President's proposals on international affairs illustrate the danger of

[35] *Ibid.*, March 4, 1921, pp. 4–6.
[36] *Ibid.*, April 12, 1921, pp. 169–73.
[37] Harding to Lodge, Dec. 29, 1920, Papers of Warren G. Harding (Ohio Historical Society, Columbus). Hereinafter cited as Harding Papers.
[38] Harding to J. Sharp Williams, May 21, 1923, Harding Papers.
[39] Transcript of presidential press conference of Dec. 23, 1921, Harding Papers.

oversimplification. His optimistic notion of rational men gathered in conference, settling international disputes, was a popular idea. Harding took a stand that Woodrow Wilson and followers could approve. If the President was not a man of creative disposition, the recently opened Harding Papers reveal that he was a lonely man desiring some "proper" and "becoming" step toward peace.

Shortly after Harding entered office members of Congress through byzantine moves gradually produced for him a situation in which the administration could propose a limitation of armaments to the leading naval powers. As noted, a resolution by Borah authorizing the President to invite the Japanese and British to disarmament negotiations had passed the lame-duck session of Congress as the Edge amendment to the Naval Appropriation Bill, but then the naval bill itself did not pass. When Congress reconvened in April 1921, Democrats and Republicans submitted new resolutions similar to the Borah proposal. The President, it seems, wanted to complete the construction program of 1916 before he called an arms limitation conference. If the United States disarmed before completing the program, its fleet might continue to be inferior to that of Great Britain. Thus, the British and Japanese would have no compelling reason to come to a disarmament conference. Representative Bourke Cockran expressed this latter view: "Second-best armament is like a second-best hand at poker. It serves no purpose except to get its holder into mischief and bring him to disaster if not ruin." [40] The administration's floor leader, Representative Martin B. Madden, revealed the President's views when he said that the administration would have no trouble negotiating a disarmament treaty when it could offer a limitation of its large navy to countries with equal navies.[41] Senators Miles Poindexter of Washington and Frederick ("Rowboat") Hale of Maine, Republican sponsors of the Senate construction bill, spoke to Harding on May 3 and reported that the President thought Congress was seeking by an arms limitation resolution to

[40] *Congressional Record,* April 25, 1921, p. 618.
[41] *Ibid.,* April 26, 1921, p. 685.

infringe on a presidential function—Harding would not appreciate any attempt to "force the hand of the executive" toward disarmament.[42] Under strong administration pressure, the House thereupon passed the Naval Appropriation Bill without the arms limitation proposal.[43]

Harding thus had a victory in the House but was apprehensive about the Senate, for Congress had the power to effect what was referred to as a "naval holiday" simply by withholding appropriations. The administration suddenly changed its mind, for Poindexter announced that the Borah resolution would not meet opposition on points of order when it came up for discussion—that is, the administration would not oppose the Borah resolution as an amendment to the Naval Appropriation Bill. The bill and the resolution together then passed the Senate by vote of 74 to 0.[44]

As the Washington *Post*, a pro-administration newspaper, was careful to point out, the resolution for an arms reduction conference was in no way binding on the President.[45] Further debate followed when the naval bill went back to the House where an arms limitation resolution had not passed. Some congressmen believed that the Harding administration still opposed the Borah resolution and had supported it in the Senate only to speed along the naval bill. They predicted that the administration would attempt to cut it out of the conference bill or to replace it with a resolution favored by Harding. Representative Stephen G. Porter introduced a resolution that the House concurred with the President's disarmament views, a general resolution which left conference arrangements to Harding. Porter had conferred with Harding and then prepared his resolution designed to give the idea "that the President is the leader in this movement." Unlike the

[42] New York *Times*, May 4, 1921.
[43] *Congressional Record*, April 28, 1921, p. 766.
[44] New York *Times*, May 18, 1921. Taft was sure that Harding had taken the wisest course. Although he hated to give a victory to Borah, he predicted, "The disarmament feature may prove to be an entering wedge for an association of nations." Taft to Wickersham, May 18, 1921, Papers of William H. Taft (Library of Congress). Hereinafter cited as Taft Papers. *Congressional Record*, May 25, 1921, p. 1758.
[45] As reprinted in the *Congressional Record*, May 27, 1921, p. 1846.

Borah resolution, it did not specify participating nations, the extent of disarmament, or the kind.[46] House debate continued over the administration-supported Porter resolution versus the Borah resolve. When it became apparent that the latter had stronger backing, Representative Mondell then made a tactical retreat for Harding by announcing that there would be no vote on the Porter resolution, easing the way for the Borah proposal.[47]

At last an arms limitation resolution—a serious disarmament proposal so desired for decades by pacific-minded Americans—stood before the House and gave every evidence of passing, for the President of the United States now was supporting it. Before the vote Harding sent a letter to Mondell which allowed administration Republicans to vote for Borah's proposal. According to Harding, he had "already been seeking information with regard to the attitude of foreign nations on the general subject of disarmament." Mondell then told Congress that for at least six weeks the President had been carrying on negotiations like those envisioned in the Borah resolution.[48] The Borah resolve thereupon passed the House by a vote of 332 to 4, and the revised Naval Appropriation Bill (containing the resolve) passed the House and Senate on July 11.[49] Harding therefore had both a naval program and an arms limitation proposal.

Thus, strong public support, intensified by the nation's embarrassment over the rejection of the League of Nations, enabled political leaders supporting limitation of arms to make way for the

---

46 Theodore Roosevelt, Jr., to Harding, June 4, 1921, Harding Papers.

47 *Congressional Record*, June 29, 1921, p. 3225. New York *Times*, June 30, 1921.

48 Letter from Harding to Mondell, June 25, 1921, as reprinted in the *Congressional Record*, June 29, 1921, pp. 3223–27; Harding and Hughes both claimed that negotiations had been taking place. Harding to Raymond Robins, May 19, 1921, and Nicholas Butler to Harding, July 13, 1921, Harding Papers. Hughes to the Sprouts, Aug. 5, 1940, as cited in Sprout and Sprout, *Toward A New Order*, 129.

49 *Congressional Record*, July 11, 1921, pp. 3526, 3569; see also 42 *U. S. Statutes at Large*, 122–41; Borah wrote on June 30, 1921, " 'I do not believe we can for a moment afford to turn this matter over to the diplomats and go about our business in the belief that it will be worked out.' " Borah to Philadelphia *Public Ledger* as quoted in Johnson, *Borah of Idaho*, 268.

Washington Conference on the Limitation of Armaments. The tireless, unceasing parliamentary activities of Senator Borah and the grudging but at least discernible support of President Harding made the proposal possible in 1921 when the climate of official and public opinion strongly favored arms limitation. Important though these influences were, however, the conference was precipitated by events taking place not in Washington, but in London.

II. THE ATLANTIC CONTEST

❦❦❦❦❦❦❦❦❦❦❦❦❦❦❦❦❦❦❦❦❦❦❦❦❦❦❦❦❦❦❦❦❦❦❦❦

MANY FORCES AND FACTORS produced the Washington Conference on the Limitation of Armaments, but chief among them was the old rivalry between the governments of Great Britain and the United States which threatened to come into the open once the World War ended and the Allies and Associated Powers had negotiated and signed the several treaties of peace at Paris. The two great Anglo-Saxon countries had argued with each other at one time or another since before the Revolution when the English-speaking peoples in North America began to consider themselves a separate nation and to challenge the government of London. After the War of 1812 the Americans tended to believe that the British were tampering with their territorial claims in the Western Hemisphere, trying to Balkanize or South Americanize the North American subcontinent. During the Civil War the Palmerston ministry behaved in unneutral fashion, so much so that the British paid dearly at the Geneva Arbitration of 1872. Only toward the end of the century, indeed almost at the numerical end (historically one could argue that the nineteenth century did not end until the banner year 1914), did the British and Americans drop their enmities and move toward friendship. It was just in time. The British sorely needed American help in redressing the balance of power against Germany, first in the years leading to the World War, then in that war itself.

But would this short-lived cooperation last into the 1920's? With American entrance into the war in 1917 a serious problem involving American naval construction had arisen almost at once. If the United States government constructed destroyers for convoy duties as the British desired and did not push its capital ship program under the Naval Act of 1916, the British fleet would remain supreme upon the high seas. At the time of the special mission of Lord Arthur Balfour to the United States in 1917 to concert the Anglo-American war effort, President Wilson's close friend and confidant, Colonel Edward M. House, suggested an odd arrangement whereby the Wilson administration might have an option to buy British capital ships after the war. On orders from London, Balfour rejected the proposal and suggested a six-power peacetime alliance (United States, Great Britain, France, Italy, Japan, and Russia) to meet a maritime attack on any of them. President Wilson took no interest in such an obvious attempt to maintain British supremacy.[1]

The British subtly continued their tactics to preserve naval supremacy. Sir Eric Geddes, First Lord of the Admiralty, came to the United States in October 1918—a month before the armistice —and warned of a great German submarine campaign to start in the spring of 1919. He urged the Wilson administration to build still more destroyers. Casting a look at the growing American merchant fleet, Geddes had the nerve to ask for an option to buy merchant vessels, in return for refitting American ships in British drydocks during the war. The United States government refused.[2] Prime Minister David Lloyd George then told Colonel House defiantly, "Great Britain would spend her last guinea to keep a navy superior to that of the United States or any other power."[3]

It was apparent by 1919 that the Americans and British had different naval objectives. Wilson had inserted in the Fourteen Points of January 1918 a proviso for freedom of the seas. The British government, fearing the end of its naval supremacy, refused to accept this point as a basis of the armistice and resisted its inclusion in the Versailles Treaty. American Admiral William S.

[1] Mary Klachko, "Anglo-American Naval Competition, 1918–1922" (unpublished Ph.D. dissertation, Columbia University, 1962), 14–20.

[2] *Ibid.*, 38–42.

[3] *Ibid.*, 77.

Benson warned the British at Paris that if they continued to insist on naval supremacy, "I can assure you that it will mean but one thing and this is war between Great Britain and the United States." [4] In this threatening atmosphere, Colonel House and Lord Robert Cecil made a temporary settlement in April 1919. The agreement called for the Wilson administration to withdraw from Congress its supplemental naval program for construction of more capital ships and the British to support a reservation of all questions pertaining to the Monroe Doctrine in the Covenant of the League of Nations then being drafted at Paris. Even so, what amounted to a gentlemen's agreement was in reality no more than a truce since the question of equality of fleets and the whole postwar naval situation remained to future negotiations.

That the size and composition of the postwar fleets would also affect the postwar commercial struggle was clear to both nations. The British obviously hoped to regain the mercantile superiority they had held in 1914. Competition in old markets, as well as the search for new ones, grew with an intensity parallel to the naval race. After the war the British began to call for "imperial preference," not only to exclude Americans but also to increase general control of world trading patterns. A wartime incident, a British mission to South America, had warned Americans of the coming British trade drive. In April 1918 Sir Maurice De Bunsen went on a warship to South America ostensibly to thank the Latin American republics for their war support. The presence of a trade expert belied the mission's stated purpose. With some effrontery—considering that the war was still on—De Bunsen then negotiated a secret trade contract with Brazil.[5] The Department of State kept the incident quiet, but did not forget it.

Failure of the United States in 1919–1920 to join the League of Nations naturally increased antagonism. Suspicion of Great Britain had permeated the League debates in the Senate. Ignoring insults, the British had announced a willingness to accept American

[4] *Ibid.*, 315; also see full memorandum from Admiral Benson in Klachko's Appendix 4.
[5] *Ibid.*, 26–27.

reservations and sent Sir Edward Grey on a special mission to Washington not only to discuss the League, but also to explore the possibility of a naval limitation agreement.[6] Grey never delivered his message to the sick President, and when it became apparent that the United States would not enter the League, the British saw no alternative to falling back on traditional power moves to protect their interests.

It was at this time that the British government publicly began to veer toward a naval race with the United States and Japan which threatened to make the Anglo-German competition of the early 1900's look like a lobster quadrille. According to the American Navy's General Board, Great Britain in 1921 had a total military tonnage of 1,753,539 tons; the United States had 1,302,-441 tons; Japan had 641,852 total tons. Using the American figures as a base, the ratio for all tonnage, including capital ships, was 13.5 (GB)—10 (US)—4.9 (J). In the crucial category of capital ships (battleships and battle cruisers) Great Britain had 1,015,825 tons; the United States had 728,390 tons; Japan had 494,528 tons. Again using American figures as a base, the tonnage ratio for capital ships was 13.9—10—6.8. The British had under construction in ships of all categories—from submarines to battleships—some 182,950 displacement tons; the Americans, 747,007 tons; and the Japanese, 706,888 tons projected or under construction. The British had just begun four capital ships totaling 172,000 tons. The United States had fifteen capital ships of 618,000 tons under construction. The Japanese had fifteen capital ships of 599,700 tons projected or under construction.[7] Upon completion of all the capital ships, when added to those existing, the capital ship ratio

---

[6] Roskill, *Naval Policy*, 216.

[7] The figures on which tonnage totals and ratios are based are from General Board Report 1088a, "Limitation of Armaments: Part II," Sept. 17, 1921, Department of State, Washington Conference Papers (National Archives, Washington, D. C.). Naval statistics are among the most misleading ever contrived, and differing sources seldom agree on tonnage totals or even total ships in active service. A convenient source is the Navy Department, *Navy Yearbook: 1920–1921*, pp. 898–907. It generally lists lower totals for the Japanese than does the General Board Report. A 1918 listing can be found in Roskill, *Naval Policy*, 71.

would change from 13.9–10–6.8 to 10.6–10–8.7.[8] The British had the biggest, most powerful fleet in 1921, but their construction program was lagging. The Americans had a smaller fleet but were building a mighty armada of capital ships which, like that of the Japanese, would approximately double by 1928. The ratio figures indicated that from 1921 to 1928 Britain's relative position would decline.

The figures, however, also contained two uncertain assumptions: first, that the projected programs would be carried out; second, that none of the powers would add programs that would further upset the projected ratio for 1928. The American building program in 1921, for example, was full of ambiguities. Congress in 1916 had enacted the great naval act providing for ten battleships armed with twelve 16-inch guns, six battle cruisers with eight 16-inch guns, and 140 supporting craft. Because of the Allied demand for destroyers, construction on capital ships lagged, and by 1921 only one new battleship was in service. The other fifteen were in various states of construction from 3.8 to 86 per cent complete. In the meantime, congressional appropriations were becoming harder to obtain. A total of $187,349,000 had gone into the ships by the end of 1921; it might take an estimated $305,503,000 to complete the program.[9]

From the beginning, as mentioned, the British had disliked the 1916 American program. There had been roars from the British lion in the person of Winston S. Churchill, who had told the House of Commons, "Nothing in the world, nothing that you may think of, or dream of, or anyone may tell you; no arguments, however specious; no appeals however seductive, must lead you to abandon that naval supremacy on which the life of our country

[8] The second ratio does not include pre-dreadnoughts, which would be well over the effective twenty years by 1928, but the first ratio does include them. The 1921 ratio without pre-dreadnoughts was 20.2–10–8.4. General Board Report 1088a, "Limitation of Armaments: Part II," Sept. 17, 1921, Washington Conference Papers.

[9] Department of the Navy, Table Showing Effect of Conference Upon Naval Vessels Under Construction, Feb. 9, 1922, Department of State, Washington Conference Papers.

depends." [10] The British government in March 1921 announced plans to resume naval construction on a "scale that would keep His Majesty's fleet equal to, or superior to, any other navy." [11]

The key to the naval situation was in private statements rather than public, for if official statements of the British government reflected confidence about the continued supremacy of the Royal Navy, private discussion at the Cabinet level did not. In November 1920 the First Lord of the Admiralty, Lord Lee of Fareham, reported that despite hints that the government did not want to engage in a naval race with the United States, no curtailment of the American program had taken place. Lee recommended a one-power standard by beginning four capital ships in 1921 and a second four in 1922. Otherwise, he warned, Britain would join the second rank of naval powers with an outdated fleet.[12] The Admiralty admitted the next month that "the utmost we can hope for in the near future is to possess a fleet as large as that of any other single power." [13]

Lloyd George had talked publicly of more capital ships; there is little doubt that he desired a large navy. But when the Standing Defence Subcommittee of the Cabinet, with the Prime Minister in the chair, met on December 4, 1920, to discuss the naval situation, he pointed out that a naval race could ruin Britain, for the country might have to repay its war debt to the Americans before starting construction, and the country was already having serious financial problems. He proposed naval spheres of influence.[14]

In January 1921 Sir Auckland Geddes, Ambassador to the United States, cabled from Washington that he believed a naval arrangement was possible but did not advise an approach to the

---

[10] Speech of Nov. 1918 as quoted in Benjamin H. Williams, *The United States and Disarmament* (New York, 1931), 137.

[11] Merlo J. Pusey, *Charles Evans Hughes* (2 vols.; New York, 1951), II, 453; Great Britain, Navy Estimates 1921–22, Command Papers 43, March 1921; see also Roskill, *Naval Policy*, 215–33, 580.

[12] Memorandum for Cabinet by Lee, "Naval Policy and Construction," Nov. 22, 1920, Cabinet Office Index 16, Group 37/2, Public Record Office (London).

[13] Roskill, *Naval Policy*, 21.

[14] Minutes of the 134th Meeting of the Committee of Imperial Defence, Dec. 14, 1920, Cabinet Office Index 2, Group 3/6, Public Record Office.

Wilson administration; such a step, he suggested, would make negotiations with the forthcoming Harding administration awkward. He advised that the Borah resolution was altogether politically inspired, designed to clear the irreconcilable group of Republicans of the charge that they were in favor of navalism and militarism and designed to help provide a Cabinet appointment for one of their group.[15] It was also reported that Senator Lodge was worried more about the Japanese than the British.[16]

Clearly, the Lloyd George government was willing to accept a capital ship equality with the United States and would not enter a naval race if there were any honorable way out.[17] For reasons of pride, and politics, the Cabinet believed that any initiative for disarmament must come from Washington. The Foreign Office was puzzled by the arms reduction talk in America which seemed to portend some proposal. Foreign Office spokesmen had to answer parliamentary questions by replying that no communications on naval limitation had come from the United States.[18] Sir Eyre Crowe, Undersecretary of the Foreign Office, doubted whether the Americans had thought out any proposal at all.[19]

The British were also perplexed by the problem of alliance policy, especially in the Far East. The major protection for British interests in East Asia had been the Anglo-Japanese Alliance of 1902, originally directed at Russia. Renewed in 1911 as a result of the German threat to Britain (Japan had defeated Russia in 1904–1905, and Russia had concluded its entente with Britain in 1908), the treaty was to end in 1921 unless extended. With each renewal

15 Telegrams from Geddes to Foreign Office, Jan. 2 and Jan. 5, 1921, F. O. Group 371, Box 5616. (F. O. refers to the unpublished papers of the British Foreign Office in the Public Record Office.)

16 Telegram from Leslie Craigie, secretary of the embassy in Washington, D. C., to Earl Curzon, Feb. 11, 1921, *ibid.*

17 Lord Lee indicated this to Adolph Ochs, publisher of the New York *Times*, on April 22, 1921; this information never reached Secretary Hughes. Eugene J. Young, *Powerful America: Our Place in a Rearming World* (New York, 1936), 48ff.

18 As late as June 15, 1921, Curzon noted, "I have received no communication on this subject from the U. S. government." F. O. A4379/18/45.

19 Comment by Crowe on May 17, 1921, on a telegram from Geddes to Foreign Office, May 16, 1921, F. O. A3715/18/45.

the Japanese government had raised the price by calling for more British guarantees. Under the cover of the treaty the Japanese had made spectacular gains in East Asia and in the process had infringed on British economic interests in North China. The British labored to keep the Japanese occupied, away from the more important British interests in South China, Tibet, Burma, India, and Australia. Earl Curzon, the Foreign Secretary, in October 1921 followed this policy in a talk with V. K. Wellington Koo, the Chinese Minister in London. Curzon asked Koo if it would not be "sound statesmanship" to steer the Japanese toward Manchuria, away from the industrial areas of China: Manchuria, he noted, was not part of China proper, and the Americans had recognized the Japanese predominance there in the Lansing-Ishii agreement. "My own inclination," he suggested, "if I were a Chinaman, would be to allow the Japanese to expand under reasonable conditions, in that direction." Koo, being a Chinaman, did not show enthusiasm.[20]

Such balancing of the British national interest was, of course, in conflict with the American Open Door policy. What the Foreign Office called a realistic act of imperial protection, the Department of State labeled a threat to China's territorial and administrative entity. British policy was in the tradition of the balance of power and spheres of influence; the Open Door policy had evolved, by 1921, into a stand against balances and spheres.

By 1921 Lloyd George's government found itself under pressure from the New World. The Canadian government called for an end to the alliance and immediate convocation of a Pacific conference. It appeared that the Canadians might even take an independent line and break with Lloyd George, but the Prime Minister was able to calm Canadian fears by promising to decide the fate of the alliance at an Imperial Conference scheduled for July 1921.[21] Many Americans, including congressional spokesmen, also

[20] Telegram from Curzon to Sir John Alston in Peking, Oct. 24, 1921, F. O. F3924/2635/10.
[21] Governor General of Canada to Churchill, Feb. 15, 1921, F. O. F1696/63/23; April 8, 1921, F. O. F1579/63/23. See also Rohan O. Butler, J. P. T. Bury, and

believed the alliance a mistake. Germany was no longer a menace, but the Anglo-Japanese Alliance remained. The Department of State believed that the alliance made the British passive partners of Japanese imperialism and left the United States government as the only check on Japanese ambitions.[22] Japan's wartime acquisition of the German concessions in Shantung and islands north of the equator were the latest results of the alliance.

The threat of a Japanese-American conflict was an embarrassing problem to the British. F. Ashton-Gwatkin of the Far Eastern Department of the Foreign Office presented some interesting possibilities. Referring to the circumstances that had brought the Wilson administration into the World War, he suggested that Great Britain might find it "equally impossible" to remain neutral in the event of an American-Japanese war. The United States "can manage without us, but Japan cannot." Geography and economics would compromise Britain in the direction of a "pro-Japanese intervention, in spite of the fact that our natural sympathies would be on the American side." Shipping munitions to Japan, American visit and search and perhaps destruction of British ships because of arms shipments, and Japanese use of Singapore and Hong Kong—all could cause conflict. "In our own material interest," Ashton-Gwatkin continued, "we should have to take action, and perhaps armed action, to prevent the United States of America from reducing Japan to complete bankruptcy." A Japanese-American war would be a "calamity to the British empire," for victory by either side would upset the Asian balance.[23]

The Foreign Office had attempted to exclude the United States

---

M. E. Lambert, eds., *Documents on British Foreign Policy: 1919–1939* (London, 1966), First Series, XIV, 271. Hereinafter cited as *British Documents*.

[22] Borah wrote that he viewed it as an unfortunate alliance "intended to cooperate against America." Borah to the debate manager of Reed College (Portland, Ore.), May 5, 1921, Papers of William E. Borah (Library of Congress). Hereinafter cited as Borah Papers. Memorandum of Hughes's conversation with Sir Auckland Geddes, June 23, 1921, Department of State 741.9411/140½. (These file numbers refer to the unpublished records of the Department of State in the National Archives.)

[23] Memorandum by Ashton-Gwatkin, "British Neutrality in the Event of a Japanese-American War," Oct. 10, 1921, F. O. F3012/2905/23.

government by name from the alliance in 1911. The Japanese had refused to approve.[24] Article 4 in the July 13, 1911, renewal was then added, stating that if either party had an arbitration treaty with a third power then nothing in the alliance "shall entail upon such contracting party an obligation to go to war with the power with whom such a treaty of arbitration is in force." A general arbitration treaty between the United States and Great Britain, signed on August 3, 1911, failed in the Senate. A modified arrangement, called the Peace Commission Treaty (one of the so-called Bryan cooling-off treaties), signed on September 15, 1914, passed the Senate, and Foreign Secretary Sir Edward Grey informed the Japanese that Great Britain regarded the Peace Commission Treaty as part of an arbitration treaty and therefore within the scope of Article 4. The Japanese government never accepted this technical evasion as a definitive interpretation of the treaty.[25]

What to do? For several years the Foreign Office had given thought to renewal of the alliance; the British had sounded ambassadors and appointed a blue-ribbon committee to study the renewal question.[26] Assistant Secretary Victor Wellesley, superintendent of the Far Eastern Department, in a memorandum of June 1920 argued that Japanese policy had become "almost diametrically opposed to the best interests of not only Great Britain and the United States but of China . . . having for its ultimate aim a complete Japanese hegemony over China, politically, economically and probably militarily." The alliance had not prevented the Japanese advance into China, and "we are already more or less helpless." He nevertheless recommended retaining the pact

24 Memorandum by Charles Bentinck of Foreign Office, "Effect of Anglo-Japanese Alliance on Foreign Relationships," Feb. 28, 1920, *British Documents*, First Series, VI, 1019.

25 Memorandum by Foreign Office, "British Commitments in the Pacific Ocean," Oct. 10, 1921, F. O. F4218/2905/23; see also memorandum by Ashton-Gwatkin, "United States and Anglo-Japanese Alliance," F. O. F2257/63/23.

26 *British Documents*, First Series, VI, 572–1074. Geddes at first called for a renewal of the alliance without including the United States; Geddes to Curzon, Nov. 15, 1920, and Dec. 3, 1920, F. O. F1057/63/23. The Foreign Office Committee called for the substitution of a tripartite pact in report by Wellesley of the Anglo-Japanese Committee, Dec. 23, 1920, F. O. F1057/63/23.

but broadening it into a tripartite agreement. On May 21, the counselor of the American Embassy in London, Butler Wright, had put out what was regarded as a feeler to Wellesley on a closer cooperation in China. The superintendent hoped for a five-year renewal of the alliance without the clause which called for military aid in the event of an attack on either power. He also recommended a separate understanding with the United States along parallel lines. Wellesley could find no better solution.[27] A friendly Japan would protect British interests more than would a hostile Japan.[28]

From the British point of view the obvious solution was the tripartite agreement. Sir Arthur Willert, Washington correspondent of the London *Times*, in May 1921 suggested such an agreement to Undersecretary of State Henry P. Fletcher. He said that when the British had a bad elephant in India they "put him between two good elephants to behave." [29]

In May 1921 Curzon suggested to the Japanese government that the alliance, to run out in July, be prolonged for three months. He warned that a notification of 1920 to the League of Nations constituted official notice of termination as required under Article 6 of the alliance.[30] To the surprise of the British the Japanese Foreign Minister refused such an interpretation.[31] The Foreign Office asked the opinion of the crown law officers who replied that the 1920 official note did serve as a proper notice. Curzon again warned the unhappy Japanese that the alliance would expire automatically in July.[32] The Foreign Office was temporarily taken

[27] Memorandum by Wellesley, June 1, 1920, F. O. F2159/199/23.

[28] Memorandum by Ashton-Gwatkin, "Present Situation in Japan," Oct. 10, 1921, F. O. F3310/3310/23; memorandum by Balfour, June 28, 1921, Cabinet Registered File 21, Group 137, Public Record Office.

[29] Memorandum by Fletcher of a conversation with Willert, May 31, 1921, Department of State 741.9411/96.

[30] Curzon to Sir Charles Eliot (Tokyo), May 11, 1921, F. O. F1797/63/23; Curzon to the Japanese Ambassador in London, Hayashi, June 8, 1921, F. O. F2025/63/23.

[31] Eliot to Curzon, June 10, 1921, F. O. F2211/63/23.

[32] Wellesley to Law Officers of the Crown, June 17, 1921, F. O. F2034/63/23; Law Officers to Wellesley, June 24, 1921, F. O. F2316/63/23; Curzon to Hayashi, June 27, 1921, F. O. F2299/63/23.

off the hook when the Cabinet asked the opinion of the Lord Chancellor, who conveniently ruled that a new one-year notification was necessary.[33]

Lloyd George opened the Imperial Conference in London on June 20, 1921, by offering to discuss with the Americans any proposal for limitation of armaments. The Prime Minister warned that sea power was the "basis of the whole empire's existence. We have therefore to look to measures which our security requires. We aim at nothing more. We cannot be content with less." [34] The conference then proceeded to the Anglo-Japanese Alliance. Prime Ministers William M. Hughes of Australia and William F. Massey of New Zealand, convinced that the alliance restrained Japan and protected their countries, believed the alliance could be modified in such a way that the Harding administration either would not object or would even make the United States government part of the arrangement. Ambassador Geddes in Washington now supported a tripartite agreement. The open opposition of Prime Minister Arthur Meighen of Canada, who wanted abolition of the treaty, remained.[35]

Curzon discussed the alliance on June 28 with American Ambassador George Harvey, who erroneously gave the impression that the American government was not interested in the Anglo-

[33] Cabinet minutes on Anglo-Japanese Alliance, June 30, 1921, F. O. F2438/ 63/23; Curzon to Hayashi, July 2, 1921, F. O. F2299/63/23.
[34] *Conference of Prime Ministers and Representatives of the United Kingdom, the Dominions, and India: Held in June, July, and August, 1921. Summary of Proceedings and Documents* (London, 1921), 13.
[35] *Ibid.*, 19, 30. See also J. Bartlet Brebner, "Canada, the Anglo-Japanese Alliance and the Washington Conference," *Political Science Quarterly*, L (March 1935), 45–58. J. Chal Vinson attempts to demonstrate that Prime Minister Hughes was not a supporter of the alliance in "The Imperial Conference of 1921 and the Anglo-Japanese Alliance," *Pacific Historical Review*, XXXI (Aug. 1962), 257–66. Balfour stated to Lloyd George, Nov. 11, 1921, that consideration must be given to "the importance which Australia and New Zealand attach to the maintenance of the Anglo-Japanese Alliance in some shape or form." F. O. F4466/2905/23. See also telegram from Geddes to Curzon, June 6, 1921, F. O. F2110/63/23. An excellent survey of the main trends in the British discussion on the Anglo-Japanese Alliance can be found in M. G. Fry's "The North Atlantic Triangle and the Abrogation of the Anglo-Japanese Alliance," *Journal of Modern History*, XXXIX (March 1967), 46–64.

Japanese pact.[36] Geddes reported this impression to Secretary of State Charles Evans Hughes, who said the Harding administration would regret any arrangement which left the British supporting the Japanese in East Asia; Hughes made it clear that the United States was against the alliance. He cabled Harvey, with some sharpness, to await "instructions before expressing opinions on policy." [37]

The Imperial Conference on July 2 formally called for a conference on the Pacific and Far East. Curzon broached the proposal to the Japanese, and Chinese, on July 4 and then to Harvey on July 5.[38]

On Thursday, July 7, Lloyd George was asked in Parliament if Britain was about to call a conference. He said he would make a statement the following Monday if replies came from the United States, Japan, and China.[39] Reporters in Washington asked Hughes if the rumor that the British were about to call a conference were true. Hughes replied that he did not know. He had not received news from Harvey of the British proposal.[40]

Then the Americans moved to halt the diplomatic confusion. At 4 P.M., Friday, July 8, 1921, Hughes sent cables to the ambassadors in Britain, Japan, France, and Italy asking them to inquire of the governments to which they were accredited if the countries would participate "in a conference on limitation of armament . . . to be held in Washington at a mutually convenient time." [41]

That same day he received the belated cable from Harvey in which Curzon proposed that Harding "invite the powers directly concerned to a conference on Far Eastern and Pacific questions,

[36] Telegram from Harvey to Hughes, July 8, 1921, Department of State, *Papers Relating to the Foreign Relations of the United States: 1921* (Washington, D. C., 1936), I, 19. Hereinafter cited as *FR*. Curzon to Geddes, June 29, 1921, F. O. F2367/63/23.

[37] Telegram from Hughes to Harvey, July 6, 1921, Department of State 741.9411/136a.

[38] Cable from Curzon to Eliot, July 4, 1921, F. O. F2446/63/23.

[39] London *Times*, July 8, 1921.

[40] Beerits memorandum, "Calling the Conference," Papers of Charles Evans Hughes (Library of Congress). Hereinafter cited as Hughes Papers.

[41] Telegram from Hughes to Harvey, July 8, 1921, *FR: 1921*, I, 18.

including the peaceful settlement of disputes and the elimination of naval warfare." [42] Harvey had held the proposal almost three days. The two cables were thus sent the same day. But in considering the question of whether the British or Americans had been the first to propose a conference, one should note that the British were primarily interested in a Far Eastern conference whereas the Americans were suggesting only a conference on arms limitation.

The Foreign Office announced on Saturday, July 9, that "no reply is expected from the United States as there is nothing to which to reply." The British proposal was "officially nonexistent." [43] Meanwhile, Hughes cabled Harvey that the proposal of the United States government must stand, for it had gone to Tokyo, Rome, and London, whereas Hughes incorrectly believed that the British had sent their proposal only to the Department of State. Hughes instructed Harvey to inquire whether the British government would agree to an enlargement of the American proposal to include Far Eastern problems, and invite China.[44] Events moved to a finish. The Secretary drafted informal invitations and a statement for the President, embodying the American proposals which Harding approved. Hughes informed other governments that the agenda also would include Far Eastern and Pacific questions, and invited China. Lloyd George read a prepublication copy of Harding's statement and told Harvey carefully that it was admirable.[45] The same day the Secretary received Harvey's report indicating British approval; he released Harding's statement to the press and cabled the informal invitations. The world knew of the proposed meeting on Monday morning, July 11, 1921.

Thus the confusions of British politics and policy impelled the

---

[42] *Ibid.*, 19.
[43] Telegram from Harvey to Hughes, July 9, 1921, *ibid.*, 22.
[44] *Ibid.*, 23.
[45] Telegram from Harvey to Hughes, July 10, 1921, *ibid.*, 25. Harvey later described the British acceptance in a speech to the Pilgrim Society. He quoted Lloyd George as saying, " 'We accept gladly; we accept gratefully. I do not need to read the telegram. It is all right; we will do everything in our power to make the conference a great success.' " New York *Times*, Nov. 1, 1921.

British government toward a conference. The British, confronted by strong public demands for a cut in government expenditures, faced by a nation that had the resources to outbuild them, and reluctant to enter a naval race they might not win, had swallowed their pride and accepted naval parity with the United States. But the primary concern that pushed the British toward the Washington Conference was not naval limitation *per se* (as it was with the American government); rather, it was the protection of vital British interests in the Pacific and East Asia. The Anglo-Japanese Alliance was about to expire and the British government recognized the danger in both a renewal or a nonrenewal; the former would cause suspicion and difficulties with the United States while the latter might turn an ally into an enemy who could directly threaten British interests from the Yangtze to Singapore. Naval limitation was only a door through which the British might enter into negotiations with both the United States and Japan. The British might even succeed in not choosing one side or the other and remain in the good graces of both. Whether the British strategy would work, only the future and the conference could tell, but the British, unable to restrain themselves, immediately attempted to emphasize Far Eastern issues and relegate naval limitation to a secondary position.

CURZON RAISED THE FIRST OBSTACLE which could have sidetracked the Washington Conference when he suggested to Harvey that a preliminary conference on Pacific and Far Eastern affairs take place in London.[1] The British proposal of July 5 had called for such a conference, but the original American proposal had not included the Far East, mentioning only limitation of arms. Receiving the British proposal, the American government decided to widen the conference by including Far Eastern and Pacific problems and duly amending its informal inquiries. Harding's statement said that the United States had invited the governments to discuss limitation of armament; because Pacific and Far Eastern questions were related to armament, the nations would discuss them to reach "common understanding with respect to principles and policies in the Far East." [2]

Hughes rejected Curzon's plan for a preliminary conference, pointing out that the American proposal combining both Far Eastern problems and arms limitation had been "specifically endorsed" in London. The Secretary argued that while Far Eastern and Pacific problems were of major importance, "it would be quite a different matter to leave the subject of limitation of armament to a second conference, the holding of which might be entirely dependent upon the success of the first." [3]

No doubt Hughes worried about Curzon's proposal. To his informal invitations he had received favorable responses from the

[1] Telegram from Harvey to Hughes, July 11, 1921, *FR: 1921*, I, 26.
[2] Telegram from Hughes to Harvey, July 9, 1921, *ibid.*, 24.
[3] Telegram from Hughes to Harvey, July 12, 1921, *ibid.*, 28.

French, Italians, and Chinese, but not the Japanese or British; the conference could not succeed without their presence. Hughes cabled Harvey and asked for a "direct expression of approval . . . which may be available for publication if desired." [4] Instead he got a reply that inclusion of Pacific and Far Eastern problems on the Washington agenda would harm the arms limitation conference. According to Harvey, Curzon "feared that it would be impracticable if not indeed impossible for the British government to take part in the conference." Yet that same day Curzon gave Harvey a formal expression of approval of a Washington Conference "for the purpose of considering the question of limitation of armaments." He said nothing about Pacific questions. [5]

A week later Sir Auckland Geddes, the British Ambassador in Washington, gave Hughes a telegram in which the Foreign Office took the preliminary conference for granted and blandly expressed some misunderstanding "in the tangle of correspondence by telegraph . . . as to the nature and locality of the preliminary consultations." Curzon suggested that Bar Harbor would be a fine place to hold a conference on Far Eastern problems and asked Harvey to arrange accommodations for August 18. In conversation with Hughes, Geddes remarked that Harvey had "warmly approved the idea" of a preliminary conference; Harvey had even suggested it take place in London or Havana. [6] The wires must have sizzled when Hughes cabled Harvey, who denied everything. Reading his answer, Hughes exclaimed, "Who is the liar?" [7]

---

[4] Telegram from Hughes to Harvey, July 12, 1921, *ibid.*, 30.

[5] Telegram from Harvey to Hughes, July 15, 1921, *ibid.*, 33–34.

[6] Memorandum from the British Foreign Office to Geddes handed to Hughes by Geddes on July 27, 1921, *ibid.*, 45; telegram from Harvey to Hughes, July 27, 1921, *ibid.*, 46; telegram from Hughes to Harvey, July 30, 1921, Department of State 500.A4/62.

[7] Telegram from Harvey to Hughes, Aug. 2, 1921, Department of State 500.A4/89; as quoted in Pusey, *Hughes*, II, 459. Pusey cites as his source the unpublished 1922 diary of William R. Castle, Jr., p. 183. That there was some confusion in Harvey's mind over the preliminary conference is reflected in his telegram of July 23 to Hughes: "Time may come when you deem it advisable to cable me in so many words . . . that . . . the President could not . . . call a conference or any part of a conference to meet in London or anywhere except in

Here the culprit was almost certainly Ambassador Harvey. A more incompetent, inept ambassador was impossible to imagine; he ignored many instructions, often took an independent line, and just plain botched negotiations. Curzon wrote that Harvey had assured him that the American government would approve a preliminary conference in London and that Harding and Hughes would attend.[8] That Hughes was against the proposal therefore came as a surprise to the British.[9]

Hughes was not to be moved, so over the protests of the Dominion ministers in London, who wanted to attend such a preliminary conference, the British government dropped the project.[10] In the course of this about-face the Foreign Office allowed itself to make a tactical error. Geddes expressed regret for the misunderstanding and wrote that Great Britain "desired the United States to take full responsibility for arrangements in order to avoid possibility of future misunderstandings." This gave Hughes the opportunity to plan the conference.[11]

The Japanese raised the second obstacle. They were hesitant about a Far Eastern conference, if indeed eager to discuss limitation of arms. The Imperial government was spending nearly half its revenue on military forces.[12] It favored the British proposal which had as its purpose the replacement of the Anglo-Japanese Alliance; the Japanese were willing, if necessary, to substitute an

United States. No occasion for doing so now but occasion may arise." Department of State 500.A4/45.

8 Telegram from Curzon to Geddes, July 14, 1921, F. O. A5169/18/45; memorandum by Curzon, July 24, 1921, F. O. A5489/18/45; Geddes to Curzon, July 30, 1921, F. O. A5551/18/45.

9 Assistant Secretary R. A. C. Sperling argued that the United States was not interested in disarmament but was attempting to score a diplomatic triumph; comment by Sperling on F. O. A5550/18/45. Geddes agreed in Geddes to Curzon, July 31, 1921, F. O. A5553/18/45. See also Curzon to Geddes, July 30, 1921, F. O. A5618/18/45. Geddes on July 29 did indicate that Hughes promised he would not reject the preliminary conference until he had talked to the President. Geddes to Curzon, July 29, 1921, F. O. A5523/18/45.

10 Telegram from the American chargé in London, Post Wheeler, to Hughes, Aug. 7, 1921, *FR: 1921*, I, 53.

11 Telegram from Hughes to Harvey, Aug. 2, 1921, *ibid.*, 50.

12 Japan planned to spend $249,318,539 on her navy from April 1921 to March 1922. *Navy Yearbook: 1921*, p. 907.

agreement to include the United States. But the question of their hard-won position in China was something else again. In reply to the American invitation the Foreign Ministry wanted to know the "nature and scope" of the Far Eastern conference.[13] Hughes inquired of the British, hoping they would consult Japanese diplomats. The Secretary suggested that conference discussion might consider the Open Door, integrity of China and Russia, status of former German possessions in the Pacific, cable and radio communications, narcotic traffic, and other Far Eastern questions. He would exclude emigration to the United States, a purely domestic matter.[14]

The Secretary knew that inclusion of Far Eastern issues had raised trouble. When a Japanese reporter asked Hughes the purposes of the conference, Hughes wisely refused to expand his comments.[15] The American naval attaché in Tokyo later reported that the Far Eastern conference came as a surprise.[16] But Edward Bell, the American chargé, reported on July 23 that Foreign Minister Uchida Yasuya indicated that the Japanese would accept.[17] Within three days they did, but they also expressed the hope that the introduction of problems "such as are of sole concern to certain particular powers or such matters that may be regarded accomplished facts should be scrupulously avoided." [18] In a manner reminiscent of John Hay's handling of the responses to the first Open Door note in 1899, Hughes released a press statement that all interested powers had accepted the American proposal. He had the Japanese reply printed, along with the American proposal that

[13] Telegram from the American chargé in Tokyo, Edward Bell, to Hughes, July 13, 1921, *FR: 1921*, I, 31.

[14] Telegram from Hughes to Harvey, July 13, 1921, *ibid.*, 31. The Republican platform of 1920 stated, "The existing policy of the United States for the practical exclusion of Asiatic immigrants is sound and should be maintained." *Republican Campaign Text-Book: 1920*, p. 163.

[15] Letter from K. Sado Hanazana to Hughes, July 14, 1921, Department of State 500.A4/56.

[16] Memorandum to the Navy Department, July 18, 1921, Department of the Navy Records (National Archives).

[17] Telegram from Bell to Hughes, July 23, 1921, *FR: 1921*, I, 43.

[18] Telegram from Bell to Hughes, July 25, 1921, *ibid.*, 44.

the two nations exchange opinions on the agenda. The Harding administration, the newspapers guessed, regarded the qualification in the Japanese note as more of a suggestion than a rule.[19]

Throughout August the State Department continued to parley with foreign ministries. Curzon suggested that the United States limit the discussions at the Pacific conference to the territorial integrity of China, Open Door, Shantung, and leased territories; the conference could ignore the opium traffic, Russia, immigration, and German possessions in the Pacific.[20] He also received a report from Tokyo that Uchida wanted to exclude the topics of Siberia and Shantung.[21] The Imperial government's position was contained in a communique which a Japanese clerk in London on August 6 gave to the press, supposedly by mistake. By this time-honored device the Japanese indicated that their Chinese and Siberian policies were not open to discussion; they believed that decisions at Paris in 1919 had settled the Yap and Shantung issues. They accused the American government of seeking to control Asia.[22] The Japanese government nevertheless had accepted the American invitation without knowing the agenda. The Japanese pointed out that their policy in the Far East was "preeminently vital"; soldiers and diplomats had devoted utmost efforts "toward securing its permanence and its maintenance might well be to her a matter of prime concern." [23]

The Chinese soon joined the Japanese in asking for a specific agenda. The Chinese Minister for Foreign Affairs, W. W. Yen, feared that at the conference the Chinese and American delegates would present the only opposition to the Japanese. For that reason, he said, the Chinese and American governments should cooperate. Hughes sympathized but believed that such a course would destroy the chance of an agreement with the Japanese on other issues. The Chinese then accused the State Department of

---

19 New York *Times,* July 28, 1921.
20 Telegram from Harvey to Hughes, July 19, 1921, *FR: 1921,* I, 36.
21 American Naval Intelligence Report, "Attitude of Japan," July 29, 1921, Department of the Navy Records (National Archives).
22 Telegram from Wheeler to Hughes, Aug. 26, 1921, *FR: 1921,* I, 52.
23 Telegram from Bell to Hughes, Aug. 23, 1921, *ibid.,* 61.

making an agreement with the Japanese that the conference would discuss no question without unanimous consent and that this procedure would prevent any discussion of Shantung.[24] Time and again in coming months Hughes had to contend with the suspicious Chinese.

The Department of State on September 10 at last announced an agenda. The first section dealt with arms and included naval disarmament, "rules for the control of new agencies of warfare," and limitation of land weapons. The second concerned Pacific and Far Eastern questions. Chinese problems were itemized: territorial and administrative integrity, concessions, monopolies, railways (including the Chinese Eastern), and a deft category entitled "status of existing commitments." Siberia's problems appeared in the second part of the second section of the agenda, and its subheads duplicated those of the Chinese section. Mandated islands of the Pacific, unless their status had been settled before the conference, composed the third subject.[25] The French and British asked about novel agencies of warfare, and Hughes included gas, submarines, and airplanes. The Chinese government wanted to bring up tariff autonomy, and Hughes approved.[26] The British Foreign Office privately was appalled by the agenda, which they thought "better calculated to make the Japanese Government withdraw from the conference than to produce any other result." The proposals, the British believed, "suggest such a complete lack of grasp of the situation on the part of the United States government that nothing short of a regular course of education seems to offer the slightest

[24] Memorandum of a conversation with Yen by the American chargé in Peking, Albert Ruddock, Aug. 16, 1921, Department of State 500.A412/18; memorandum by John V. A. MacMurray, chief of the Far Eastern division of the Department of State, of a conversation with the Chinese Minister, Sao-ke Alfred Sze, on Aug. 31, 1921, Department of State 500.A4/128.

[25] Telegram from Hughes to Harvey, Sept. 10, 1921, *FR: 1921,* I, 67; "Electrical Communications in the Pacific" was added to the agenda in telegram from Hughes to Harvey, Sept. 28, 1921, *ibid.,* 75.

[26] Prince Louis Bearn, the French chargé in Washington to Huges, Sept. 16, 1921, *ibid.,* 69; the British request, Department of State 500.A4/109½; telegram from Hughes to Bearn, Sept. 20, 1921, *FR: 1921,* I, 70; memorandum of a conversation with Sze by Hughes, Nov. 5, 1921, *ibid.,* 82.

chance of the matter being put on anything like a rational basis." [27]

The Japanese Foreign Ministry wished to know what was
meant by the "status of existing commitments." Hughes replied
that he wanted to clarify the respective position of the powers in
China.[28] Former Secretary of State Robert Lansing, a paid consul-
tant to the Chinese, predicted privately that if the Japanese refused
to discuss the China problem they would appear to have bad motives: "they hate to come in and they can't stay out." He guessed
that the Japanese had "wasted a lot of unclassical language on the
situation." [29] The Japanese ambassador to the United States, Baron Shidehara Kijuro, did get Hughes to agree that the conference would not discuss settled treaties.[30] The Japanese then accepted the agenda on October 17, with the understanding that
they could raise questions during the conference.[31]

Another dispute arose between the State Department and the
Foreign Office when Harvey, acting on instruction from Harding
that had not been communicated to Hughes, suggested that Canada's position in the new Panama Canal tolls bill under consideration by the Senate could be the same as that of the United States—
coastwise vessels of neither country would pay. Curzon reported
this course unacceptable and suggested that all nations have the
same rate. Harvey noted that he told Curzon that he, Curzon,
spoke only for Britain and that Curzon became upset.[32] Harding
and Harvey had unwittingly reopened a touchy subject. Geddes
then told Hughes that the British approved the agenda but wanted
to discuss Panama tolls, yet because Hughes was unaware of the

[27] Comments on agenda by Sperling and Williams on Sept. 13 and 16, 1921,
F. O. A6675/18/45.
[28] Telegram from Bell to Hughes, Sept. 12, 1921, *FR: 1921,* I, 68; telegram from
Hughes to Bell, Sept. 12, 1921, *ibid.*
[29] Lansing to Norman Davis, Oct. 4, 1921, Papers of Robert Lansing (Library
of Congress). Hereinafter cited as Lansing Papers.
[30] Memorandum by Hughes of a conversation with Shidehara, Sept. 12, 1921,
Department of State 793.94/1316.
[31] Memorandum by the Japanese Embassy in Washington to the Department
of State, Oct. 17, 1921, *FR: 1921,* I, 78.
[32] Copy of letter from Harvey to Harding, Sept. 19, 1921, Department of State
811F.8123/91.

conversation between Harvey and Curzon, Hughes could not understand why the British raised the tolls issue. Harvey then told Hughes of his private communications from Harding and informed his superior that he thought it desirable for him to have that information.[33] Hughes reported that he had not received any word from President Harding and did not approve putting the subject on the agenda because it should go no further than bilateral negotiation between the two nations.[34] Finally, Harding sent to Hughes a letter from Harvey, with a note that he had requested Harvey to feel out the British on the subject and that it looked to him as if Harvey's activities had made the British irritable.[35] The Secretary wrote Harding explaining his own instructions to Harvey.[36] It is indeed interesting that Harding would be so careless in writing to Harvey without consulting the Secretary of State. Hughes might have resigned but probably realized that the President was not so much undercutting him as simply committing a *faux pas*. Hughes knew Harding well enough, by this time, to know that the President meant well, whatever he did. Incidentally, the tolls bill passed the Senate on October 10, but the House ignored it and so it died.

Immediately following Harding's statement that the United States planned an arms control conference dealing also with Far Eastern problems, the Department began to receive inquiries from uninvited nations with interests in the Far East. The administration decided to invite the Belgian and Netherlands governments after gaining approval of the other powers. The Portuguese thought their claims as good as the Belgian and Dutch and asked for an invitation. Hughes extended one.[37]

Russia was not so easy. A representative of the Russian Socialist

33 Harvey to Hughes, Sept. 20, 1921, Department of State 500.A41a/15.

34 Hughes to Harding, Sept. 29, 1921, Department of State 811F.8123/63.

35 Copy of letter from Harvey to Harding, Sept. 19, 1921, Department of State 811F.8123/91; letter from Harding to Hughes, Oct. 10, 1921, *ibid.*

36 Hughes to Harding, Oct. 13, 1921, Department of State 811F.8123/92a.

37 Circular telegram from Hughes to American legations in Paris, London, Rome, and Tokyo, Sept. 3, 1921, *FR: 1921*, I, 66; circular telegram from Hughes to American legations in Paris, London, Rome, and Tokyo, Sept. 27, 1921, *ibid.*, 75.

Federalist Republic in Sweden protested Russia's exclusion, declaring that the Bolshevik government would not recognize any decision at the Washington Conference affecting its interests. Foreign Minister George Chicherin made a similar announcement.[38] The Russians asked to come, but Hughes replied through a press statement that since the United States government did not recognize the Bolshevik regime he could not invite them.[39]

From China came a protest that Dr. Sun Yat-sen, who headed the Canton government, would not recognize decisions at the conference affecting China unless Hughes invited the Canton as well as the Peking government.[40] Pro-Canton agitators in the United States began to press congressmen. To an inquiry from one senator, Hughes replied that the Department could not well ask Canton because neither the United States nor any other government invited to the conference had recognized Canton's claim, whereas all recognized Peking.[41] Protests continued to come from Sun Yat-sen's agent in Washington, Ma Soo.[42]

The delicacy of selecting the American delegates was also a sort

[38] American chargé in Stockholm, Sheldon L. Crosby, in a telegram to Hughes, July 21, 1921, Department of State 500.A4/38; telegram from Crosby to Hughes, July 22, 1921, *FR: 1921*, I, 40.

[39] Telegram from Hughes to Ruddock, July 28, 1921, Department of State 500.A4/63; telegram from Hughes to Harvey, Sept. 17, 1921, *FR: 1921*, I, 69. It is interesting that Elihu Root, shortly to receive appointment to the American delegation to the Washington Conference, wrote, "Evidently no conference undertaking to deal with the subject of general disarmament would be likely to leave the Russian condition and probable future out of consideration. . . ." Root to S. R. Bertron, Aug. 10, 1921, Papers of Elihu Root (Library of Congress). Hereinafter cited as Root Papers.

[40] Telegram from the American consul general at Canton, Leo A. Bergholz, to Hughes, Sept. 9, 1921, Department of State 500.A4/222.

[41] Hughes to Senator La Baron Colt, Sept. 17, 1921, Department of State 500.A4/174.

[42] Ma Soo wrote Henry Cabot Lodge that the Canton government wanted the withdrawal of recognition from the Peking government, foreign noninterference in China's internal political affairs, open diplomacy, review of all treaties pertaining to China, Japanese withdrawal from Shantung, Mongolia, and Manchuria, remission of the Boxer indemnity, and gradual abolishment of consular jurisdiction. Letter from Ma Soo to Lodge, Dec. 7, 1921, Papers of Henry Cabot Lodge (Massachusetts Historical Society, Boston). Hereinafter cited as Lodge Papers. Memorandum of MacMurray, "Self-Constituted Government of China at Canton," Sept. 28, 1921, Department of State 893.00/4080. See also Hughes to Levi Cooke, Oct. 4, 1921, Department of State 500.A4p81/4.

of diplomatic problem, albeit within the United States. Hughes was the natural choice for chairman of the delegation. But who else should be selected? And in particular, should the Senate be represented? President William McKinley had set a precedent when he put senators on the delegation to the Paris Peace Conference in 1898. The Republicans had criticized Wilson when he did not send senators to the Versailles Peace Conference. Thus the Harding administration decided for senatorial representation, in effect a senatorial blessing, before formal advice and consent.

Hughes and Harding had to decide whether they should choose Senator William E. Borah, who had sponsored the arms limitation resolution. Borah received backing from friends in the Senate and from many private peace groups. Senator "Pat" Harrison of Mississippi believed that Borah deserved a place. Robert M. Lovett, editor of *The New Republic,* Oswald Garrison Villard, editor of *The Nation,* and Norman Thomas all urged Harding to appoint Borah.[43] But one of Harding's advisers, Charles D. Hilles, Republican national committeeman from New York, after several discussions with the President, came out strongly against Borah. He felt that Harding should emphasize the conference as part of the plan for an association of nations rather than a result of pressure by the Borah resolution. Because on many occasions Borah had shown an independent attitude, Hilles warned that he might not work with other delegates.[44] Borah himself was enough of a realist to see that Harding would not select him as a delegate, although there is little doubt that he would have accepted. He wrote his brother that Harding had not asked him, at least "not loud enough for me to hear it, although I wasn't expecting to hear anything of that kind and I might have overlooked it." He advised that he would find something to do in connection with the limitation of armaments; he would have opportunity to discuss and vote upon the treaties.[45] In a later letter Borah pointed out that he had "in-

---

[43] *Congressional Record,* Aug. 17, 1921, p. 5096; letter to Harding, Aug. 18, 1921, Washington Conference Papers.

[44] Copy of letter from Hilles to Harding, Aug. 17, 1921, Root Papers.

[45] Borah to Frank Borah, Aug. 23, 1921, Borah Papers.

curred the displeasure of some in high places because of my persistent urging of the resolution. Besides I am not supposed to be able to work in double harness. And it is no doubt feared that I would not be amenable upon all programs." [46] Borah told friends that he understood the situation from the first and was not disappointed when passed over. [47]

The next obvious Senate choice was Lodge, and Hilles told Harding that this selection was "universally expected." [48] In the twilight of a long career (he died in 1924), the senator from Massachusetts, chairman of the Foreign Relations Committee, was the first delegate appointed after Hughes. Delighted, old Lodge wrote privately to a friend that the President "had only decided on two members of the delegation—the Secretary of State and me—and I naturally was very much gratified by his doing so." [49] Lodge was to become a familiar figure at the conference; the small, slender aristocrat of the Senate, who gloried in his reputation as a scholar, used public occasions to display his learning and sprinkled his speeches with classical allusions. His self-assured presence reminded one observer of a bewhiskered cat about to eat a canary. [50] But Ambassador Geddes reported to London that Lodge was "crotchety, old and cold, and thoroughly disillusioned. I know of nothing that he believes in except himself." [51] Yet Lodge proved of great importance when the conference treaties went up to the Senate.

The third member of the American delegation was Elihu Root, perhaps the outstanding Republican not directly connected with the Harding administration. He proved to be a popular choice. Root had served under Theodore Roosevelt first as Secretary of

---

[46] Borah to Charles P. McCarthy, Aug. 23, 1921, *ibid.*
[47] Borah to W. G. Scholtz, Aug. 24, 1921, *ibid.*
[48] Copy of letter from Hilles to Harding, Aug. 17, 1921, Root Papers.
[49] Lodge to Henry White, Aug. 31, 1921, Lodge Papers. Lodge was very pleased with Hughes as Secretary of State. He wrote, "I think Secretary Hughes is doing extremely well. He and I are on most excellent terms and have had many talks together, and he seems anxious to consult and advise with me, which is, of course, very pleasant." Lodge to Langdon Mitchell, May 5, 1921, Lodge Papers.
[50] Mark Sullivan, *The Great Adventure at Washington* (New York, 1922), 207.
[51] Geddes to Curzon, Sept. 1, 1921, F. O. A7148/18/45.

War and then as Secretary of State; he had more diplomatic experience than any other member of the American delegation. Lloyd George viewed Root very favorably.[52] At the time of the convention, however, Root was seventy-six years old (he lived to be ninety-two) and was beginning to demonstrate signs of his age —he did not always understand what was taking place and he looked at issues in a narrow legal way. But, as one historian has written, Root had "an instinct for order and for the way power can be used, with restraint but also with assurance, to introduce order in a system." [53] In 1921 Root favored an amended League of Nations and especially the World Court. He had had much experience with the Far East and, unlike other delegates, did not regard the Japanese as a menace. During the Washington Conference, Root's chief activity was to be in the negotiations over the Nine-Power Treaty concerning China.

The fourth position on the delegation proved hard to fill. Hughes and Harding decided that the Democratic party must have representation, but politics excluded the leading Democrats —Woodrow Wilson, James M. Cox, William Jennings Bryan, Robert Lansing, and Thomas Marshall. Then Harding wavered for a moment and wanted to appoint Republican Senator Philander Knox, Secretary of State under President Taft; at the last minute, however, Harding offered the post to Oscar W. Underwood, Senate minority leader, who accepted.[54] He had been a candidate for the Democratic presidential nomination in 1912, but later supported the policies of Wilson and sponsored the Tariff of 1913. Fifty-nine years old in 1921, Underwood was nominal head of the leaderless Democratic party. He had developed a friend-

[52] Lloyd George told Harvey that he "regarded Mr. Root most favorably, but in that respect he was only voicing the universal sentiment here to the effect that in Mr. Root the British have a very strong and favorable friend in any court. He grieved sorely and shook his head sadly, at his own mention of the anti-British proclivities of Senator Lodge and literally raised his hands in horror at the thought of Borah . . . ." Harvey to Hughes, Sept. 26, 1921, Hughes Papers.

[53] Elting Morison, *Turmoil and Tradition: A Study of the Life and Times of Henry L. Stimson* (Boston, 1960), 53.

[54] Telegram from Hughes to Harvey, Aug. 29, 1921, *FR: 1921*, I, 65. Knox died shortly before the conference began.

ship with Harding when the latter had served in the Senate. Overshadowed by Hughes, Root, and Lodge, Underwood was not of great importance at the conference but did support the treaties in the Senate so strongly that he incurred the intense displeasure of his former leader, Wilson, who angrily remarked to an intimate, "If Underwood is a Democrat, then I am a Republican." [55]

Such were the members of the delegation (it must be noted that the Secretary of the Navy, Edwin Denby, was not appointed as delegate to a conference that was to discuss naval limitation). Many groups felt that Harding should have appointed a more representative set of citizens—other than professional politicians. Besieged by petitions and letters from women's groups, labor unions, and veterans' organizations, the Harding administration conceived the idea of an advisory commission. One of its members, Secretary of Commerce Herbert Hoover, later wrote that Hughes had asked him to serve on "this subsidiary committee which was a political repository for some twenty persons who thought they ought to be on the main delegation." Hoover's task was to keep this group happy. Some members rebelled at being window dressing, and it became a large task "to get them back home without their exploding in public." [56] Headed by ex-Senator George Sutherland, it included among its members John L. Lewis, Samuel L. Gompers, General John J. Pershing, Governor John Parker of Louisiana, Congressman Stephen G. Porter, and Theodore Roosevelt, Jr.

Having met the British and Japanese challenges on the preliminary conference and agenda and having chosen the American delegation, Harding and Hughes had made a good beginning, but the Secretary was well aware of the need for more hard work. Every wise diplomat knows, but sometimes forgets, that successful negotiations at a conference depend on preparation. The Americans, conscious that delegates with specific goals more often succeed at a conference, began to draw up a plan.

[55] Quoted in Thomas A. Bailey, *The Great Betrayal* (New York, 1945), 347.
[56] Herbert Hoover, *The Memoirs of Herbert Hoover: The Cabinet and the Presidency: 1920–1933* (New York, 1952), 179.

IV. THE AMERICAN PLAN

AMID THE BUSTLE of preparation for the conference, Hughes started to hold meetings of the American delegation. Unnoticed at first, this small group generally met in the Secretary's office at the Department. Lodge later claimed that he, Root, Underwood, and Hughes had twelve sessions before the conference, and out of those discussions came a full plan for naval limitation.[1]

The American delegation decided to concentrate on limitation of naval armaments rather than Far Eastern questions, and this procedure eventually placed the Harding administration at the front of the world movement in support of arms limitation. Hughes knew the American people were much more interested in a dramatic pursuit that promised results directly affecting peace and the electorate's pocketbook, rather than in mysterious Far Eastern political problems.

Far Eastern problems nonetheless were important, if only because of the Japanese, who favored naval limitation but were apprehensive about questions relating to their area of the world. Approaching such issues through naval limitation made it easier to compromise on Asian problems. But finally the tactic of concentrating on naval limitation gave the United States much more to bargain with, for in 1921 the nation had a huge postwar fleet under construction. The American government had something to offer.

Once the decision was made to concentrate on naval limitation, the next move was to formulate a plan. Hughes mobilized almost

---

[1] *Congressional Record*, March 28, 1922, p. 4677.

all of the departments of the government; the result was several thousand pages of reports covering the conference agenda.[2]

The American Navy, of course, had a plan of sorts. The American delegates had not been the first to suggest that Secretary of the Navy Edwin Denby's department draw a plan of limitation, for as early as June 10, a month before the informal invitation issued by Harding, Professor George Grafton Wilson of Harvard had suggested that the Navy start on draft proposals in the event Harding called a conference. The Navy replied, in the best Washington manner, that it would take no action until requested by the Department of State.[3] It was not until three weeks after Harding's invitation that Assistant Secretary of the Navy Theodore Roosevelt, Jr., asked the General Board for a preliminary investigation and report by September 20.[4] The General Board was composed of Rear Admirals William L. Rodgers (chairman), Harry P. Huse, Robert M. Jackson, William V. Pratt, Harry S. Knapp, and Robert E. Coontz and Captain Frank H. Schofield. While members of the General Board had informal discussions, circulated memoranda, and sent out questionnaires to other naval officers, the Board did not begin formal meetings until August 29.[5]

The Board reflected a fear of Japanese intentions in the Pacific, and Pratt suggested that the United States have a navy equal to that of Great Britain and double that of Japan, and that the most important step to take at the conference was an accord with the British. The Anglo-Japanese Alliance was at best a temporary solution for problems that could be "*better* and more *permanently* solved in the interest of peace in the hands of an undivided Anglo-Saxon race." Schofield and Rodgers came out for a 2:1 ratio over

[2] Studies made for the American delegation, Washington Conference Papers; the requests for information are in the State Department Index 500.A41a.

[3] Rear Admiral Robert E. Coontz, Chief of Naval Operations, to Wilson, June 17, 1921, Navy Department Records, 3809–959:15 (National Archives).

[4] Letter from Roosevelt to the General Board, June 27, 1921, General Board Papers, Naval History Division, Department of the Navy.

[5] Roosevelt to Denby, Aug. 8, 1921, Papers of Edwin Denby (Detroit Public Library) and General Board Papers, Naval History Division, Department of the Navy. The Papers of Edwin Denby hereinafter called Denby Papers. Also Coontz to Sims, Aug. 23, 1921, Navy Department Records, 3809–959:20.

the Japanese. Huse and Knapp called for "preparedness in the Pacific." [6]

Replies to the questionnaires sent to twenty-six naval officers reflected the same suspicion of the Japanese. Opinions varied far more on the British; three correspondents were willing to give Great Britain more naval power than the United States, but the majority wanted equality with the British. Retired Admirals William F. Fullam, Hugh Rodman, and James Oliver would not limit naval arms at all although Rodman had no objection to cutting down the size of armies. Oliver could see neither "the possibility nor the propriety of our tieing [*sic*] of our hands." The British and Japanese were coming to the conference as allies, and one could not "deny or forget that Great Britain has an evil record as regards her treatment of rival traders—Spain, Holland, France, and Germany." [7]

When on September 1 Secretary Hughes asked the Navy Department to submit recommendations as soon as possible ("What standard or yardstick can be determined by which to measure existing armaments or any future plan of reduction?"), the General Board submitted the first part of its proposal. It contended that traditional American foreign policy—no entangling alliances, the Monroe Doctrine and Open Door policy, control of the Panama Canal, exclusion of Asiatics—was well known. If the United States intended to protect its interests, it must have a fleet at least equal to that of Great Britain. The Board believed that the Anglo-Japanese Alliance was a threat; renewal would force the Americans to build a navy equal to that of the British and Japanese combined. As a minimum, the Board felt, the American Navy should equal that of the British and be double that of the Japanese. [8]

[6] Memorandum by Pratt, Aug. 8, 1921; memorandum by Schofield, Aug. 22, 1921; memorandum by Rodgers, Aug. 20, 1921; memorandum by Huse, Aug. 20, 1921; memorandum by Knapp, Aug. 6, 1921, in "Policy and Discussion" binder on Washington Conference, General Board Papers, Naval History Division, Department of the Navy.

[7] Memorandum by Rodman, Sept. 6, 1921; memorandum by Fullam, Sept. 10, 1921; memorandum by Oliver, Sept. 25, 1921; these and other replies are in the "Opinions" binder on Washington Conference, *ibid*.

[8] Report of the General Board of the Navy, "The Limitation of Armaments:

Soon the Board recommended quotas so that by 1928 the United States and Great Britain each would have approximately 1 million tons of capital ships while Japan would have 600,000 tons; auxiliary ships—cruisers, destroyers, submarines—would follow the same ratio. The three nations would reach these totals by completing their naval construction programs, except that construction not under way by 1921—keels laid—would not be permitted from 1922 to 1928; the British, however, could complete four *Hoods*, while the Japanese could complete four ships under construction plus two more not yet laid down. Such a proviso struck at the Japanese because eight more ships were authorized but not under construction.[9] The Board was willing to depart from its "safe" 2:1 ratio since the United States would complete its vessels and have a million tons.[10] In practice the Board plan would give the advantage to the nation with the largest program in progress in 1921: the United States.[11]

The Secretary of State's legal adviser, J. Reuben Clark, noted that the plan had not received the sanction of the Navy Department, and Assistant Secretary Roosevelt intimated to Clark that Denby would not approve it; a letter from Denby to Hughes shortly confirmed this fact.[12] Clark informed Hughes that a modi-

---

Part One," Sept. 12, 1921, General Board Reports, Washington Conference Papers; Report of the General Board of the Navy, "The Limitation of Armaments: Part Two," Sept. 17, 1921, *ibid*.

[9] Report of the General Board of the Navy, "Capital Ships," Oct. 3, 1921, and Report of the General Board of the Navy, "Auxiliary Combatant Ships," Oct. 8, 1921, *ibid*.

[10] William Howard Gardiner to Hilary P. Jones, "Memorandum on Naval Matters connected with the Washington Conference on the Limitation of Armaments, 1921–1922," Oct. 25, 1924, Papers of the Naval Historical Foundation (Library of Congress).

[11] According to General Board figures, the United States had (not counting pre-dreadnoughts) 500,650 tons of capital ships in 1921; Great Britain had 1,015,825 tons; and Japan had 419,600 tons. In 1928 with the completion of all authorized building programs the figures would be United States—1,118,650; Great Britain—1,187,825 tons; and Japan—974,950 tons; General Board Report, "The Limitation of Armaments: Part Two," General Board Reports, Washington Conference Papers.

[12] Memorandum by Clark, "Navy Plans," Oct. 11, 1921, Hughes Papers; Denby to Hughes, Oct. 10, 1921, Denby Papers.

fied proposal was in preparation which would include not a limit
but a reduction.[13]

The modified plan appeared: it assumed abrogation of the
Anglo-Japanese Alliance, and navies of 820,000 tons each for the
United States and Great Britain, with 410,000 tons each for Japan,
Italy, and France—a return to a 2:1 ratio. The United States
was to stop construction on four capital ships (two battleships,
two battle cruisers) and scrap 350,000 tons of older ships so it
might complete the other eleven capital ships. The Japanese and
British were to make corresponding reductions.[14] Again the United States Navy would emerge with a stronger, more modern
fleet than the Japanese or British.

At this time a special naval advisory board made up of Assistant Secretary Roosevelt and Admirals Coontz and Pratt began
to function. Roosevelt, the key figure on the Board, was, like his
father, a man of culture and much charm. The junior Roosevelt
enjoyed the social whirl, which was of some importance because
he derived a good deal of information from the foreign delegates.
A devoted bridge player, he paid his highest compliment by calling
someone a "trump" of a person. Coontz and Pratt must have had
difficulty resisting him because in rapid succession this small group
submitted three plans, although none received the support of the
General Board.[15] Plan one would have the three powers contin-

[13] Memorandum by Clark, "Navy Plans," Oct. 11, 1921, Hughes Papers.

[14] Report of the General Board of the Navy, "Modified plan designed to meet
a specific demand for reduced expenditures with condition that no inimical alliances against the U. S. exist," Oct. 14, 1921, General Board Reports, Washington
Conference Papers; Great Britain was to complete the four *Hoods* and Japan
was to complete two battleships. Included with this report was an analysis pointing out that $332 million had been spent on the fifteen capital ships and that it
would take $216,300,000 to complete them. Report of the General Board of the
Navy, "Analysis of Plan for October 14, 1921," *ibid.*

[15] Roosevelt wrote, "Admiral Coontz of course is in a very difficult position
for he has got to divorce himself from the traditions of a lifetime in relation to a
strong navy, and place himself where he will unquestionably meet with active
antipathy from a large number of the commissioned personnel." Diary of Theodore Roosevelt, Jr., Oct. 27, 1921, Papers of Theodore Roosevelt, Jr. (Library of
Congress). Hereinafter called Roosevelt Papers. Gardiner conducted an investigation into the evolution of the naval plan of the Washington Conference in
1924 for Admiral Hilary P. Jones and interviewed both Coontz and Pratt. He

ue construction of all ships on which the keels had been laid. Plan two, least favored by the group, would cut out eight American ships under construction, the four British *Hoods*, and six Japanese ships. Plan three was like two, but scrapped more old ships to make way for new ships. All three plans suggested a higher ratio than the 10:5 of the General Board.[16]

After consideration by Denby, plan two was put forward as the proposal of the Navy Department.[17] Work was to stop on eight American capital ships (two battleships, six battle cruisers), and seventeen old capital ships (268,000 tons) would be scrapped. Great Britain was to build no capital ships during the agreement, and Japan could complete the *Mutsu* and *Kaga*. It would leave the United States with a capital ship fleet of twenty-three, thirty-four for Great Britain, and fourteen for Japan. The American fleet would be more modern.[18]

On the afternoon of October 24 the American delegation led by Hughes decided that the Navy proposal was not enough; during the previous week Hughes had thought of a plan far more

concluded that they favored the original General Board Plan and not the "stop-now" plan; they contended that they simply carried out orders from the American delegation to fill in the technical details. Memorandum by Gardiner, Naval Historical Foundation. A note attached to the folder of plans submitted by the Advisory Committee and signed by L. C. Sims, chairman of the executive committee of the General Board, stated, "The General Board had nothing to do with their preparation and had no formal and very little informal knowledge of them." In General Board Papers, "Advisory Book Number One," Washington Conference, Naval History Division, Department of the Navy.

[16] Naval Advisory Committee, "Explanation of Plan Number One," n.d., *ibid.*; the United States was to stop construction on four ships, while Japan and Great Britain were to complete four ships apiece. Naval Advisory Committee, "Explanation of Plan Number Two," n.d., *ibid.* Naval Advisory Committee, "Explanation of Plan Number Three," n.d., *ibid.*; U. S. was to finish eight ships, Great Britain two, and Japan three. The tonnage at the beginning of each program before reaching the desired ratio on the replacement year follows for the above three plans: Plan one, US—809,600, GB—925,250, and Japan—482,600; Plan two, 731,250—882,425—439,650; Plan three, 722,300—839,250—440,200.

[17] For Denby's statement see the Washington *Post*, Oct. 13, 1921. Roosevelt wrote, "The Secretary decided definitely on Plan No. 2." Diary of Theodore Roosevelt, Jr., Oct. 21, 1921, Roosevelt Papers.

[18] Memorandum to Hughes signed by Denby, "Navy Department Plan," n.d., Washington Conference Papers; memorandum to Hughes signed by Denby, "Explanatory of Navy Department Plan," n.d., *ibid.*

drastic.[19] He proposed to scrap the entire American building program and ask the British and the Japanese to discontinue theirs. The Secretary would set the fleets of the United States, Great Britain, and Japan at a ratio (expressed in capital ship displacement tonnage) of 5—5—3, using the existing American fleet as a base. Limitation on the basis of existing strength would end the problem of inventing a ratio that would consider the naval requirements of each country. It was also a true limiting of armaments: ships scrapped, programs stopped, fleets limited, and ever-increasing naval costs ended. It would serve as an ideal way to gain Far Eastern concessions because the American fleet would not be a threat to Japan.[20]

Through Reuben Clark, Hughes had asked the General Board how the navies would compare if the United States government scrapped all its program, or vessels less than 60 per cent completed, with the British and Japanese to make corresponding reductions; and the Board replied by listing ships which would make up the three fleets if the American delegation adopted either plan; it recommended neither.[21] The Secretary had taken this information to the White House and convinced Harding of the possibilities of the "stop-now" proposal. After that meeting Senator Lodge predicted "that neither Japan nor England could possibly accept the proposition . . . and then we should have to fall back on the less extensive reduction, using the recommendations prepared by the navy." [22] Roosevelt said it looked as if the plan "could not possibly be accepted by the other nations." But Lodge

[19] Diary of Henry Cabot Lodge, Oct. 24, 1921, Lodge Papers; Diary of Theodore Roosevelt, Jr., Oct. 24, 1921, Roosevelt Papers.

[20] Beerits memorandum, "The Five-Power Treaty," Hughes Papers; Elihu Root later claimed that he had independently conceived the same idea. Philip C. Jessup, *Elihu Root* (2 vols.; New York, 1938), II, 450.

[21] General Board of the Navy, "Scrapping of the United States New Construction with Corresponding Reductions by Great Britain and Japan," Oct. 21, 1921, General Board Reports, Washington Conference Papers.

[22] Diary of Henry Cabot Lodge, Oct. 24, 1921, Lodge Papers; Harding had told Lodge he wanted to complete the six battle cruisers. *Ibid.*, Oct. 12, 1921.

that same evening told Roosevelt that it was now the "President's plan and as such would go through." [23]

Next day Hughes asked Denby what reductions the American delegation could ask of the British and Japanese if the United States government abandoned its building program.[24] Denby passed the query to the General Board which, now that it realized Hughes was considering a halt to all construction, predicted disaster: "Fifteen capital ships brought Japan to the conference. Scrap them and she will return home to pursue untrammeled her aggressive program." [25]

In the few remaining weeks the delegation polished the "stop-now" proposal. Roosevelt and the advisory group presented a proposal which they believed would leave the United States safe; the Japanese, they predicted, would accept but the British might complain. The United States, Great Britain, and Japan were to stop work on all ships under construction or authorized, and were not to build during the term of the agreement. The United States would halt fifteen ships (618,000 tons) under construction on which it had spent $322 million; in addition the United States would scrap fifteen old capital ships (227,740). Great Britain was to discontinue the four *Hoods* (172,000), which were not under construction but on which money had been spent, and to scrap fourteen capital ships totaling 322,275 tons (this was later changed to twelve at 302,075 and finally to nineteen at 411,375). Japan was to stop eight ships authorized but not under construction and seven under construction (289,100); in addition it would scrap ten older vessels totaling 159,828 tons. Japan was to have a total of 330,000 tons of capital ships with 550,000 tons for the United States and Great Britain during the term of the agreement; this tonnage was later lowered by another tenth.[26] The

[23] Diary of Theodore Roosevelt, Jr., Oct. 25, 1921, Roosevelt Papers.

[24] Hughes to Denby, Oct. 25, 1921, General Board Papers, Naval History Division, Department of the Navy.

[25] General Board of the Navy to Hughes, Oct. 26, 1921, State Department Index 500.A41a/178.

[26] Memorandum on "stop-now" proposal by Naval Advisory Committee, Oct.

proposal retained the 10:6 ratio rather than the 10:5 suggested by the General Board, which continued to forecast disaster for 10:6.[27]

Logic, consistency, and accuracy were not hallmarks of the "stop-now" proposal adopted by the American delegation and later presented by Hughes to the conference. The claim was made that the United States government already had spent $332 million on the fifteen capital ships under construction; that sum does not agree with the total of $187,349,000 found on a Navy Department chart of February 1922.[28] Hughes accepted and used the larger figure supplied by the General Board. Second, both Great Britain and Japan had fewer keels laid than the proposal may have indicated. The Japanese were given credit for seven ships whereas the actual figure was five; the four British *Hoods*, for which materials had been gathered, were also counted. It appears that this procedure was followed in part to make the Japanese and British totals more respectable in comparison with the American fifteen. It is true, also, that four of the American ships were less than 11 per cent completed, while four others were less than 30 per cent finished.[29] Finally, the "stop-now" proposal included

---

26, 1921, Naval History Division, Department of the Navy; memorandum from Denby to Hughes, "A Limitation and Reduction of Armaments on the Principle of Stop Now," Oct. 26, 1921; and memorandum from Denby to Hughes, "Explanatory of the Proposal to Limit and Reduce Armaments on the Basis of Stop Now," Oct. 26, 1921, Washington Conference Papers.

[27] W. L. Rodgers to Hughes, "Arguments in favor of maintaining the relative strength of the American and Japanese ratio of two to one," Oct. 28, 1921, State Department Index 500.A41a/145.

[28] Department of the Navy, Chart on Naval Construction, Feb. 1922, Washington Conference Papers (also in the Harding Papers). The higher figure is still not reached even if one adds the total cost not to complete of $43,300,000 estimated by the General Board. General Board, Analysis of Plan of Oct. 3 and Oct. 8, serial 1088e, Oct. 14, 1921. The cost of labor on construction of a capital ship amounted to approximately 90 per cent.

[29] For Japan it was the *Amagi, Akagi, Koga, Tosa,* and *Mutsu.* Memorandum by the American naval attaché in Tokyo, J. W. McClaron, to the Director of Naval Intelligence, Aug. 26, 1921, in General Board, Policy and Discussion on Washington Conference, General Board Papers; for the United States on Oct. 1921—*Massachusetts* 10.4 per cent, *Ranger* 2.7 per cent, *Constitution* 11.1 per cent, *United States* 10.7 per cent, *Montana* 27.7 per cent, *Iowa* 29.5 per cent, *Lexington* 25.5 per cent, and *Saratoga* 28.5 per cent. Navy Department, *Navy Yearbook: 1920–21,* 884.

—among older capital ships to be scrapped by the United States and Great Britain—vessels already deactivated, decommissioned, scrapped, or slated for those actions. Nine of the nineteen British ships were in this category; five of the American fifteen qualified for the same distinction.[30] While the addition to the British total may have recognized the voluntary scrapping by the Admiralty of thirty-eight capital ships between the Armistice in 1918 and the conference in 1921, it is possible that it was an attempt to make the proposal more acceptable. To count ships out of service or so destined would make the sacrifice publicly greater, but privately easier.

The American delegation thereupon decided not to make an opening proposal to France and Italy, for the navies of both countries were weak. A promise also was given the Navy Department that the American proposal would not in any way prohibit fortification of the Pacific island naval bases deemed so necessary by the General Board.[31]

While the American delegation was evolving its plan, the Japanese and the British were active, although both groups expected the Americans to make some proposal that would form a basis of negotiation. Both were eager to end the naval competition with honor and, if possible, advantage to themselves; but there is no

[30] Denby told Geddes, "Five obsolete battleships—*Virginia, Rhode Island, Nebraska, Georgia,* and *New Jersey*—are being scrapped but it is expected that although mentioned in treaty they would in any case have been condemned." Quoted by Geddes in Geddes to Curzon, Sept. 26, 1922, F. O. 6001/2/45. An Admiralty report of Nov. 1921 listed: *Commonwealth*—paid off, *Agamemnon*—fleet target service, (*Dreadnought*—not listed but paid off), *Bellerophon*—paid off, *St. Vincent*—paid off, *Inflexible*—paid off, *Superb*—experiments, *Neptune*—paid off, *Hercules*—paid off, *Indomitable*—paid off, *Temeraire*—paid off, *New Zealand*—reserve, *Lion*—reserve, *Princess Royal*—reserve, *Conqueror*—reserve, *Monarch*—reserve, *Orion*—seagoing gunnery training ship, *Australia*—in Australia, *Agincourt*—reserve. British Admiralty, Ship Report, Nov. 1921, Adm. 116/2149. Lord Lee on March 10, 1922, said, "Of the 20 completed capital ships to be scrapped under the terms of the Washington naval treaty, nine have already been so disposed of." Great Britain, Command Papers 1922, Command 1603, XIII (Navy Pensions) in Naval Estimates 1922–23.

[31] Minutes of the American delegation, meetings of Nov. 2 and 3, 1921, Washington Conference Papers.

evidence that these two governments consulted each other on their naval plans.

When the Japanese Ministry of Foreign Affairs, advised by its military consultants, had begun discussion of a possible plan, it stressed the advantage of avoiding a treaty; it recommended making any limitation under a gentlemen's agreement which would leave each nation freedom of action. It was willing, if necessary, to limit not only the navy but also the army.[32] Discussion narrowed to two modes of naval limitation on September 1, 1921. In their first plan, the Japanese shrewdly predicted that the Anglo-Saxon nations would attempt to equalize each other's power. In that event the Japanese were to propose naval limitation to begin in 1924, which would allow completion of ships under construction in 1921 as well as replacements during the proposed eight-year life of the arrangement (1924–1932). This plan would not strike at the 1921 programs but would attempt to prevent future programs; such a procedure would favor the Japanese and Americans, with large fleets under construction, and operate against the British. The second Japanese alternative was an uncomplicated proposal to spread the 1921 programs over twice the time planned; this too would favor the Japanese who were having difficulty financing construction, but for the same reason it would have appealed to the Americans and British.

The Japanese demonstrated considerable interest in American Pacific bases. The American delegates had relegated bases to a position of secondary importance, but both Japanese alternatives emphasized the base question.[33] This fact was not unknown in

[32] Memorandum by Japanese Foreign Ministry, n.d., Archives of the Japanese Ministry of Foreign Affairs (microfilmed by the Library of Congress), reel MT 306, pp. 156–73. The Foreign Ministry Archives will hereinafter be cited with reel numbers and pages only. For more detailed references, see *Checklist of Archives in the Japanese Ministry of Foreign Affairs, Tokyo, Japan, 1868–1945*, comp. Cecil H. Uyehara *et al.* (Washington, D. C., 1954).

[33] Memorandum of Sept. 1, 1921, to Yamakawa (Division Chief), reel MT 306, pp. 174–88.

the American government, for public statements from Tokyo hinted of the importance of bases.[34]

Whatever the Japanese government may have thought in the summer of 1921, its shaky financial condition could not help but give pause to expansive tendencies. Japan during the World War not only had taken over German possessions in East Asia and conducted an expedition into Siberia, but also had enjoyed a great economic boom. Exports had increased with the absence of competing European products; trade with the United States also had gone up markedly.[35] With the end of the war the Europeans returned; it was apparent that the Japanese could not sustain the wartime level of production, and a severe economic recession had taken place by 1921, so that the Japanese government was looking for ways to cut expenditures.

A substantial part of the Japanese budget went for naval arms. The General Board of the United States Navy estimated that 32 per cent of the Japanese national budget went for naval expenditures in 1921–1922, whereas the comparable figure in the United States was 12 per cent. Many people in Japan and elsewhere doubted the ability of the Japanese to continue the large naval program. It is instructive to note that nations bent on acquiring armaments have seldom let financial problems deter a continued acquisition of arms, but this was before the age of Keynesian economics and especially before the fiscal experience of World War II showed governments the world over that what they previously had considered impossible national budgets were quite possible. The important point, though, is not what Japan might have done fiscally but what people of the time thought the Japanese could do, and Japanese leaders undoubtedly—in accord with much foreign opinion—considered their nation in fi-

[34] Telegram from Eliot to Curzon, Aug. 18, 1921, F. O. A6099/18/45, contains a naval attaché report; Eliot to Curzon, Oct. 9, 1921, F. O. A6953/18/45.
[35] W. W. Lockwood, *The Economic Development of Japan* (Princeton, N. J., 1954).

nancial trouble by 1921. The navy seemed to cost an almost prohibitive sum.

The British naval proposal made in advance of the grand conclave at Washington was much more carefully thought out. The Admiralty sent its proposal to the Committee on Imperial Defence. The British concerned themselves first with politics, by calling for an international guarantee of the status quo in the Pacific to prevent the Japanese from developing a base south of Formosa that might threaten British interests in the South Pacific. No conference treaty was to receive British assent if it interfered with development of Hong Kong and Singapore. Admiralty officials were reluctant to let the Japanese any farther into the British sphere of influence. The report recommended that the British delegates allow the American group to make the initial proposal on naval disarmament. This procedure would demonstrate interest and open-mindedness. Delegates were always to argue that the naval needs of the British empire were greater than those of any other nation, that "although the government has accepted a position of equality in naval strength with the United States this is a concession to which their naval needs do not really entitle them." At the conference British delegates, therefore, were to oppose any naval holiday proposals. The Royal Navy was already reduced, and to agree to a holiday "would place us in a position of permanent inferiority." A system of foreign inspection was to be resisted, as were any attempts to limit navies by budgets, personnel, tonnage, total warships, size, or on a basis of total tonnage of capital ships.[36]

The Admiralty plan was to concentrate on limiting the number of capital ships. The Royal Navy was large enough to protect itself in European waters, but to meet any challenge from Japan in the Pacific a superiority of three post-Jutland British capital ships to two Japanese ships was necessary. Would the

[36] Memorandum 277B by the Admiralty to the Committee on Imperial Defence, Oct. 5, 1921, British Cabinet Papers 21/218.

Americans accept such a ratio? A substitution of a tripartite pact for the Anglo-Japanese Alliance would help the Americans agree to equality with the British and thus a 3:2 ratio over the Japanese. What margin of inferiority were the Japanese willing to accept? The Admiralty suggested that British delegates try to convince the Japanese to accept the lowest standard.[37]

When the Standing Subcommittee of the Committee of Imperial Defence, composed of Cabinet members and high-ranking military officers, considered the Admiralty proposals, the Prime Minister, Lloyd George, accepted its conclusions on national security. Churchill called for a paper program of naval construction as a bargaining device which, he pointed out, had worked on the Germans and might work on the Americans. Of course, there was always the possibility that the Americans might call the bluff; in that event the British must build the ships if the national interest demanded it.[38]

The subcommittee on October 24 sent its final proposals to the Cabinet. Great Britain's financial troubles were so great, it reported, that unless the government could secure a considerable reduction in military spending its political as well as economic life would be in jeopardy. The report supported the Admiralty proposals on maintenance of the Pacific status quo and limitation of naval arms. It supported the Admiralty suggestion that other delegations first put forward proposals. "The result of this is likely to be the adoption of the admiralty plan." [39]

The Cabinet on November 1 decided that the report of the subcommittee, based on the Admiralty report, was to serve the British delegation as a guide. The Cabinet recommended Churchill's paper program as a bargaining device. And, of some importance, it said that if renewal of the Anglo-American guarantee to France should come up—that is, a revival of the nonratified

37 *Ibid.*
38 Minutes of the Standing Defence Subcommittee, Oct. 21, 1921, *ibid.*
39 Memorandum 280B by the Committee on Imperial Defence to the Cabinet, Oct. 24, 1921, *ibid.*

treaties of guarantee included with the Treaty of Versailles, which the Senate had failed to consider—the delegates should ask for ratification.[40]

All three of the major naval powers came to Washington with a carefully designed plan to end the naval race; each, of course, hoped to advance its own national interest and restrict that of its competitors. The United States, with an unfinished capital ship construction program that faced, in all probability, further cuts in congressional appropriations, decided to make a bold proposal that would turn that liability into an asset in order to achieve a relative balance of power that favored its position. Great Britain, having weathered many a storm that appeared to threaten its naval dominance, had previously decided to accept a naval parity with the United States; at the conference the British hoped to maintain superiority even though they would talk of equality. Japan wanted to slow up the pace of the race but keep intact its position in the western Pacific and East Asia. Each country was prepared to sacrifice some of its naval strength (actual or potential), and perhaps even a degree of its political influence, to end the naval competition with honor, for none at that time was prepared to push the race. The only problem was to arrive at a balance of naval power that each could accept in the belief that it protected its own particular political interests.

[40] Minutes of Cabinet meeting, Nov. 1, 1921, F. O. A8366/18/45.

V. THE SPEECH

IN THE PRESENT hectic era of diplomacy it may seem odd that the Washington Conference on the Limitation of Armaments was the first major international conference to meet in the capital of the United States. At the time some observers believed it a long overdue recognition of American prestige and influence. The conference served as a belated indication of the American desire to take a serious part in international relations.

Excitement filled America's capital as the Washington Conference delegates arrived. Capital society was agog over the arrival of the many important diplomats. Welcoming committees appeared from everywhere, and there were soirees, receptions, bands, and other attractions.[1] Critics such as former Secretary of State Robert Lansing thought the entertainment provincial —"just as if there was to be a convention of Chiefs of Fire Departments or the annual meeting of the G.A.R." [2] His was a minority view, however, for residents of Washington anticipated history in the making.

Foreign delegations approached the United States from west and east; European members generally had a pleasant trip by liner to New York and thence by train to Washington, whereas the Chinese and Japanese had to make a long voyage across the Pacific. Japan's chief delegates landed in Seattle rather than California, to avoid unpleasant episodes; then they made the long trip across the country by transcontinental railroad, frequently stopping to greet local dignitaries.

[1] "Golf May Aid Success of Parley," Washington *Post*, Oct. 30, 1921.
[2] Lansing to Alexander Kirk, Oct. 1, 1921, Lansing Papers.

Delegates had their first view of Washington from Union Station where they were met by Assistant Secretary of State Robert Woods Bliss, who performed the welcoming honors accompanied by a brass band. Hughes came down to meet important delegates such as Prince Tokugawa Ieyesato of Japan and Premier Aristide Briand of France. In early November 1921 the concourse of Union Station was a colorful sight with bands playing, steam hissing in clouds at the end of the sidings, dignitaries descending from their long coaches, top hats shaking and wobbling as the great men shook hands, and aides hovering nearby carrying portfolios or translating. Behind the police lines surging crowds caught sudden glimpses of "our people" and "the foreigners."

One would expect that individuals from six European and two Asian countries would display marked differences of language and culture, but other differences distinguished most of the delegates. Many men present had either military or legal backgrounds. In attendance were military officers: First Lord of the Admiralty Arthur Lee and Admiral David Beatty of Great Britain, Admiral Ferdinand de Bon of France, Baron Kato Tomasaburo of Japan, together with Generals John J. Pershing and William Mitchell of the United States. But some observers dubbed the meeting the "lawyers' conference": Baron Shidehara Kijuro of Japan, Sir Robert Borden of Canada, Senator Carlo Schanzer of Italy, and all of America's delegates (Hughes, Root, Lodge, and Underwood). At times it seemed that the conference was a struggle for control between the diplomats and military advisers, although any adviser knew that the lawyers would usually have the better of it.

Many of the foreign delegates had lived in the United States. The principal members of the Chinese delegation had graduated from American universities. Lord Balfour, chief delegate of Great Britain, had headed the British mission to the United States in 1917. Lord Lee, a crony of the elder Theodore Roosevelt, had married an American and served as observer for the Royal Navy during the Spanish-American War. Prince Tokugawa had visited the United States in 1910, and his aide Hanihara Masanao had spent years at the Japanese Embassy. And all the countries except Portugal had their regular envoys in Washington as members of their delegations. The nonmilitary delegates were leading statesmen in their respective countries. Only three political leaders were noticeably absent. The Japanese Prime Minister, Hara Takashi, had been shot in Japan on November 4, and was hovering near death. Lloyd George of Great Britain and his Foreign Secretary, Lord Curzon, were not present, and their excuse was the Irish situation, which they felt might cause the fall of their government at any moment.[3] There are indications that Lloyd George, who had lost to Hughes on the preliminary conference dispute, realized that the Secretary of State would not be an easy person to lead; understandably, Lloyd George would have preferred to deal with Harding.[4] Until the last minute he did not say that he was not coming.

Premier Briand, arriving in New York on the *Lafayette*, was the leading European delegate, and the French hoped that their seven-time premier (before his death in 1932 he was to serve four more times) would dominate the conference. Powerful of frame with a shaggy head, heavy brows, and a bushy, downward-curving mustache—all set off by a white choker collar—he was a striking person. Known throughout the world as an orator, he was somewhat a vocal virtuoso, ever ready to improvise on the emotions of an audience. A fighter in debate, he was never more dangerous than when he or his beloved France was in a difficult position. No one could plan on leading Briand easily at the conference; he warned that he would view questions in relation to the security of France.[5]

When Briand returned to France after a short stay at the con-

---

[3] Geddes to Hughes, Sept. 19, 1921, Department of State 500.A41a/15.

[4] Harvey to Hughes, Sept. 28, 1921, Hughes Papers.

[5] Briand had said, "France must remain armed as long as her security has not been assured. . . . If guarantees of security are granted France, she will be among the first nations to enter into a policy of disarmament, for France loathes war and imperialism." Washington *Post*, Oct. 10, 1921.

ference, the polished René Viviani, twice premier, took charge, assisted by Albert Sarraut. Viviani was not an emotional speaker. Although often the obstructionist, he was a capable person.[6] His compatriot Sarraut had been selected because of his knowledge of the Far East, gained as colonial minister and governorgeneral of Indo-China.

To the average American the most familiar foreign delegate was the perennial French Ambassador, Jules Jusserand, who had served in Washington since 1902. Dean of the diplomatic corps, he was perhaps the most popular Frenchman ever to serve in the United States. The French delegation received the benefit not only of Jusserand's experience but also of his friend Philippe Berthelot, Secretary of the Foreign Ministry, who, like a walking archives, knew all the details of past negotiations.

Balfour, of course, headed the British delegation, and he often made decisions without asking permission from London, a fact which seemed to reflect the eagerness of Great Britain to come to an agreement. One American noted that compliments rolled from Balfour's tongue "as collar buttons from a bureau." [7] A believer in Anglo-American amity, he won many friends. Tall and ungainly, with long white hair, he was an impressive man. His habit of jotting comments on the backs of envelopes was duly noted, and the American delegation made sure that he had an ample supply.

The Ambassador, Sir Auckland Geddes, was the secondranking British delegate. A brother of Sir Eric Geddes and a former professor of anatomy at the Royal College of Surgeons in Dublin, Geddes had experience in diplomacy that dated back to 1878 when at the Congress of Berlin he had served as secretary to Lord Salisbury. Lord Lee, Sir Robert Borden, the Prime Minister of Canada from 1911 to 1920, and the Australian Minister of Defense, George F. Pearce, completed the British delegation.

[6] Theodore Roosevelt, Jr., wrote, "He is as impossible a French bourgeois as I have ever seen." Diary of Theodore Roosevelt, Jr., Dec. 13, 1921, Roosevelt Papers.

[7] *Ibid.*, Jan. 14, 1922.

The Japanese who left Yokohama on the *Kashima Naru* reached Washington by rail nearly three weeks later. Prince Tokugawa, president of the House of Peers and last representative of the famous Japanese ruling family, did not take an important part in the conference. Baron Kato, Baron Shidehara, who was Ambassador to the United States, and Hanihara Masanao, Vice-Minister for Foreign Affairs, handled negotiations. Difficulties in communicating with Tokyo handicapped the delegation, for it took several days to send a message and receive an answer. Because the delegation seldom made an independent decision, this delay sometimes held up the negotiations for days.

In practice Kato was the head of the Japanese delegation. He represented the military group which, if it did not control the government, was important in party cabinets of the period. He stood for the older military officers with samurai backgrounds who did not display the eagerness toward war which marked the young officer class. The latter had representation at the conference in the person of Major General Tanaka Kunishige, chief of the intelligence department of the Japanese general staff and a member of the technical staff; Tanaka reported back to Tokyo on his own.

Shidehara, a lawyer, proved a capable negotiator but took his lead from Kato; just prior to the conference Shidehara had said that a naval agreement would be a "comparatively simple matter." [8] Hanihara, the last of the Japanese delegation, had served twelve years in the United States, and in 1924 was to be Ambassador to the United States at the time of the act excluding Japanese from immigration.

Then there was the Chinese delegation—Sao-ke Alfred Sze, Minister to the United States; Chung-hui Wang, Chief Justice of the Supreme Court; and V. K. Wellington Koo, Minister to Britain. They proved to be an exasperating trio. Their demands were not only unrealistic, but quarrels among their subordinates often led to open bickering. At first the American public, tradi-

8 Washington *Post*, Nov. 9, 1922.

tionally friendly to the Chinese, favored their position, but by the end of the conference the Chinese had lost much support.

With the exception of the Italian delegation headed by Senators Carlo Schanzer, Vittorio Rolandi-Ricci, and Luigi Albertini, the other delegations did not have much to do with negotiation.[9] Ever the bridesmaid, Italy was willing to vote on the side of the United States, but the Italians had little in the way of ships or imperial power to bargain with.[10]

Although the Washington Conference opened on November 12, 1921, ceremonies began the previous day at Arlington National Cemetery. Three years before, on November 11, 1918, the German government had accepted the Allied armistice in the railway car at Compiégne. It seemed appropriate to begin a conference on arms limitation by marking the end of a war caused in part by an earlier armament race. The United States took this occasion to bury its Unknown Soldier. The horse-drawn caisson headed a two and one-half hour procession of dignitaries and citizens (including former President Wilson) from the Capitol, where the body had lain in state, to Arlington. In a short address at the cemetery Harding glorified the American fighting man and dwelt on the sacrifices that war demanded. He said that he sought a "rule under which reason and righteousness shall prevail." He took the opportunity to remind delegates that the hopes of the world centered on them. "The commanding voice of a conscious civilization against armed warfare" was calling for a "new and lasting era of peace on earth." [11]

Then came the first session of the naval assemblage, open to those persons with special invitations, the following morning in

[9] A complete list of all the delegates can be found in the Department of State's *Conference on the Limitation of Armament* (Washington, D. C., 1922), 12–41. This is the official printed record of the plenary sessions and committee meetings with parallel French and English texts. Hereinafter cited as *C. L. A.*

[10] Ambassador Rolandi Ricci told Hughes on Nov. 3 that he had "full instructions from his government to see that the delegation supported the American position." Memorandum by Hughes of a conversation with Rolandi-Ricci, Nov. 3, 1921, *FR: 1921*, I, 81.

[11] New York *Times*, Nov. 12, 1921, and a fuller description in the Washington *Post* of the same date.

Continental Hall,[12] the white marble building owned by the Daughters of the American Revolution which stood a few blocks from the White House. (Nearby were the Navy building which contained the delegates' offices and the Pan American building where committee meetings took place. Within easy walking distance was the Department of State building where the American delegation held most of its meetings.) Remodeled for the conference, Continental Hall seated about a thousand persons. The main floor had been planked over to bring it to the height of the stage; the floor was a large platform covered by a dark green carpet. In the center were some tables in the form of a blocked inverted "U" around which sat the thirty-two chief delegates. Flanking the table were chairs for technical advisers and newsmen. In the galleries at the two sides and front were permanent seats for the Cabinet, Supreme Court, Senate, House of Representatives, and diplomatic corps.

The galleries rapidly filled on that morning of November 12. On one side, seated in an overhanging box, were Mrs. Harding and the Vice-President, Calvin Coolidge. Other prominent public figures were in attendance: Oliver Wendell Holmes, William Jennings Bryan, Louis D. Brandeis, Albert Fall, Will Hays were there and took the momentary attention of the crowd. H. G. Wells, acting as a reporter for the occasion, wrote, "It was difficult at first to imagine the conference as anything more than an admirably well managed social occasion." [13] Soon the main delegates arrived around the tables, and the first incident of the conference followed. When the delegates started to take their chairs

---

[12] Continental Hall should not be confused with Constitution Hall at the opposite end of the block. Continental Hall has now been converted into a reading room and library rather than a convention hall.

[13] Herbert G. Wells, *Washington and Riddle of Peace* (New York, 1922), 68. This is a reprint of articles written by Wells at the conference for the Chicago *Tribune*. Among other reporters of note who covered the conference were Ida Tarbell, Mark Sullivan, Stephen Bonsal, H. W. Nevinson, H. Wickham Steed, Stephen Lauzanne, and William Allen White. For a complete list see Department of State, Press Bulletin, Oct. 31, 1921, Washington Conference Papers. Mark Sullivan's *The Great Adventure at Washington* (New York, 1922) contains a brilliant description of the opening session.

at the table, Premier Briand could not find a seat at the top of the inverted blocked "U" arrangement of tables; American and British delegates occupied all the chairs. Briand's displeasure was obvious as he sat down in a chair around the corner of the top table. At the following sessions, Briand, who so desired a seat at the *table d'honneur* (as he called it), took a chair there when Sir Auckland Geddes diplomatically moved.[14]

Only one seat remained empty by 10:30 A.M.—that of Harding. When the President appeared there was a demonstration of shouts and applause led by old friends from the Senate. Wells thought the conference resembled a first-night premiere.[15] A prayer opened the meeting. Secretary of State Hughes then announced, "The President of the United States."

Harding made a set speech which in his earlier days he might have described as a bloviation, but which in his impressive late middle age was appropriate for a grand international meeting. He declared that "the conclusions of this body will have a signal influence on all human progress, on the fortunes of the world." He said the burial of the Unknown Soldier was a symbol of the tragedy of war. He knew "all thoughtful peoples wish for real limitation of armaments and would like war outlawed." Convoking the conference, the United States government was not trying to serve devious ends but to secure peace: "Our hundred millions frankly want less of armament and none of war." The President hoped for "understanding which will emphasize the guarantees of peace, and for commitments to less burdens and a better order which will tranquilize the world." Amid applause he bowed and retired from the conference. Hughes thereupon took the floor as permanent chairman.[16]

At fifty-eight years of age, the Secretary of State indeed looked like a statesman. His tall, straight-backed figure was in contrast to that of Harding. Although Hughes was slightly bald, with a fringe of gray hair, his trimmed mustache and short beard, now

[14] Beerits memorandum, "Calling the Conference," Hughes Papers.
[15] Wells, *Riddle of Peace*, 69–70.
[16] *C. L. A.*, 44–48.

almost gray, made him appear immensely distinguished. His face seemed rigid as he started to address the conference, but the delegates settled back for another ceremonial welcome. Then followed the most notable scene of the entire conference.

As everyone now knows, the Secretary of State was to be anything but perfunctory. It was the most dramatic occasion of Hughes's long life and has gone down in the annals of American diplomacy as the major effort of a great American statesman. Yet he began his address in an ordinary way, and no one except a few American officials suspected what was to be the most startling proposal ever heard in the opening speech of an international meeting. The Secretary noted that the world was looking to the conference to reduce the arms burden—"It is the view of the American government that we should meet that expectation without any unnecessary delay." He proposed that the conference consider limitation of arms immediately, leaving Far Eastern problems to committees. He paused and started an involved description of efforts at disarmament from the time of the first Hague conference, called by the Czar of Russia twenty-three years before. As he droned on, the spectators glanced around contentedly.

Speaking with emphasis, Hughes by this time was saying that "competition in armament must stop." Chin whiskers bristling, the Secretary declared that the time for resolutions was past; it was time for action. There was only one way to stop naval competition and "that is to end it now." Here was a speech, delegates must have thought—but nothing more—in the manner of forceful American diplomacy.

At this moment Hughes moved out of the area of platitudes. He came suddenly to a proposal, a ten-year naval holiday. The President, he said, had authorized him to set out four principles:

(1) That all capital ship building programs, either actual or projected, should be abandoned;
(2) That further reduction should be made through the scrapping of certain of the older ships;

(3) That in general, regard should be had to the existing naval strength of the powers concerned;

(4) That the capital ship tonnage should be used as the measurement of strength for navies and a proportionate allowance of auxiliary craft prescribed.

Everyone in the hall was alert. The rustling in the seats, creaking of chairs, scuffling of shoes, and coughs and sneezes had ended.[17]

Hughes explained that his proposal, if adopted, would make the United States scrap fifteen capital ships under construction and fifteen older battleships—thirty vessels totaling 845,740 tons.[18] Almost everyone thought Hughes's speech was over, but he now proposed, with shocking specificity, that Great Britain stop construction on four battleships and scrap nineteen others—a total of twenty-three ships of 583,375 tons.[19] At this remark Admiral Beatty came forward in his chair and looked at Hughes with astonishment, "in the manner of a bulldog, sleeping on a sunny doorstep, who had been poked in the stomach by the impudent foot of an itinerant soap canvasser seriously lacking in any sense of the most ordinary proprieties or considerations of personal safety." [20] Lord Lee "turned the several colors of the rainbow, and behaved as if he were sitting on hot coals." [21]

The Japanese remained unmoved, for at least Hughes was not tossing their ships on the scrap heap, but their turn came.[22] The Secretary said that the Japanese should not start eight capital ships

[17] Diary of Theodore Roosevelt, Jr., Nov. 12, 1921, Roosevelt Papers.

[18] C. L. A., 50–52. This included fifteen new ships (varying from 3.8 to 86 per cent complete) with a tonnage of 618,000 and fifteen old ships with a tonnage of 227,740.

[19] Ibid., 62. This included four new ships not yet laid down with a tonnage of 172,000 and nineteen old ships with a tonnage of 583,375.

[20] Sullivan, The Great Adventure, 27.

[21] Diary of Theodore Roosevelt, Jr., Nov. 12, 1921, Roosevelt Papers; Wells wrote, "we were a little stunned . . . we wanted to go away and think." Wells, Riddle of Peace, 73. Colonel Charles A'Court Repington noted in his diary, "it took us off our feet. We seemed spellbound." After the War: A Diary (Boston, 1922), 433.

[22] Diary of Theodore Roosevelt, Jr., Nov. 12, 1921, Roosevelt Papers.

and should scrap seventeen others—448,928 tons.[23] If the Japanese did not show emotion, they must have received the American proposal with uncertainty, for it would handicap Japan's offensive power.

One commentator remarked, "Hughes sank in thirty-five minutes more ships than all the admirals of the world have sunk in a cycle of centuries."[24] The American proposal would leave the United States with eighteen capital ships (500,650 tons), Great Britain with twenty-two older, more lightly armed battleships and battle cruisers (604,450 tons), and Japan with ten capital ships (299,700 tons). Replacement tonnage could not be laid down for ten years and would be limited by a total maximum capital tonnage of 500,000 tons for the United States and Great Britain and 300,000 for Japan—that is, a ratio of 10—10—6.[25]

The American Secretary of State became a national hero. Hughes had concluded by remarking that the American proposal could lift the burden of armaments and release enormous sums for the progress of civilization. "Preparation for offensive war will stop now," he concluded.[26] Newspapers headlined the proposal.[27] The speech made a deep impression on all those who heard it. William Allen White later wrote that Hughes's speech was the most dramatic talk he had ever witnessed.[28] Ironically, Joseph P. Tumulty, whose memoirs of Wilson were running serially in the newspapers, had just written that Hughes would never do anything to capture the public imagination.[29] Another and

[23] *C. L. A.*, 62–64. The tonnage of the eight proposed ships was not included; included were seven new vessels with a tonnage of 289,000 and ten old ones with a tonnage of 159,828.

[24] Repington, *After the War*, 432; Hughes, *C. L. A.*, 64, incorrectly said sixty-six ships at 1,878,043. It was either seventy ships with a total tonnage of 1,878,043, or sixty-six ships with a tonnage of 1,706,043. Hughes counts the tonnage but not the ships projected by the British *Hoods*.

[25] The entire American plan as handed to the delegates immediately after Hughes's speech is printed in *C. L. A.*, 78–92. For an original mimeographed copy see First Plenary Session, Washington Conference Papers.

[26] *C. L. A.*, 66.

[27] For a collection of headline stories see the Washington *Post*, Nov. 13, 1921.

[28] *Autobiography* (New York, 1946), 598.

[29] New York *Times*, Nov. 13, 1921.

more important figure of the recent Wilson administration, Lansing, confided to his diary that Wilson should have used Hughes's method at Paris.[30] Senator Borah saw a "splendid beginning." [31] General Pershing was impressed, Justice Holmes thrilled, and Theodore Roosevelt, Jr., thought the speech one of the great documents of American history ("I never felt so much in my life before that a page had been turned in world events").[32]

It remained for Henry Cabot Lodge to sum up the feelings of the American delegation with Bostonian restraint: "We opened our conference yesterday and made some very straight and drastic proposals about disarmament . . . ." [33] Hughes had played his trump card and stolen the lead from his opponents. He clearly won much support within the United States through the dramatic starkness of his proposal. The Secretary's unprecedented opening speech also centered the attention of the world on the Washington Conference, and any delegation that had the courage to combat the American proposals would be forced to do so under intense public scrutiny both in the United States and, more important, back home.

[30] Memorandum by Lansing, "Opening Session of the Washington Conference," Lansing Papers.

[31] Washington *Post*, Nov. 12, 1921.

[32] Nov. 12, 1921, Diary of John J. Pershing, Papers of John J. Pershing (Library of Congress), hereinafter cited as Pershing Papers; Holmes to Hughes, Nov. 13, 1921, Hughes Papers; Roosevelt to Hughes, Nov. 12, 1921, *ibid*.

[33] Lodge to Archibald Collidge, Nov. 14, 1921, Lodge Papers.

VI. THE PACIFIC CONTEST

ONE OF THE REASONS Secretary Hughes's speech had so dramatic an impact on the watching world was that observers were acutely aware of the growing tension and the deepening mutual suspicion between the United States and Japan. Indeed, naval competition between the two nations was becoming so intense that talk of war was widespread. Whatever might come of Hughes's specific proposals—and only long and difficult negotiations over naval ratios in the months ahead would settle that—his speech did much to clear the air, to reassure those who had begun to fear that war was inevitable, by making it clear that national leaders intended to take direct action to prevent or at least to bring under control the causes of war.

Before the involved maneuverings of the delegates over the details of the Five-Power Naval Treaty can be fully understood, one must first understand something of the history of Japanese-American relations in the western Pacific and the Far East. Moreover, one must also understand that the delegates of the two nations were conducting their negotiations in a climate of intense national and racial emotions, evidenced by—and to some extent caused by—popular and widely read books published in both countries, all speculating on the possibility of war in the Pacific. All in all, it was a situation to try the most skilled statesmen.

Japanese-American antagonisms over the future of China and control of the western Pacific reached back into the late nineteenth century when both had demonstrated that their nations were indeed world powers (Japan in the Sino-Japanese War of 1895 and the United States in the Spanish-American War of

1898) capable of influencing events in the Far East. Neither was certain of the intentions of the other, and the United States, especially after the Russo-Japanese War ended in 1905, became increasingly distrustful of and uneasy about Japanese ambitions. For the Japanese, having allied themselves with Great Britain in the Anglo-Japanese Alliance, had thoroughly defeated the Russians and began to display alarming expansive tendencies: Korea was annexed in 1911; Japanese economic interests penetrated farther and farther into Manchuria; German interests in Shantung were taken over in 1914; the Twenty-One Demands were presented to China in 1915; and Japanese troops marched into Siberia in 1919. The American government, which by 1921 had vacillated between a tacit recognition of Japanese ambitions (as in the Taft-Katsura, Root-Takahira, and Lansing-Ishii agreements) and strong protests (as against the Twenty-One Demands), was unsure of how to deal with the Japanese.[1] The United States had not yet backed up its protests with military force, but the American naval program of 1916 and the stationing of a powerful fleet in the Pacific after the World War indicated that perhaps a change might take place.

The Japanese navy, however, had become an important element in the Far East since its easy conquest of Chinese forces in 1895. But it was the decisive and surprising victory over the Russians in 1905 that made the Japanese navy famous; from that time on the size and strength of the Imperial Navy was taken into consideration by the Far Eastern powers. Germany's small naval force in the western Pacific was easily overwhelmed by the Japanese in the early days of World War I; as a result the Japanese not only moved into Shantung but also occupied Germany's Pacific islands which they later received as League of Nations' mandates. These islands, when added to those already in Japanese possession, gave the Japanese a strong position along the ocean routes to Japan, China, and the Philippines. As indi-

[1] See Paul H. Clyde and Burton F. Beers, *The Far East: A History of the Western Impact and the Eastern Response, 1830–1965* (4th ed.; Englewood, N. J., 1966), pp. 274–90, for an excellent survey.

cated previously, the Japanese regarded the American naval program as a direct challenge to their interests and had begun to build their own fleet of capital ships.[2]

The Japanese-American naval race had caused a great deal of journalistic speculation about war. Armchair strategists saw each naval construction program stimulating the other. The fleets had to be ready if war came. Book after book which sold thousands of copies both represented the public's apprehension about war and aroused more apprehension.

Writer after writer predicted trouble. In 1921 the British naval critic, Hector C. Bywater, published *Sea-Power in the Pacific*, a description of the strategic problems such a war would bring to the Japanese and Americans. In the preface to his second edition in 1934 he wrote that "in the winter of 1920–21 the situation in the Far East was so ominous that well-informed observers believed war between the United States and Japan to be only a question of time, and no long time at that." [3] Bywater had predicted that in the event of war the American Asiatic fleet and the Philippines would fall quickly to the Japanese. He was critical of the decision in 1919 which stationed half of American naval strength in the Pacific and half in the Atlantic, and even more biting about the failure to increase the strength of American Pacific bases; he advised the United States to build up the defenses of Guam immediately before the Japanese entrenched themselves in the former German islands.[4]

A former Tsarist general, Nikolai Nikolaevich Golovin, in *The Problem of the Pacific in the Twentieth Century* concluded that rumblings were a sign of an "impending struggle between the yellow and white races" with the former led by the "warlike" Japanese. He counseled that the "only means of averting war with Japan in the twentieth century was for the United States

[2] William R. Braisted, *The United States Navy in the Pacific, 1897–1909* (Austin, 1958), 236–45.

[3] *Sea-Power in the Pacific: A Study of the American-Japanese Naval Problem* (2nd ed.; Boston, 1934), ix.

[4] *Ibid.*, 22, 245, 256, 261.

to evacuate the Philippines and to renounce her interests in Eastern Asia." Since these moves were unlikely, Golovin saw war as inevitable and concluded that naval disarmament would not even delay war, much less prevent it.[5]

Racial speculation appeared in Lothrop Stoddard's *The Rising Tide of Color: Against White World Supremacy* with its emphasis on the population of China and Japan. In time, he predicted, both nations would create a great racial imperialism. Stoddard disliked any white nation that consorted with what he considered the enemy. He could not write a kind word about Great Britain, which had concluded the Anglo-Japanese Alliance, or Bolshevik Russia—"the traitor within the gates, who would betray." The West, he warned, must retreat from East Asia and conserve its strength.[6]

Along a similar line was Sidney Osborne's *The New Japanese Peril*, which took the view that the United States had become isolated as a result of the Versailles Treaty and now stood alone before Japan. He called on the governments of the United States, Great Britain, Germany, and Russia to form a great alliance to save China from Japan. As the leading exponents of democracy and liberal institutions, Americans had a moral obligation to block Japanese moves into China. Osborne warned that unless the Western nations stepped in, they would "once again see an Attila leading his hordes into their capitals and quartering his beasts in the pews of their cathedrals."[7]

A more prominent American writer was Thomas Millard, publisher of *Millard's Review* in Shanghai, who launched a tirade against the Japanese. In the Far East, he reported, Japan stood for militarism and autocracy whereas China was "genuinely democratic." Unless China was relieved of the Japanese pressure, a war involving the Western powers, including America, was "inevitable." He adroitly drew a comparison with Germany before the World War. Both countries were militaristic. It was true, he

5 Copenhagen, 1922, pp. 20, 87, 88.
6 New York, 1921, pp. 30, 203, 221, 233.
7 New York, 1921, pp. 104, 146, 164.

wrote, that there were good reasons for Americans to stay on friendly terms with the Japanese, but "this desire is secondary in importance to maintenance of the independence and integrity of China vis-á-vis Japan." The United States had obligations, responsibilities "to maintain the territorial integrity and administrative autonomy of China." [8] Millard's voice often reached to the Far Eastern division of the Department of State.

Must We Fight Japan was the eye-catching title of a volume published in 1921 by Walter B. Pitkin. To him it was clear that the "government and the people of Japan dislike us." In part he blamed this reaction on the distorted picture the American newspapers and movies presented to the Japanese, and on the comparable ignorance by Americans of things Japanese.[9] His arguments found support in the writings of a retired Japanese army officer, General Sato Kojiro, who rattled his samurai sword in *If Japan and America Fight* by demanding an end to the temporizing and by insisting that war with the North American giant was not to be feared.[10]

But what was the position of the Japanese government? The Japanese not only had to defend their continental interests in East Asia, with which they closely identified their national security and economic prosperity, against potential land threats, but also had to defend their Pacific possessions against the leading sea powers. As James B. Crowley's study has emphasized, Japan became a world power at a time when its naval security "was absolutely dependent on the good will of the British fleet," which was secured by astute statesmanship in 1905.[11] This achievement was followed by the formulation of a "National Defense Policy" whose naval clauses designated the United States as its "sole imag-

---

[8] *Democracy and the Eastern Question* (New York, 1919), 3, 14–15, 17–18, 34, 342; in 1921 Millard predicted a war with Japan at any moment; Jan. 29, 1921, Department of State 711.94/431.

[9] New York, 1921, pp. 6, 8.

[10] Tokyo, 1920, pp. 4–20.

[11] *Japan's Quest for Autonomy: National Security and Foreign Policy* (Princeton, N. J., 1966), 4. The material in this paragraph and the next is based on Crowley's excellent study.

inary enemy" and called for the continuation of parity in capital ships with the United States, which was achieved from 1905 to 1914.[12] But during the World War the United States Navy had greatly expanded and had a large building program on the stocks. Japan, on the basis of the battle of Jutland, decided that parity with the United States was no longer necessary; but, in order to protect its naval security, it needed to have a 10:7 ratio. To maintain such a ratio in the face of the American naval program, however, was expensive, and by 1921 almost half of the Japanese budget went for military expenditures. And if Japan continued to strive for the 10:7 ratio, Great Britain might decide that the Japanese fleet was becoming a threat to New Zealand and Australia. This in turn might just force Great Britain into the arms of the United States with results calamitous to Japanese security. For these reasons, the naval ministry hoped to secure some sort of arrangement with the United States in 1921 that would not bring about an Anglo-American Alliance against Japan and perhaps even retain Japanese naval superiority in the western Pacific.[13]

During the previous two decades a struggle for control of foreign policy and national security had been taking place among the rising parliamentary parties, the military services, and the old extralegal advisory group of Japanese statesmen, the Genrō. The conflicts and alliances among the various groups shifted, as did their goals, but the army in 1911 finally precipitated a crisis which by 1913 led to the beginning of cabinet responsibility to the majority party. Okuma Shigenobu, premier from 1914 to 1916, allied his party with the military services and attempted to gain further control away from the Genrō, who argued that foreign policies were too important to be entrusted to the care of politicians. From 1916 to 1922, it was not the Genrō but a Foreign Policy Deliberative Committee, composed of members

[12] *Ibid.*, 6–7.
[13] *Ibid.*, 25–27.

of the leading political parties, that advised the cabinet on questions of foreign policy and national security. But more party responsibility did not restrain Japanese expansive tendencies, and it became obvious that the Japanese movement into Siberia and the dispute over Shantung and the Pacific islands at the Versailles Conference had aroused the American government. Hara Kei, representing the Seiyūka party, had criticized the government for not paying enough attention to American relations; he succeeded in winning the support of the Genrō, and in 1918 he became premier of Japan. Although he was committed to the territorial acquisitions of previous cabinets and could not easily move away from them, he was willing to make an accommodation with the United States; it was Hara who was premier when Japan accepted the invitation to the Washington Conference.[14] By no means had the Japanese ruling groups given up maintaining and securing a position of political hegemony in Northeast Asia, but there was a strong consensus that it was time for a consolidation, and perhaps the government, faced by a serious naval race, could secure its goals by diplomatic means rather than by war.

When the American military had drawn war plans against Japan and other nations in 1904, a color of the rainbow designated each nation, and orange denoted Japan. In 1913, the conclusion of the Orange Plan was that the Philippines would be the first Japanese objective; defenders, according to the plan, were to hold there for three or four months, until the United States Navy could send reinforcements. A dispute over the location of a strong base in the western Pacific (Guam or the Philippines) clouded the issue, as did promises of independence for the Philippines in Congress. Admiral William S. Sims in 1920 warned that any plan based on retention of Manila was in error, and the Army came to the same conclusion about Guam.[15] It was clear that the Unit-

---

[14] *Ibid.*, 14–22.

[15] Louis Morton, "War Plan Orange: Evolution of Strategy," *World Politics,* XI (Jan. 1959), 221–50. It might be noted that a careful study of public opinion from 1914 to 1917 in a midwestern state, Indiana, observed that "since 1905,

ed States would face serious problems if a war came with Japan in the western Pacific.

Given the fact that there was widespread conviction that real trouble was brewing in the Far East, it was inevitable that after the Secretary's famous speech on November 12, 1921, the delegates at Washington would come under intense public scrutiny. World reaction was overwhelmingly favorable. From London the editorials were enthusiastic. "Never in the history of mankind has the world been nearer its dream of brotherhood." "The World has been shown a way of salvation . . . . its challenge is direct and cannot be avoided." "A noble and dramatic stroke which staggers humanity." From Paris "we wish every success"; "a revolt of human consciences against war." In the United States the address was thought "a master stroke," "a plain business statement," an "exhibition of American horse sense." [16]

But what did the governments and delegations think of a proposal that would scrap forty of their capital ships and prevent construction of others for ten years? Indication of their positions came at the second plenary session on Tuesday, November 15, when Balfour and Kato accepted the American proposal in principle but mentioned modifications. Schanzer and Briand were more restrained; Hughes had rankled both by not mentioning proposals for their nations.[17] Some observers thought the statesmen had accepted Hughes's propositions and that the impossible had become a fact, subject only to putting it in treaty form, but the American delegation recognized that a diplomat who accepts in principle has a great deal more to say.[18] Indeed, on the next day the Japanese naval delegate demanded a higher ratio.

At the first meeting of the Subcommittee of Naval Advisers,

American suspicion of Japan had been mounting until war with her would have been more popular than with any other major country in the world." Cedric Cummins, *Indiana Public Opinion and the World War: 1914–1917* (Indianapolis, 1945), 18.

[16] New York *Times*, Nov. 14, 1921.

[17] *C. L. A.*, 96–110.

[18] New York *Times*, Nov. 16, 1921; General Pershing wrote that the powers "voiced their acceptance in substance of the American programme for the re-

Admiral Kato Hiroharu, under orders from Baron Kato, argued that a ratio of 70 per cent, not the 60 proposed by Hughes, was the lowest the Japanese could accept. The Japanese, then, were stirring in disagreement. Kato also wanted to retain the *Mutsu*, scheduled for scrapping under the American plan; he claimed it was not under construction, as indicated, but was actually completed.[19] If these modifications were allowed, they would certainly strain the spirit if not the principle of the American proposal. The American delegation discussed the question and came to the tentative conclusion that the ratio was not one of importance compared to the principle of no construction beyond existing strength. Hughes at this time surprisingly went so far as to say that he would even accept a 10:8 ratio to preserve the principle, but more reflection changed his mind.[20] From the American Ambassador in Tokyo, Charles B. Warren, came encouraging news: a report that Foreign Minister Uchida had told him the Japanese government had approved the American proposal in general but was leaving the details to Baron Kato. Hughes ordered Warren to use his influence so that the Japanese would not insist on a higher ratio; otherwise there would be naval competition. Warren reiterated the government's desire for an agreement and predicted that Baron Kato would not receive support even though newspapers in Tokyo had mounted a demand for 10:7.[21]

---

duction of naval armament." Diary of John J. Pershing, Nov. 15, 1921, Pershing Papers. Diary of Theodore Roosevelt, Jr., Nov. 15, 1921, Roosevelt Papers; minutes of the American delegation, Nov. 15, 1921, Washington Conference Papers.

[19] A description of the subcommittee meeting was included in a dispatch from Tokyo to the Japanese ambassador in Washington, July 31, 1936, *FR: 1922*, I 69n; Diary of Theodore Roosevelt, Jr., Nov. 29, 1921, Roosevelt Papers.

[20] Minutes of the American delegation, Nov. 16, 1921, Washington Conference Papers.

[21] Telegrams from Warren to Hughes, Nov. 17 and 19, 1921, and telegram from Hughes to Warren, Nov. 19, 1921, *FR: 1922*, I, 61, 64. Baron Kato later said that he had received no definite instructions on the ratio before coming to the conference. Tokyo Embassy to Hughes, translation of Kato's speech before the Imperial Diet on March 15, 1922, Department of State 500.A4b/14. Telegrams from Warren to Hughes, Nov. 23 and 30, 1921, *FR: 1922*, I, 67, 68.

Baron Kato continued to push for more vessels, but Uchida (although he had sent orders on November 22 to support 10:7) recognized the growing opposition not only of the Americans but also the British.[22] Continued declarations in favor of 10:7 could lead to unpopularity in the world press; they might also jeopardize Japanese interests at the conference. Clearly, a demand for a 10:7 ratio was an ideal bargaining device. Kato wanted a 10:7 but if he could not achieve it he would accept a 10:6. At Kato's own suggestion, Uchida telegraphed provisional permission on November 28 to fall back to 10:6 in exchange for a quid pro quo; this was to ask, at the proper moment, of course, for a Pacific islands fortifications agreement.[23] The delegation reported to Uchida on December 1 that Great Britain clearly had decided to support the United States, and the 10:7 ratio demand was not gaining any support from the other delegations; it warned that if Japanese newspapers continued to push for the 10:7 ratio, they would make it very hard for the delegation to accept a 10:6 no matter what the quid pro quo.[24]

Japanese naval representatives under Admiral Kato's direction tried to prove to other conference naval advisers that Japan deserved the higher ratio. The American and Japanese delegations, with the British supporting the former, talked over the definition of existing strength which was the base of the American proposal. American experts headed by Assistant Secretary Roosevelt believed that in measuring existing strength "ships under construction as well as ships in active service must be counted in proportion to the extent of their completion." [25] Japanese experts would not

[22] Telegram from Uchida to the delegation, Nov. 22, 1921, reel MT 312, p. 114.
[23] Telegram from Uchida to the delegation, Nov. 28, 1921, reel MT 313, p. 204. Herbert O. Yardley, *The American Black Chamber* (Indianapolis, 1931), 313, incorrectly translates it as a retreat to 6:5.
[24] Telegram from the delegation to Uchida, Dec. 1, 1921, reel MT 314, p. 072; telegrams from Uchida to the delegation, Dec. 4 and 7, 1921, reel MT 313, pp. 301, 352.
[25] Memorandum by American naval experts, *FR: 1922*, I, 72; Diary of Theodore Roosevelt, Jr., Nov. 21, 1921, Roosevelt Papers; telegram from delegation to Uchida, Dec. 2, 1921, reel MT 317, p. 644.

count ships under construction.[26] The American proposal measured existing strength at a 10:6 ratio. The Japanese claimed it was actually somewhere between 10:6.9 and 10:8.6 The American delegation supported their advisers' figures and refused to accept the Japanese computation as justification for a 10:7 ratio.[27]

While Hughes was putting direct pressure on the Japanese government and delegation, Elihu Root was using indirect pressure. Root's legal adviser, Chandler P. Anderson, arranged a meeting between Root and Fred Kent, an American banker who was on good terms with Japanese financiers Baron Mitsui and Baron Shibusawa Eiichi, both at that time in the United States. Root explained to Kent that the conference would likely break up if Japan did not consent to the naval treaty. He predicted a naval race, possible war, and economic disaster for Japan; there was even the possibility that the United States might lead the nations into an economic blockade. Kent promised to report to the Japanese. He was to explain that newspaper reports of economic consequences to Japan had caused him some concern. Root, of course, hoped Mitsui and Shibusawa would press the Japanese government.[28] The result of the meeting between Kent and the Japanese is, however, uncertain.[29]

It was time for maneuvering. Baron Kato and Balfour had a long and important talk on the naval situation on December 1, in which the Navy Minister told Balfour that Japanese opinion and the government were strongly behind 10:7, and that unless there were good reasons the Japanese could not retreat. Good reasons

[26] Memorandum by Japanese naval experts, Nov. 26, 1921, General Board Papers, Naval History Division, Department of the Navy. British Rear-Admiral Alfred E. M. Chatfield concluded, "it was a matter of national pride and honor rather than logic that is at the bottom of their case." Nov. 30, 1921, F. O. A115/2/45.

[27] Minutes of the American delegation, Nov. 30, 1921, Washington Conference Papers.

[28] Diary of Chandler P. Anderson, Nov. 30, 1921, Papers of Chandler P. Anderson (Library of Congress). Hereinafter cited as Anderson Papers.

[29] Kent reported back to Anderson, but the latter does not indicate in his diary what Kent did or said; Dec. 5, 1921, *ibid.*

number one and two, he said, were an agreement on Pacific fortifications and retention of the *Mutsu*. He implied that the Japanese
would then accept 10:6.[30] Balfour reported the proposal to
Hughes, who agreed to confer with his colleagues and Harding.[31]
Kato, reporting to Tokyo, said Balfour had argued that Japanese
insistence on 10:7 would wreck the conference, and the British,
desirous of world peace, could not support the Japanese demand
for 70 per cent. It was apparent to Kato that it was imperial defense and not world peace that interested Balfour. Faced with
such opposition, the Japanese delegation, pleased with the scrapping of American battleships, had warned that revival of the
naval race was likely.[32]

Finally on December 10 Uchida ordered the delegation to accept the Hughes plan. Because of the persistence of the Americans,
backed by the British, the Foreign Minister saw no alternative.
The Japanese did not want to appear as militarists. But before giving final approval the delegation was instructed to secure the status quo in fortifications, which would reduce the anxiety of the
Japanese public. The delegation was to try to preserve the *Mutsu*
and in its place sacrifice the *Settsu*.[33] With these instructions in
hand, Kato entered the crucial phase of his negotiation with the
Anglo-Americans. Hughes, Balfour, and Kato discussed the two
Japanese proposals through December. Kato argued that he could
not justify scrapping of the *Mutsu*, and Hughes argued that there
was justification enough in the example set by the United States,
which was scrapping more nearly completed ships than Japan.
The Japanese surely could destroy one ship.[34] Hughes again attempted to press Kato through the government in Tokyo, to no
avail because Kato still refused.[35] The Secretary on December 12

[30] Telegram from the delegation to Uchida, Dec. 5, 1921, reel MT 317, p. 731.

[31] Memorandum by Sir Maurice Hankey, secretary to the British delegation,
of a conversation between Hughes and Balfour, Dec. 1, 1921, *FR: 1922*, I, 74.

[32] Telegram from delegation to Uchida, Dec. 2, 1921, reel MT 317, p. 644.

[33] Telegram from Uchida to the delegation, Dec. 10, 1921, reel MT 313, p. 420.

[34] Memorandum by Hankey of a conversation between Hughes, Kato, and
Balfour, Dec. 2, 1921, *FR: 1922*, I, 80.

[35] Telegram from Hughes to Warren, Dec. 3, 1921, *ibid.*, 84; Diary of Theodore Roosevelt, Jr., Dec. 12, 1921, Roosevelt Papers.

asked the naval experts to consult on revising tonnage estimates and shuffling the scrapping arrangements so that the *Mutsu* could be retained. Preservation of the 10:6 ratio was the basic instruction under which the experts were to proceed.[36]

Theodore Roosevelt, Jr., acting on Hughes's suggestion, presented a revised plan in which the United States would scrap two of its oldest dreadnoughts and complete two of the battleships under construction if the Japanese retained the *Mutsu* (35,000 tons) and scrapped the *Settsu* (21,400 tons). American total tonnage would rise to 525,000 tons, Japan's to 313,300, but the number of ships scrapped and retained would remain as in the original plan. The 10—10—6 ratio was intact.[37]

As for the ten-year naval holiday, the British delegation—unknown to the Americans—was divided. Admiral Beatty had convinced his colleagues that a slow replacement of obsolete capital ships was preferable to an orgy of building at the end of the period. He worried about the unpreparedness of British shipyards after ten years without work. Beatty also wanted to apply the 10—10—6 to numbers of ships rather than tonnage and to have an active status for two-thirds of the remaining capital ships, with reserve status for the others. Borden of Canada and George Pearce of Australia disagreed.[38] Back in London the Committee on Imperial Defence and Lloyd George decided to support the ten-year holiday. Churchill thought the American proposal fair, but suggested a ship-by-ship replacement by each nation at the end of the treaty. The Committee supported Beatty's other propos-

[36] Memorandum by Hankey of a conversation between Kato, Hughes, and Balfour, Dec. 12, 1921, *FR: 1922*, I, 97. Hughes received a letter from an American Legion commander in New York City which said, "Must the delegates of our government bargain with the delegates of Japan? . . . Why not tell them to reduce their fleet to a basis of 5—5—3, if they refuse, why not blow up their fleet?" Letter to Hughes, Dec. 2, 1921, Washington Conference Papers.

[37] Minutes of the American delegation, Dec. 13, 1921, *ibid.*; Diary of Theodore Roosevelt, Jr., Dec. 13, 1921, Roosevelt Papers. Increase in tonnage would result since the uncompleted ships were larger than those scrapped.

[38] Telegram from Balfour to Curzon, Nov. 13, 1921, F. O. A8447/18/45; memoranda by Borden and Pearce, Nov. 14, 1921, Cabinet 30/1B; Roskill, *Naval Policy*, 312–19.

als.[39] Lloyd George, stressing economy, approved the holiday and kept to this opinion despite appeals from Beatty and Balfour.[40] The split within the British delegation, and between Balfour and London, was kept quiet.

Balfour, eventually surrendering to orders, then attacked on another front. He argued that his government would have to build two ships if the Japanese retained the *Mutsu* and the United States increased its fleet. Obviously, a sort of escalator had appeared. The British wished to construct two battleships approximately 50,000 tons apiece, 15,000 tons more than the maximum set for battleships by the American proposal. Such a plan would upset the computations of the American plan which gave Great Britain twenty-two capital ships to America's eighteen; addition of the two largest ships in the world would change the relative situation in Great Britain's favor since American calculations had given the British more vessels because of age and smaller size.[41] To the amazement of Roosevelt, Root at this time suggested that England receive a far greater tonnage than the United States. Roosevelt noted that Hughes pushed Root's proposal aside, "as if unworthy of notice." [42] Hughes, supported by Kato, resisted the British proposal; and Balfour, acting without instruction from London, thereupon compromised and agreed to building two new 35,000-ton ships, and scrapping of four older capital ships to make up for the difference in tonnage.[43] Thus, the 10—10—6 (or 5—

[39] Minutes of the 149th meeting of the Committee of Imperial Defence, Nov. 14, 1921, Cabinet 2–3/6; telegram from Curzon to Balfour, Nov. 18, 1921, F. O. A8589/18/45.

[40] Telegram from Balfour to Curzon, Nov. 17, 1921, F. O. A8585/18/45; telegrams from Curzon to Balfour, Dec. 1 and Dec. 9, 1921, F. O. A8863/18/45 and F. O. A9204/18/45.

[41] Memorandum by Hankey of a conversation between Kato, Hughes, and Balfour, Dec. 13, 1921, *FR: 1922*, I, 103. Balfour had been given orders in Curzon to Balfour, Dec. 1, 1921, F. O. A8863/18/45; see also Admiralty Staff report, Dec. 14, 1921, Admiralty 116/2149.

[42] Diary of Theodore Roosevelt, Jr., Dec. 15, 1921, Roosevelt Papers.

[43] Memoranda by Hankey of conversations between Kato, Hughes, and Balfour, Dec. 14 and 15, *FR: 1922*, I, 113, 125; Balfour explained himself to Curzon in a telegram, Dec. 15, 1921, F. O. A9338/18/45.

5—3) ratio was preserved but with the addition of 25,000 tons to the American and British totals, and 13,600 to Japan's.

With the signing of the Five-Power Naval Treaty a substantial portion of the American naval proposal was accepted by Great Britain and Japan. But several points must be noted. First, parity with Great Britain in capital ships was not secured at the Washington Conference, for the British maintained a superior number of capital ships; this superiority continued throughout the 1920's. Second, the United States did not scrap all fifteen of its unfinished capital ships; only eleven were scrapped since the United States received permission to finish two of them and turn two others (as will be noted in Chapter Eight) into aircraft carriers. The American sacrifice was considerably less than originally proposed. Third, thus there was no ten-year naval holiday since under the terms of the treaty itself both the United States and Great Britain built capital ships, as indeed did Japan and France. But the race was certainly changed from a fast gallop to a slow trot. One could argue, however, that three major hallmarks of the proposal—the scrapping of the American construction program, the 5: 5 ratio between the United States and Great Britain, and the ten-year naval holiday—existed in theory but certainly not in reality.

The naval situation in the western Pacific became primarily a defensive one for both the United States and Japan. Restricting capital ships, the chief offensive weapon of the era, prevented either power from easily attacking the other, and it certainly stopped the talk of war between the two nations, relieving, at least temporarily, potentially dangerous tensions. In fact, Japan, deprived of the support of the Anglo-Japanese Alliance, began an era of cooperation with the Anglo-American powers and attempted to adhere to the Washington Conference treaties in the hope of best protecting both the empire and Japan's hard-won position on the Asian mainland. The end of the naval race in capital ships made this new situation possible.

VII. PACIFIC FORTIFICATIONS

ACQUISITION OF PACIFIC ISLANDS by the United States and Japan had taken place simultaneously over a span of years. American expansion had started slowly, with the addition of the Aleutians in 1867 as part of the Alaskan purchase and annexation of Midway in that same year; then the explosion of the Spanish-American War in 1898 extended sovereignty over Guam, Wake, the Philippines, and Hawaii. Within five years Samoa was brought within the American empire. The Japanese had acquired the Kurile Islands in 1875, annexed the Bonins the next year, and then added Formosa, the Pescadores, and Ryukyus in 1895 as a result of the Sino-Japanese War. After Japan defeated the Russians in 1905, Southern Sakhalin became part of the Japanese empire. Both powers had thus expanded into the Pacific at approximately the same time, but whereas American expansion had ended in 1903, the Japanese received the Carolines, Marshalls, and Marianas as mandates under the Versailles Treaty of 1919. The two nations by 1921 faced each other from their island outposts, each watching the other's possessions.

The proposal of Baron Kato that the United States halt construction of fortifications in its Pacific islands was not easy to meet. In previous years proposals by congressional committees that the government reinforce the fortifications on Guam and the Philippines had raised much apprehension in Japan. The Japanese construed strong American naval bases on the doorstep of Japan as a hostile act, designed to cut their lines of communication. Captain Mahan had written, "Guam held securely, with a navy superior to that of Japan, threatens every Japanese interest from Dalny and Korea to Nagasaki and Yokohama." [1]

Japanese participation in the World War had brought about a drastic change in the strategic position of American posts in the western Pacific. At the Paris Peace Conference the Japanese had received as mandates the former German islands—Marshalls, Carolines, and Marianas. The Japanese thus occupied positions virtually surrounding the Philippines and Guam. While the League mandate specified nonfortification, in the event of war the Japanese government surely would ignore the letter of the law. American posts were isolated. Even had the American government spent millions to build western Pacific naval bases, whether it could hold those posts in the event of war was at least questionable. In a highly interesting memorandum the Naval Advisory Committee had concluded:

> The military importance attached to our holdings in Guam and the Philippines has already been vastly discounted by the strategic position which Japan has already obtained in the ex-German mandated islands; so much has this military importance, once so prominent, been affected, that in the minds of some of the naval men it is now open to question whether the military importance of our holdings in the Far East have not become entirely subordinated to other greater needs. [2]

A British naval expert, Stephen Roskill, has argued that the "truth was that the Wilson administration had virtually surrendered to Japan the dominance of the central and western Pacific" when it did not block the Japanese acquisition of the mandates. [3] Any island the Japanese did not further fortify was a strategic assistance to the United States; Captain Dudley Knox, for ex-

[1] Quoted in a memorandum by George Blakeslee, "The Islands of the Pacific Ocean," n.d., Washington Conference Papers; the London *Daily News* said that "war between the United States and Japan is almost certain to take place in 1923 unless the United States agrees not to fortify Guam." *Ibid.*

[2] Memorandum by American naval advisers, "Reasons why it might be advisable for technical naval advisors to be present at the discussion of Far Eastern problems," n.d., General Board Papers, Naval History Division, Department of the Navy.

[3] Roskill, *Naval Policy*, 88–89.

ample, believed that the Pescadores were more of a threat to the Philippines than were the Philippines to Japan.[4]

In preparing materials for the American delegation before the conference, the General Board had recommended no discussion of naval bases in the Pacific; if bases did appear as the subject of negotiation, the delegates were to reject all proposals.[5] The General Board was willing to sacrifice ships if necessary, but not naval bases. A War Department memorandum also had stated that "the outcome of a war waged by America against Japan is at least doubtful so long as Guam and the Hawaiian islands are not developed into first class naval bases." [6] A postwar mission to Japan by General Leonard Wood and W. Cameron Forbes reported that Japan coveted the Philippines and recommended an increase in Pacific island fortifications.[7]

Hughes knew that military opinion was "strongly against" any proposal on the islands. But there were other considerations. The special adviser to the Department of State on Far Eastern affairs, Professor George H. Blakeslee of Clark University, pointed out that the Pacific islands were a cause of naval expansion and encouraged mistrust between the United States and Japan. He suggested either neutralizing possessions in the Pacific or making an agreement not to fortify further these islands for ten years. This plan, he predicted, would remove the mistrust, preserve the status quo, and make it difficult for either power to attack the other. The chief of the Far Eastern division of the Department, John Van Antwerp MacMurray, concurred but advised techni-

[4] Dudley W. Knox, *The Eclipse of American Sea Power* (New York, 1922), 51.

[5] Report of the General Board of the Navy, "Naval Bases," Oct. 20, 1921; "Ex-German Islands in the Pacific," Oct. 22, 1921; and "Ex-German Islands," Oct. 27, 1921, General Board Reports, Washington Conference Papers. The General Board wanted the United States to either neutralize or even take over the mandated islands; how, it did not say.

[6] Memorandum by B. H. Wells to the Chief of Staff, Sept. 22, 1921, Department of State Papers, 43–93, No. 277.

[7] Forbes to Harding, Nov. 10, 1921, Harding Papers.

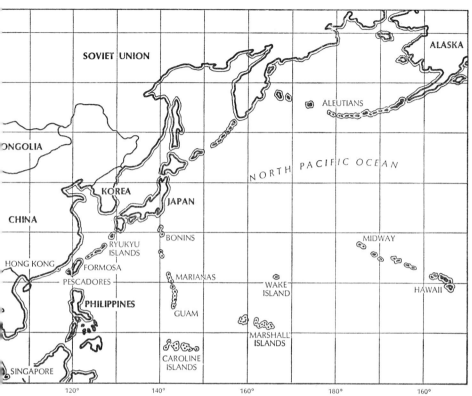

THE NORTH PACIFIC

cal consultation with naval advisers to discuss the naval problems created.[8]

Before the conference the Japanese had given much thought to fortification. All evidence indicates that they planned to discuss it at the first opportunity.[9] The Japanese military had drawn up two proposals. The first called for the Americans to abolish fortifications in Hawaii, the Philippines, and Guam; the British were to follow suit at Singapore and Hong Kong; the Japanese, to do

[8] Memorandum by George Blakeslee, "The Pacific Islands in Relation to Limitation of Armament," n.d., Department of State 500.A41a/103; letter from Mac-Murray to Hughes and Root, Oct. 26, 1921, Department of State 500.A46/26.

[9] A convenient listing of Japanese public statements can be found in Blakeslee, "The Islands of the Pacific Ocean," Department of State Papers.

the same in the Bonin, Oshima (Loochoo or Ryukyu) Islands, and Formosa. In the event of a partial abolition the United States would be asked to include Guam and the Philippines or Hawaii, the British only Hong Kong, and the Japanese would include the Bonins, or Oshima or Formosa; a second partial alternative was to include Guam, Hawaii, Hong Kong, Ogasawara, and Oshima. The Japanese military clearly preferred abolition although they were willing to accept a status quo.[10]

Kato in conversation with Balfour on December 1 had mentioned the outline of the first alternative, so he later reported to Uchida. The British Foreign Office record of the talk makes no mention of the Bonins and substitutes the Pescadores, whereas Kato's record now in the Japanese archives mentions both the Bonins and Pescadores.[11] The Japanese delegate regarded his proposal as tentative, mentioning islands but not intending to include all in the final agreement.[12] Balfour and Hughes were both to misunderstand this point, and perhaps the Japanese translator was in part to blame for the confusion. Balfour talked to Hughes about the Japanese proposal and the Secretary of State displayed reluctance; he then made a quick suggestion. On his own Hughes suggested that if either the United States or Japan wished to fortify an island, that nation might give notice to the opposing party, which then should have the right to cancel the whole naval agreement. This was rather a strange *démarche* and indicates that Hughes had not given serious thought to the problem. When Balfour pointed out that this would leave the British in a bad spot and introduce instability for other nations, Hughes promised to

[10] Instructions to Tanaka, "Lists of Alternative Plans for the Abolition of Pacific Fortifications," n.d. (but obviously preconference), reel 131, p. 49031 of Japanese Army and Navy Archives. For more detailed references see John Young, comp., *Checklist of Microfilm Reproductions of Selected Archives of the Japanese Army, Navy, and Other Government Agencies, 1868–1945* (Washington, D. C., 1959).
[11] Telegram from Balfour to Curzon, Dec. 1, 1921, F. O. A8939/18/45; see also letter from Hankey to Hughes, Jan. 17, 1921, *FR: 1922*, I, 247; telegram from Kato to Uchida, Dec. 27, 1921, reel MT 318, pp. 1627–35.
[12] *Ibid.*

discuss the problem with Harding and the American delegation.[13]

After talking with Harding about the Japanese proposal on Pacific fortifications, the Secretary reported to the delegation that the President approved such a course if the result would be adoption of the American naval proposal. Any island agreement would not prevent the United States from enlarging the fortifications in Hawaii, which were part of the defense of the American mainland.[14] At a previous meeting of the delegation Root had asked if there were any possibility of Congressional authorization of funds to continue the naval program and build bases in the Pacific. Senators Lodge and Underwood both felt no hesitation in making the agreement pertaining to Guam and the Philippines "since Congress would never consent to spend the vast sums required in adequately fortifying these islands." Root agreed.[15]

Hughes later wrote that the prospect of making Guam a strong base against Japan was "nothing but a picture of the imagination." Congress never had authorized the funds, and even if it did "the challenge would have been taken up [by Japan] and the issue forced before it would have been possible to develop it into a base of any great military value." [16]

With Harding's approval, that of both senators, and the knowledge that in all probability Congress would not vote funds to fortify the islands, the Secretary told Kato that he was willing to consider a fortification proposal but made a distinction between offensive and defensive bases and then excluded Hawaii. Hughes also wanted the addition of France, Britain, and the Netherlands as signatories to any agreement. Hughes put a special price for any American concession on bases: the United States could not

13 Telegram from Balfour to Curzon, Dec. 1, 1921, F. O. A8939/18/45; minutes of the British Empire Delegation, Dec. 1, 1921, Papers of Robert Borden (Public Archives of Canada—Ontario).

14 Minutes of the American Delegation meeting, Dec. 1, 1921, Washington Conference Papers.

15 Hughes to the Sprouts, Aug. 5, 1940, as quoted in Sprout and Sprout, *Toward A New Order*, 175; Jessup, *Root*, II, 449; Beerits memorandum, "Five-Power Treaty," Huges Papers.

16 Hughes to Secretary of War Weeks, April 11, 1922, Department of State 500.A4/425.

consider the Japanese proposal "except as part of the acceptance by Baron Kato to a general agreement which would also embrace the proposed quadruple entente in the Pacific [for which, see below], as well as the proposals of the American delegation on the limitation of armaments." [17]

Kato asked time to cable the Foreign Office for instructions, and General Tanaka, reporting directly to the Army Ministry, telegraphed that if the Japanese government accepted the 60 per cent ratio it must have a fortifications agreement to save face. He did not want to include France and the Netherlands but circumstances at Washington might make it impossible to protest. The delegation agreed with Tanaka's position; too many countries might cause a more complicated agreement.[18]

When Uchida on December 10 sent the order to give in on the 10:7 ratio, he had sent instructions to put through an agreement maintaining fortifications at the status quo. If the American delegates wanted to include other nations as signatories, Uchida had no objection. He approved exclusion of the mainland of Japan as well as Hawaii. Final consent to the naval treaty awaited a fortifications agreement.[19]

Hughes entered into further discussion with Kato and Balfour on December 12, after the Secretary had received a report from the American Ambassador in Tokyo that in the minds of the Japanese the fortification issue was the key to the whole situation.[20]

17 See Chapter IX for the Four-Power Treaty. Diary of Theodore Roosevelt, Jr., Dec. 21, 1921, Roosevelt Papers; memorandum by Hankey of a conversation between Kato, Hughes, and Balfour, Dec. 2, 1921, *FR: 1922*, I, 75–83.

18 Telegram from Tanaka to Army Minister, Dec. 5, 1921, reel 131, pp. 49565–68, Army and Navy Archives; telegram from delegation to Uchida, Dec. 8, 1921, reel MT 317, pp. 857–58.

19 Telegram from Uchida to the delegation, Dec. 10, 1921, reel MT 313, pp. 420–22.

20 Telegram from Warren to Hughes, Dec. 3, 1921, *FR: 1922*, I, 83. American naval intelligence in Tokyo had written Hughes that the key to the Japanese position at Washington would be "prevention of the fortification of Guam and the dismantling of defenses at the Panama Canal, Philippine Islands, and Hawaii"; General Board Papers, Naval History Division, Department of the Navy. M. K. Mochizuki, a member of the Japanese parliament who had come to the conference, said, "You should destroy your fortifications in Hawaii, the Philippines and Guam, while we in turn should raze ours in Formosa, and other island ap-

Kato said the Japanese would accept the 10–10–6 ratio if there would be agreement on fortification. Hughes replied that he must exclude Hawaii but that the United States government was willing to enter an agreement preserving the fortification status quo in the Pacific.[21] Three days later Kato, Balfour, and Hughes announced that they had reached an agreement in a press announcement based on a Japanese draft; they agreed to maintain the status quo on fortifications and naval bases in the Pacific region except for Hawaii, New Zealand, Australia, and "the islands comprising Japan proper, or, of course, to the coasts of the United States and Canada."[22]

The Japanese government and delegates began to attempt to clarify among themselves just what "Japan proper" meant, a wise decision, for Hughes unbeknown to them was awaiting their definition before he made a counterproposal. Uchida asked for definition of the Japanese islands, and Kato replied that the delegation had not yet given a clear statement.[23] Tanaka and Kato on January 9 agreed they would prefer not to specify, but it appeared that the Americans and British wanted a list.[24]

The Americans and British were drawing up proposals that did

---

proaches to Japan. If that is impossible, let us at least stop where we are. God did not make the Pacific to be disturbed by conflict, but to be a 'holy water.' " Blakeslee, "Islands of the Pacific," 95.

21 Memorandum by Hankey of a conversation between Kato, Hughes, and Balfour, Dec. 12, 1921, *FR: 1922*, I, 90–99; telegram from Kato to Uchida, Dec. 14, 1921, reel MT 317, pp. 1238–50.

22 Press statement issued Dec. 15, 1921, *FR: 1922*, I, 127–30.

23 Memorandum, "Treaty for Abolition of Pacific Fortifications and Islands to be Placed Outside of its Application," Dec. 17, 1921, reel MT 314, pp. 552–59; telegram from Uchida to the delegation, Dec. 22, 1921, reel MT 313, pp. 561–62; telegram from Kato to Uchida, Dec. 27, 1921, reel MT 318, pp. 1627–35.

24 On December 12, however, Kato had written, "I will start a proposal to stabilize the fortifications of the Philippines and Guam, according to the U. S. Ambassador's suggestion, and try to avoid touching on the fortifications of the Japanese islands. If the U. S. does not accept it, and Britain and France insist on stabilizing the fortifications on Taiwan, Ogasawara, and Amami islands, I will have as my alternate plan, the U. S. stabilize the fortifications on the Philippines and Guam and in return I will offer to stabilize the fortifications of Keetung, Hoko Islands (Pescadore group), and Ogasawara. I intend to throw in the Amami islands if necessary." Telegram from Kato to Uchida, Dec. 12, 1921, reel MT 317, pp. 1073–77.

not name islands but included them within exact longitude and latitude. The first American draft included most of the western Pacific. This was refined to include west of 180°E and north of the equator, to a line of 30°N latitude just south of Japan's home islands.[25] Such definition left the British free to act in their possessions south of the equator; in fact, it was so favorable that their naval section later suggested almost the same position in a neat parallelogram on January 3 (with the exception of drawing a line at 110°E and including everything west to 180°E).[26] Both countries desired the Japanese to include as many islands as possible, other than Formosa and the Pescadores.[27]

At a meeting of the conference's drafting committee on January 7 each nation presented its wording of the fortifications agreement, using as a basis the understanding of December 15. The British proposed 110°-180°E, but said nothing about Japan proper; the American draft abandoned latitude and longitude but did limit the statement of December 15; the Japanese draft referred to the broader Pacific and did not attempt to define Japan proper.[28] Lord Lee assailed the Japanese for not specifically including the Bonins and Ryukyus. Kato argued they were part of Japan proper and that the British were attempting to limit the broad Pacific.[29] Lee continued to argue and the whole problem went to Hughes, Balfour, and Kato on January 10. Roosevelt called on Kato before the meeting and attempted without success to get him to support the British proposal.[30]

Uchida sent instructions from Tokyo to Kato that now was the

[25] Five-power draft, Dec. 20, 1921, Chandler P. Anderson Papers; proposed Article 19, by naval advisers, Jan. 1, 1922, General Board Papers, Naval History Division, Department of the Navy; five-power draft, Jan. 3, 1922, Chandler P. Anderson Papers.

[26] Five-power draft, Jan. 3, 1922, Borden Papers.

[27] Memorandum by Undersecretary Fletcher to Hughes, Jan. 5, 1922, Hughes Papers.

[28] Drafts of Article 19, Jan. 9, 1922, Borden Papers; Diary of Theodore Roosevelt, Jr., Jan. 7, 1922, Roosevelt Papers; drafts of Article 19 in telegram from delegation to Uchida, Jan. 13, 1922, reel MT 318, pp. 2221-29.

[29] Telegram from the delegation to Uchida, Jan. 13, 1922, reel MT 318, pp. 2182-93.

[30] *Ibid.*, 2194-2202.

The official United States delegation to the Disarmament Conference posed with Basil Miles, secretary of the delegation, for this first photograph. Left to right: Elihu Root, Oscar Underwood, Charles Evans Hughes, Henry Cabot Lodge, and Miles. —*Wide World photos.*

Shown above is the after deck of the *USS Michigan* dismantled for sale. —*U. S. Bureau of Ships photo no. 13728 in the National Archives.*

time to define Japan proper. The Foreign Minister interpreted it to mean inclusion of the Bonins and Ryukyus; these islands were not under the status quo agreement; included were the areas of Formosa and the Pescadores.[31] The Japanese delegates privately were willing to suspend fortifications in the Bonin and Ryukyu islands but could not make an open agreement because they feared hostile public reaction at home.[32]

Warned of these Japanese difficulties, Hughes did not offer a text for Article 19 but on January 10 yielded the floor for suggestions. Repeating to Hughes and Balfour his instructions from Tokyo, Kato argued for the December 15 statement. Both said that they did not understand the Japanese purpose in accepting such a vague and imperfect document. Kato said that he was willing to name the islands in a separate agreement, but both Hughes and Balfour refused to go along with that proposal and asked for a statement within Article 19.[33]

Prepared for just such an impasse, Balfour now produced a map on which the British delegation had marked a parallelogram of latitudes and longitudes enclosing the Pacific islands. It would cover all islands between the equator and 30°N, and between the meridians of 110° (including French Indo-China) and 180°E. This proposal had the virtue of not naming the islands but including them. Kato argued that the original proposal had covered the entire Pacific and the British proposal did not. Such a plan would have left the British free to continue their fortifications south of the equator, especially at Singapore where the British Admiralty had just decided to create a major naval base. Hughes accepted the British proposal, but Kato declined, explaining that again he had to ask for instructions.[34]

[31] Telegram from Uchida to the delegation, Jan. 10, 1922, reel MT 313, pp. 704–707.

[32] Diary of Theodore Roosevelt, Jr., Jan. 8, 1922, Roosevelt Papers.

[33] Memorandum by Hankey of a conversation between Kato, Hughes, Balfour, Sarraut, and Schanzer, Jan. 10, 1922, *FR: 1922*, I, 150–55; Kato and Tanaka had agreed on tactics the day before. Telegram from Tanaka to Army Minister, Jan. 9, 1922, reel 131, pp. 49575–76, Army and Navy Archives.

[34] Memorandum by Hankey of a conversation between Kato, Hughes, Balfour,

Kato sent a long cable to Tokyo. He accused the American and British delegates of untrustworthiness but regretfully advised Uchida to accept the British proposal now supported by the Americans. Failure to get a fortification agreement, he advised, would not hurt the Anglo-Saxon powers but would be disadvantageous for Japan. He had gotten the Americans to agree to a stabilization of the Philippines and Guam, worth more than any fortifications Japan might have to include.[35] Tanaka, at the same time, cabled the Army Minister and suggested that the lines run at 29°N and 150°E; this would include more islands in Japan proper but would have placed the American island of Wake (19°N, 167°E) outside the exclusion area.[36] The internal Japanese discussion continued. Uchida instructed the delegation to reject the British-American proposal. The Foreign Minister lectured the delegation on the virtues of standing firm. The 10:6 ratio would make enough trouble.[37] In a spirited exchange Kato argued that the naval treaty was in jeopardy and that there was not a chance that Hughes or Balfour would accept voluntary stabilization. The Navy Minister preferred to sign the pact and weather domestic political storms.[38] Uchida said the American-British plan was acceptable as a question of national defense, but there now was a much more serious problem of national morale. Too many Japanese would conclude that naval limitation was not an attempt to secure peace, but a plot against Japan. The fate of the government was at stake since the Privy Council would oppose ratification. Hughes was to be told that Japan would reject the treaties unless

---

Sarraut, and Schanzer, Jan. 10, 1922, *FR: 1922*, I, 155; when Balfour had previously approached Kato on the British proposal, Kato had told him he could not support it. Yamato Ichihashi, *The Washington Conference and After* (Stanford, Cal., 1928), 86; Roskill, *Naval Policy*, 347.

[35] Telegram from Kato to Uchida, Jan. 12, 1922, reel MT 318, pp. 2212–13.

[36] Telegram from Tanaka to the Army Minister, Jan. 11, 1922, reel 131, pp. 49577–78, Army and Navy Archives.

[37] Telegrams from Uchida to the delegation, Jan. 12, 1922, reel MT 313, pp. 720–22, 732–42; Kato told his interpreter, Yamato Ichihashi, that the instructions were a deliberate attempt to embarrass him by his enemies in the Japanese government and put him in an impossible position. Ichihashi, *The Washington Conference*, 84–85.

[38] Telegram from Kato to Uchida, Jan. 13, 1922, reel MT 318, pp. 2260–65.

the fortification issue was settled on the basis of Japanese inter-pretations.[39]

Kato, who had told Hughes he had advised acceptance of the British-American proposal, now had to say he had received in-structions to reject the offer. He did ask for more time.[40] The delegates appealed to Uchida. They would have to refuse to sign the naval treaty, a step with serious consequences. If they had to carry out Uchida's orders, they then would resign.[41] The appeal moved Uchida to approve inclusion of the Bonins and Amami-Oshima but to make clear that the unnamed islands were part of the Japanese homeland.[42] Kato then presented Hughes with a new draft which named—for the first time—the Bonins, Pescadores, Formosa, and Amami-Oshima as the islands that would be covered in the nonfortifications clause.[43]

Hughes wanted to make sure that the United States had the right to fortify Alaska and the Panama Canal; he also wanted to include Okinawa-Oshima (a second group within the Ryukyus) and exclude Samoa (the latter because the United States might someday want to build a naval base to guard the approaches to the canal). Approval came quickly from Balfour on the first two points, but the Britisher argued that a base in Samoa could become a threat to British islands in the South Pacific. Later that afternoon the American delegation advised Balfour it would withdraw the Samoa proposal but would insist on including Okinawa and a clause to extend the status quo to any islands the three powers might acquire in the future.[44]

---

[39] Telegram from Uchida to the delegation, Jan. 15, 1922, reel MT 313, pp. 766–73.

[40] Diary of Theodore Roosevelt, Jr., Jan. 14, 1922, Roosevelt Papers; memoran-dum of Kato's conversation with Hughes, Jan. 16, 1922, *FR: 1922*, I, 245–46.

[41] Telegram from the delegation to Uchida, Jan. 18, 1922, reel MT 318, pp. 2395–2404.

[42] Telegram from Uchida to the delegation, Jan. 21, 1922, reel MT 313, pp. 820–22.

[43] Telegram from Kato to Uchida, Jan. 22, 1922, reel MT 314, pp. 396–400.

[44] Memorandum of Hughes-Balfour talk, Jan. 23, 1922, F. O. A796/2/45; Amami-Oshima is closer to the home islands than Okinawa, thus making it hard to include the former and leave out the latter.

A new American draft which included the above two points then went back to the Japanese.[45] An appeal from the delegation to Uchida, along with concurring recommendations from Shidehara and Hanihara, pointed out that Japanese intransigence was prolonging the conference; the latter two statesmen advised immediate acceptance of the American draft including all the Ryukyus—Okinawa if necessary.[46]

Final instructions came on January 28 from Uchida, who approved the inclusion of Okinawa. He also offered to include the Kuriles if the American delegates would add the Aleutians.[47] This was accepted. The British reintroduced the 110° line, thus excluding Singapore, and the American draft became the basis of the final statement of Article 19 of the Five-Power Naval Treaty.[48]

The long controversy over Pacific island fortification was over, and, predictably, each of the powers had attempted to protect its own major bases while restricting the offensive power of the others. Each to a large degree succeeded. The American delegation, of the three delegations perhaps the least aware of the value of its Pacific outposts, chose not to challenge the Japanese position in the western Pacific and East Asia by building advanced bases in the Philippines or Guam. Without an active and interventionist Far Eastern policy, backed by a large, powerful navy, the United States government decided that it was wiser to stem the Japanese ambitions by diplomatic rather than forceful means. Even if one grants, under the prevailing circumstances, the wisdom of the decision, it is nonetheless true that the value of the bases as a bar-

---

[45] Telegram from delegation to Uchida, Jan. 25, 1922, includes a copy of the American draft. Reel MT 319, p. 2889.

[46] Telegram from Shidehara to Uchida, Jan. 25, 1922, reel MT 314, pp. 433–40; telegram from Hanihara to Uchida, Jan. 25, 1922, reel MT 319, pp. 2899–901; telegram from Shidehara to Uchida, Jan. 26, 1922, *ibid.*, pp. 2962–65.

[47] Telegram from Uchida to the delegation, Jan. 28, 1922, reel MT 313, pp. 843–45; Diary of Theodore Roosevelt, Jr., Jan. 29, 1922, Roosevelt Papers; see also entries of Jan. 23, 30.

[48] *FR: 1922*, I, 252–53; Roosevelt concluded that it left the United States "in a slightly better position than Japan . . . . we trade certain fortifications which we never would have completed, for fortifications which they would have unquestionably completed." Diary of Theodore Roosevelt, Jr., Jan. 29, 1922, Roosevelt Papers.

gaining device with the Japanese was far greater than the American government realized. The Japanese should have paid a higher price in capital ships (say, a 10:5 ratio) than they actually did, although the abandonment of the Anglo-Japanese Alliance (in the Four-Power Treaty) in part compensated for the American failure to demand a lower ratio from the Japanese in return for the fortification agreement. On the important fortification issue the American delegation, in a clear mistake, had not weighed its alternatives and let others lead when it should have presented a positive proposal.

VIII. ARMS LIMITATION

AT THE CONFERENCE the French government had one objective—
to acquire further security against the Germans. The French plan
at Washington was to improve, if possible, their position against a
renewal of German aggression by a treaty of assistance from the
British and Americans; in return the French would agree to a reduction in land armaments. As long as the German threat existed,
in fact or fancy, the French did not intend to disarm. Lloyd
George and Wilson at Paris in 1919 had offered Premier Georges
Clemenceau guarantee treaties as a condition for giving up the
idea of a buffer state along the Rhine. Then the British and Americans had reneged, the British refusing to go ahead because the
Americans had not ratified their treaty. Thereafter the French
looked to their military might as security against Germany and
would not consider a reduction in land forces unless they could
obtain a diplomatic equivalent.

At the Washington Conference the French apparently hoped
for a deadlock between the United States and Great Britain, after
which the Anglo-Americans would turn to discussion of land armaments whereupon the French would state their position and ask
for a new guarantee.[1] To the amazement of the French, who
could not believe that the British would give up supremacy of
the seas without a struggle, the British from the outset of the conference accepted the principle of approximate naval parity with
the Americans. Excluded from the preliminary negotiations by
Hughes until the three major naval powers reached agreement,

---

[1] Sprout and Sprout, *Toward A New Order*, 182.

the French were at first spectators. Hughes in the early days did not even mention land armament. In a talk with Geddes and Balfour, Briand stated that he believed the Washington Conference had come about as a result of domestic politics. It was, he believed, largely an attempt by the Harding administration to lighten taxes and acquire prestige. Hughes would settle for some measure of disarmament and "something" for China. For the rest, he concluded, the Secretary of State "knew nothing of Europe or its difficulties and less if possible of the Far East." In a private memorandum on the talk, Balfour wrote that it appeared to the French that their "Lafayette credit" was running out.[2]

Suspecting that the French position was not clear, Briand felt compelled to plead France's case at the third plenary session on November 21, and there described a Germany that overnight could mobilize millions of soldiers. Behind Germany loomed Bolshevist Russia. Only the French Army protected western Europe. The French government had already reduced its army by a third and planned more reduction. Briand said that if only someone would say, "We see this danger as well as you do; we appreciate it, we are going to share it with you; we offer you every means of security that you can desire," the French government would not hesitate to take another position on land disarmament.[3]

This speech reverberated in London where Curzon charged privately, and then openly, that Briand did not have a leg to stand on. Curzon guessed that the Premier was hoping for an American guarantee. If the French at the conference did not take some measure to reduce either their sea or land power, Curzon concluded, the British government could not afford to diminish its own strength, nor could any of the powers reduce naval forces.[4] Curzon's statements preceded those of Lloyd George, who advised Balfour that Europe, led by France, was again becoming an armed camp. He also felt that the military statistics used by Briand were

[2] Report of a Briand conversation with Geddes and Balfour, Nov. 20, 1921, F. O. A8616/18/45.

[3] *C. L. A.*, 116–34.

[4] Telegram from Curzon to Balfour, Nov. 22, 1921, F. O. A8711/18/45; *ibid.*, Nov. 23, 1921, F. O. A8711/18/45; New York *Times*, Nov. 25, 1921.

"faked and disingenuous" and that the French were in no danger of a German invasion.[5]

Although there are some indications that the Japanese might have been willing to limit their army and that the British government was willing again to sign the guarantee treaty with the French if the American delegates would follow suit, the conference never seriously discussed land armaments again.[6] Briand's proposal was clear, but the price still seemed high. At no time did the American government appear willing to guarantee French security. Nor would a reduction of the American Army have brought a large saving or evoked as dramatic a response as naval limitation.[7] There were no compelling political or economic reasons for anyone but the French delegates to push the issue, and their bargaining power at a conference on naval affairs and Far Eastern issues was small indeed.

What was the French position on naval affairs? The French nation had found itself in a poor situation in the early years of the twentieth century. Unwilling to participate in the Anglo-German naval race, the French had taken refuge behind a system of alliances and a large land force. During the World War, in part because of the large naval contribution of Britain, the French had spent their national substance on building an army. After the war the French government continued to do this. The French Navy of 1921, approximately the size of the navy of 1914, was fourth-

[5] Telegram from Lloyd George to Balfour, Nov. 27, 1921, F. O. A8763/18/45.

[6] Japanese Foreign Ministry memorandum, Sept. 1921, reel MT 306, p. 185; minutes of British Cabinet meeting, Nov. 1, 1921, F. O. A8366/18/45.

[7] Hughes pointed out that the United States had already reduced its army to less than 160,000. *C. L. A.*, 114. The War Plans division of the War Department suggested to General Pershing on November 29 that a one-third cut in armies be proposed. This would have given France 400,000 troops and the other four nations 200,000 men apiece (the United States had authorized 280,000 but had only 150,000). This plan was never suggested at the conference. Memorandum by the War Plans division, "Limitation of Land Armaments," Pershing Papers. The Land Armaments Subcommittee of the Advisory Committee, also headed by Pershing, recommended that the private manufacture of munitions be regulated, chemical warfare be abolished, and an international code of civilized warfare be drawn up; it noted that the size of armies was a question of domestic politics. This also was never read at the conference. Land Armaments Subcommittee report by Pershing, Nov. 20, 1921, Washington Conference Papers.

rate.[8] The French delegates came to the Washington Conference without a plan. Two weeks before the conference Assistant Secretary Roosevelt had discussed the situation with the French Ambassador, who stated that since France had no navy he did not believe the French Navy could be discussed.[9]

Hughes had left the French and Italians out of his opening naval proposal, and Jusserand had protested the omission, but to no avail.[10] The French delegation began to suspect the Americans and British of collusion. One can argue that Hughes could have eliminated this suspicion if he had invited the French to the early discussions. But if the French had attended and raised objections, the delegates of the United States, Britain, and Japan would not have reached their provisional agreement so easily.

At this time there was, of course, considerable French antagonism toward the British. Interests had clashed at Paris on almost every European issue. A belief that the British had deserted the French after the war was an assumption of French diplomacy. A sensational report in the New York *Times* of November 22, 1921, disclosed that the French intended to ask for equality with Japan in capital ships (300,000 tons).[11] The American delegation was not surprised.[12] In its preconference planning the first proposal of the General Board had given France and Italy the same capital tonnage as Japan (600,000 tons). This figure went down to 410-000 tons in the modified plan also rejected by the American dele-

---

[8] According to the figures of the General Board presented to Hughes, France had a total tonnage (all ships) of 372,064 in 1921. The United States had 1,074,701 tons, Great Britain had 1,753,539 tons, and Japan had 566,924 tons. General Board Report, "Limitation of Armaments," Sept. 17, 1921, Washington Conference Papers; see also a memorandum by the French Delegation, "Naval Situation in France," Nov. 19, 1921, Naval History Division, Department of the Navy.

[9] Diary of Theodore Roosevelt, Jr., Oct. 27, 1921, Roosevelt Papers.

[10] Memorandum by Hughes of a conversation with Jusserand, Dec. 5, 1921, *FR: 1922*, I, 86–88.

[11] New York *Times*, Nov. 22, 1921.

[12] Just before the conference, Vice-Admiral Grasset, Chief of Staff of the French Navy, had told American Vice-Admiral Albert Parker Niblack that France wanted a navy equal to Japan's and that this was the only condition on which a limitation of armaments could be made. Naval Intelligence Report to the General Board, Oct. 3, 1921, Navy Department Records (National Archives).

gation.[13] The decision by the delegates to adopt the "stop-now" proposal did not provide quotas for France and Italy; discussion of their tonnage was to come later, and considering the well-known sensitivity of the two Latin nations with regard to national honor, it was a mistake not to attempt to pacify them as soon as possible by an exchange of views.[14] After the opening session the American naval advisers had tried to work out acceptable quotas. The Italians did not care what their tonnage figure was as long as they secured parity with France.[15] The British wanted a navy equal to that of the Japanese and French combined.[16] When the British accepted the 5:3 ratio with the Japanese, the problem was to persuade the French to accept 200,000 tons or less.

American naval advisers finally produced a figure of 175,000 tons.[17] The French would not have to scrap ships, nor would the Italians. Hughes realized that the French might not assent to the American proposal and sent Assistant Secretary Roosevelt to see Admiral de Bon.[18] The latter refused to state a figure. Jusserand quizzed Hughes on the possible French quota; the Secretary replied by asking carefully what the Ambassador thought a fair figure; Jusserand said the French were waiting for the American proposal. When Hughes suggested 175,000 tons, Jusserand said nothing.[19]

[13] Report of the General Board of the Navy, "Capital Ships," Oct. 3, 1921, Washington Conference Papers. It should be noted that the American naval officers questioned by the General Board generally gave France a naval ratio equal to that of Japan. General Board Papers, Naval History Division, Department of the Navy, "Modified Plan," Oct. 14, 1921, *ibid.*

[14] Roosevelt claimed he had been against leaving France and Italy out but was overruled by the American delegation. Diary of Theodore Roosevelt, Jr., Nov. 3, 1921, Roosevelt Papers.

[15] Memorandum by Undersecretary of State Fletcher of a conversation with Senator Albertini, Nov. 23, 1921, *FR: 1922*, I, 65–66; telegram from Balfour to Curzon, Nov. 23, 1921, F. O. A8738/18/45.

[16] Diary of Theodore Roosevelt, Jr., Nov. 16, 1921, Roosevelt Papers.

[17] *Ibid.*, Nov. 19, 1921. See also memorandum by American naval adviser, "A Proposal for the Limitation of Armaments of France and Italy," n.d., in General Board Papers, Naval History Division, Department of the Navy.

[18] Beerits memorandum, "Treaty for the Limitation of Armaments," Hughes Papers.

[19] *Ibid.* See also memorandum by Hughes of a conversation with Jusserand, Dec. 16, 1921, *FR: 1922*, I, 134.

The British government and delegation were uneasy, for discussion by the Admiralty had resulted in a recommendation to retain enough pre-Jutland ships to deal with France and Italy.[20] Although the two nations were of minor importance in the American naval equation, to the British they were of more importance. Balfour and Beatty cornered Hughes on November 18, but the Secretary declined to raise the subject until the Japanese negotiations were finished. According to Balfour, he did promise that the number of British capital ships would depend on what happened to the French and Italian allotments.[21] The Committee of Imperial Defence decided not to oppose French and Italian navies equal to the navy of Japan. This would give the two nations a 12:10 combined ratio over Britain, which the committee was willing to accept if it could include in the treaty a limit on the number of submarines for the two nations.[22]

Balfour was not sure he wanted to press the French too hard on capital ships. As he understood his instructions, he was

> to induce the French to agree to a very small battle fleet so as to leave us free to accept American proposals without modification. Having persuaded them to deprive themselves of their form of naval defence I am to persuade them that they really require no submarines because a war between France and England is unthinkable. This task being successfully accomplished, I am then to ask them to reduce the number of their aircraft seeing that we cannot sleep securely in our beds lest in a war with France, London should be burned to the ground.[23]

The whole problem of the French quota came out when on December 15, the day of the final provisional naval agreement between the United States, Britain, and Japan, the Secretary presented the American proposals to the French and Italians. The

---

[20] Committee of Imperial Defence, "The Washington Conference," Oct. 5, 1921, Cabinet 21/218.

[21] Telegram from Balfour to Curzon, Nov. 18, 1921, F. O. A8604/18/45.

[22] Committee of Imperial Defence Minutes, Nov. 26, 1921, Cabinet 2–3/6.

[23] Telegram from Balfour to the Foreign Office, Nov. 24, 1921, F. O. A8763/18/45.

latter accepted, but Sarraut and Jusserand demanded 350,000 tons of capital ships.[24]

The American position was that the French would not have to scrap ships while the British, Americans, and Japanese were scrapping more vessels than there were in the entire French fleet. If the French were to reduce in the same proportion as the three major powers, they would retain 136,500 tons. The French possessed 164,500 tons of capital ships in 1921. On the basis of the existing ratio Britain and the United States were 6:1 over France, but if the French would accept the 175,000 tons of the American proposal the ratio would drop to 3:1, the same as in 1914; the French would not suffer for wartime inactivity, having not only the opportunity to economize by not building more ships, but also the possibility of doubling their relative strength. The French could probably never finance a building program of their own to match that of the three great powers. The fruits of victory without the toils of labor were available, but the French insisted on increasing their navy.[25]

"Steeped in a profound French calm," the French delegates regarded the American argument as unthinkable.[26] The French delegates, Sarraut said, had been out of the early naval negotiations and never had the opportunity to explain. Other powers, not France, had settled on the 175,000-ton quota. Admiral de Bon rejected the tonnage unit and demanded ten ships. "France was willing to limit her armament, but she did not propose to disappear from the seas," he rejoined as he promised that the 175,000-ton

[24] Minutes of the American delegation, Dec. 16, 1921, Washington Conference Papers.

[25] Department of State, *Conference on the Limitation of Armaments: Sub-committees* (Washington, D. C., 1922), 24–32. Hereinafter cited as *Subcommittees*. According to a chart by the American naval advisers, if the American proposals were accepted, the United States would retain 62 per cent of its capital ship strength, Great Britain 56 per cent, Japan 75 per cent, and France and Italy 100 per cent. General Board Papers, Naval History Division, Department of the Navy.

[26] Diary of Theodore Roosevelt, Jr., Dec. 15, 1922, Roosevelt Papers. The Assistant Secretary next day wrote, "I have seen many an excited Frenchman in my day, but never such emotional, wild-eyed individuals as those . . ."; *ibid.*, Dec. 16, 1921.

limit "would never be accepted by his country." Sarraut and de Bon described a France which had sacrificed for the Allies during the World War, now being crucified on the altar of naval limitation.[27]

The American naval advisers thought the British should make a *beau geste* and allow the French 210,000 tons.[28] William R. Castle, Jr., head of the Division of Western European affairs, wrote Hughes that the French might have planned on the American delegation's leaving them out of the naval settlement. To remain a fourth-rate naval power would put the French at a disadvantage with the British and perhaps the Germans. Castle believed the American delegation could not force the French to give in, but he predicted that the French might withdraw from their position if provision were made for a future conference at the time the French planned to increase their navy.[29]

Hughes did not want to delay to some indefinite future. He knew he could gain the support of the British and Japanese who could not reduce their fleets until the French agreed. Aware that neither Sarraut nor Jusserand could speak with authority, he prepared a cable to Briand which the American delegation debated on December 16. Underwood thought the proposal a little too forceful in one or two sentences, but Lodge and Root believed that Hughes had to state candidly the American position; he must point out that criticism of France and perhaps failure of the conference would result if the French refused. Hughes favored, and polished, the more forceful statement.[30] That night he informed Jusserand of his intention and in his capacity as chairman of the conference sent the cable to Briand. He described the provisional agreement between the delegates of the United States, Britain, and Japan and indicated that the Italians were willing to accept the suggested quota. "You will observe that the attitude of France will determine the success or failure of these efforts to reduce . . .

[27] *Subcommittees*, 12, 34, 48.
[28] Diary of Theodore Roosevelt, Jr., Dec. 20, 1921, Roosevelt Papers.
[29] Memorandum by Castle to Hughes, Dec. 16, 1921, Department of State 500.A41a/108.
[30] Diary of Henry Cabot Lodge, Dec. 16, 1921, Lodge Papers.

naval armament." The American government was willing to help the French rebuild their economic life, but Americans would be disappointed if the French government was spending millions on naval construction.[31]

Hughes now considered a proposal to leave the French out of the naval treaty in the event Briand refused to cooperate, and at the meeting of December 17 the American delegation decided that if the French did not change their position the delegation would propose a Four-Power Naval Treaty with a clause that if any other power built beyond 175,000 tons a new conference would give the signatory powers an opportunity to increase their tonnage.[32] Hughes planned to make sure that the responsibility for the failure of the Washington Conference would accrue to the French.[33]

From Ambassador Myron Herrick in Paris came word that Briand would arrive at an agreement with Hughes on capital ships. Briand also told Herrick that the French Chambers would never agree to great reductions in auxiliary ships.[34] Ambassador Harvey saw the French premier in London and said that Briand "accepts your proposal in regard to capital ships and has instructed the French delegation to inform you to this effect." [35] That same day, December 19, Jusserand presented Briand's message to Hughes expressing the desire of the French to make the conference a success. "With regard to the tonnage of capital ships," he wrote, "I have instructed our delegates in the sense you desire." But with regard to defensive ships of the auxiliary type, he believed it impossible to take a correponding reduction.[36]

It soon became evident that there were two different interpretations of Briand's letter. Hughes concluded it was unconditional

[31] Hughes to Herrick in Paris, Dec. 16, 1921, *FR: 1922*, I, 130–33.

[32] Minutes of the American delegation, Dec. 17, 1921, Washington Conference Papers. See also the diary of Henry Cabot Lodge, Dec. 16, 1921, Lodge Papers.

[33] Copy of Hughes letter to Chandler P. Anderson, Dec. 18, 1921, Hughes Papers.

[34] Telegram from Herrick to Hughes, Dec. 17, 1921, *FR: 1922*, I, 134.

[35] Telegram from Harvey to Hughes, Dec. 18, 1921 (received Dec. 19), *ibid.*, 136.

[36] Briand to Hughes, Dec. 19, 1921, *ibid.*, 135–36.

acceptance of the 175,000-ton quota for capital ships and had nothing to do with the rest of the treaty. The French delegation believed Briand had accepted the 175,000-ton quota, but with the condition that the French government have as many auxiliary ships and submarines as it wished.[37] The French delegation finally accepted the 175,000-ton quota, but not before a heated debate that led to the omission of any limits on submarines and auxiliary ships.

At the opening session of the conference Hughes had not mentioned quotas for submarines. Copies of the American proposal explaining all quotas in detail, given the delegates after the speech, assigned 90,000 tons to the United States and Britain, with Japan receiving 54,000 tons. There was nothing about the French and Italian limits.[38]

In planning for the conference the General Board had made two suggestions regarding submarines. First, the United States and Britain were to have 100,000 tons with 60,000 tons for Japan, France, and Italy. In the final plan a further reduction was made, as noted above, and the proposals for the French and Italian quotas were omitted. Still, Hughes was recommending, as suggested by the General Board, an increase in existing tonnage of the leading powers, not a reduction.[39]

Second, the General Board with reference to the agenda topic, "Rules for the control of new agencies of warfare," recommended clear rules for submarine warfare. The submarine was a legitimate weapon of war as long as it conformed to the same maritime rules as a surface raider. The Board believed submarines effective

[37] Memorandum of a conversation between Hughes, de Bon, Jusserand, and Sarraut, Dec. 19, 1921, *ibid.*, 137–41.

[38] C. L. A., 86. In 1921 the United States had 50,522 tons of submarines with 51,577 tons more to be built by 1928; Great Britain had 82,464 tons and none projected; Japan had 12,990 tons and 26,868 tons projected; France had 28,826 tons and 14,024 tons projected; Italy had 20,108 tons with 120 tons projected. General Board Report, "Limitation of Armaments," Sept. 17, 1921, Washington Conference Papers.

[39] General Board Reports, "Auxiliary Combatant Ships," Oct. 8, 1921; "Submarines," Nov. 15, 1921; and "Minimum of Submarine Tonnage," Dec. 12, 1921, Washington Conference Papers.

against warships as well as merchant ships; Britain during the war had lost forty-one warships, including five battleships and five cruisers, to submarines as well as 7,648,223 tons of merchant ships.[40]

The delegation thought the submarine quotas were too high. While recognizing that the submarine, even if legally used, was a cheap defensive weapon, Balfour said that the British would prefer to abolish it. He believed abolition was probably impossible or undesirable; he did think it possible to ban large submarines that were suitable only for offensive purposes.[41] For the British government had clear memories of the submarine campaigns of the World War. The Germans had destroyed so many merchant ships that the British were in danger of running out of supplies. They were fortunate in that many people, filled with antisubmarine propaganda during the World War, felt horrified at the inhuman aspects of submarine warfare, and an offer to abolish submarines would find support throughout the world.[42]

But the French, who had only 28,826 tons of submarines, intended to build more, for if France could not have capital ships an equalizer lay at hand in the form of 90,000 tons of submarines, a cheaply produced weapon that could perhaps force the British to support French policies or at least not oppose them in European politics. The French had used the threat of building torpedo boats in the 1880's with some success. Perhaps it would work again.

This dispute left the American delegates right in the middle. As the controversy increased the American delegation was unsure of what to do. They did forestall a request for 45,000 tons by the Netherlands.[43] When Roosevelt's group had proposed 175,000 tons of capital ships for France, they had set up a submarine limit

40 *Ibid.*; Admiralty Report, n.d., Admiralty 116–2149 (Public Record Office).

41 Lord Lee on December 5 told Roosevelt that the British knew abolition was impossible; the most that they hoped for was reduction. Diary of Theodore Roosevelt, Jr., Dec. 5, 1921, Roosevelt Papers.

42 William Howard Taft, for example, wrote that he sympathized "deeply" with the British proposal to abolish submarines. Taft to Mrs. Bellamy Storer, Dec. 26, 1921, Taft Papers.

43 Diary of Theodore Roosevelt, Jr., Dec. 7, 1921, Roosevelt Papers.

On January 30, 1924, this shot was taken of the dismantling of the
USS Delaware. —*U. S. Bureau of Ships photo no. 19–N–13726 in
the National Archives.*

Pictured here is the Disarmament Conference in progress on November 21, 1921. —*U. S. Signal Corps photo no. 111–SC–80631 in the National Archives.*

of 31,500 tons.[44] This proposal got lost in the shuffle. American naval advisers continued to stress submarines even though they regarded the capital ship as the mainstay of the fleet. The American people apparently favored abolition. In preparation was a report by the American Advisory Committee. Until its publication the delegates hoped to keep the controversy in committee where a compromise might develop.

The British delegation thereupon decided to bring the submarine debate out in the open. Lord Lee, setting out the inconsistency of the American proposal, trained the guns of the British Admiralty on the French submarines in the Committee on Limitation of Armament meeting of December 22. Lord Lee pointed out that it was ironic that a conference for limiting naval armament should allow submarine tonnage to increase: "what was required was not merely restrictions on submarines, but their total and final abolition." Lee said that the submarine used against a fleet was almost powerless; it was against merchant ships that the submarine had its greatest success. German submarines took the lives of 22,000 noncombatants and destroyed over a billion dollars in ships. He admitted the danger of the submarine to England and asked if the French could risk disaster to their only certain ally if the conditions of 1914 reappeared. If England could rid the sea of submarine murderers, it would scrap its submarine fleet, then the largest in the world at 82,464 tons.[45]

While the argument raged, Hughes presented the submarine report by a subgroup of the Advisory Committee headed by Rear Admiral William Rodgers. The report adopted the position of the General Board, approving the use of submarines against warships and merchant vessels but asking for limited submarine warfare since submarines were to act under the same rules as surface raid-

[44] American Naval Advisers, "A Proposal for the Limitation of Armaments for France and Italy," General Board Papers, Naval History Division, Department of the Navy.

[45] *C. L. A.*, 474–86; Hughes tried to head off open discussion by appealing to the British not to bring it up. Telegram from Balfour to Curzon, Dec. 18, 1921, F. O. A9501/18/45.

ers.[46] The report caused a sensation. Most people believed that President Harding had appointed the Advisory Committee to sample public opinion for the use of the American delegation as a sort of referendum diplomacy at the conference. But the submarine report, dated December 1, did not mention the overwhelming public disapproval of submarine warfare. No work of the Advisory Committee met with as much public disapproval as this report.[47] The Advisory Committee thought it detected an attempt by antisubmarine supporters to deluge the committee with protests. By January 4 it had received 422,488 expressions for abolition of submarines and 4,149 for retention (albeit with restrictions on their use).[48] But the committee had chosen to consider matters of national policy which, it felt, the average man did not understand. The committee had evidently decided that it represented a cross section of the American population and needed no poll to confirm its opinions.

As the argument wore on, Hughes proposed that the Americans (who had 50,522 tons) and British reduce their quotas to 80,000 tons and the French, Italians (20,108 tons in existence), and Japanese (12,990 tons) retain their present tonnages.[49] All chance of limitation of submarines disappeared on December 26 when Sarraut announced that the Cabinet and Supreme Council of National Defence had decided on quotas for the French Navy of 175,000 tons of capital ships. But they could not go "below that of 330,000 tons for auxiliary craft and 90,000 tons for submarines, without impairing the vital interests of the country and of its colonies and the safety of their naval life." [50]

Defeated on its attempt to apply submarine quotas, the Ameri-

[46] *C. L. A.*, 490–502.

[47] Hoag, *Preface to Preparedness*, 134.

[48] Letter of the American Advisory Committee, Jan. 4, 1922, Washington Conference Papers; Advisory Committee reports, Jan. 15, 1922, *ibid.*; an additional report of Jan. 6, 1922, recognized the public demand but still argued against abolition. Hughes chose to think that the committee represented public opinion. Diary of Theodore Roosevelt, Jr., Dec. 24, 1921, Roosevelt Papers.

[49] *C. L. A.*, 556. Roosevelt claimed that he originated the proposal; diary of Theodore Roosevelt, Jr., Dec. 24, 1921, Roosevelt Papers.

[50] *C. L. A.*, 570.

can delegation then turned to a series of resolutions, offered by Elihu Root, defining and restricting submarines.[51] Submarines had to visit and search in the same way as surface raiders. If the submarine commander attacked a ship without following the traditional procedures, it was to be considered an act of piracy; the commander was then subject to trial as a pirate. Root told Admiral Rodgers that to meet the expectations of the public it was "necessary to do something striking and vivid that could be easily grasped by the man in the street." [52] Delegates from France, Italy, and Japan tried to send the measure to a committee of jurists. Root, battle-scarred from many a legal skirmish and interested in the measure, recognized the motion as an attempt to destroy the issue.

The crux of the controversy over the so-called Root resolutions lay in the interpretation or definition of an armed merchantman. If it were legal to arm a merchant ship, supporters of submarine warfare could hardly agree to visit and search because a surfaced submarine was highly vulnerable. A disguised armed merchantman could blow a submarine out of the water. Controversy went on for days over whether the term "merchant ship" in the Root resolutions included armed merchant ships; a decision was made on January 6 when Schanzer interpreted it to mean unarmed vessels. Lord Lee rose from his seat and said that Schanzer surely was not suggesting they change international law by taking away the right of a merchant ship to defend itself. After some debate the delegates, including the American group, supported the British, leaving the rules unchanged.[53]

Nine nations eventually signed a treaty which included the Root resolutions in almost their original form, a serious breach at

[51] Minutes of the American delegation, Dec. 20, 1921, Washington Conference Papers.

[52] Notation in a letter from Rodgers to Root, Dec. 31, 1921, General Board Papers, Naval History Division, Department of the Navy; Roosevelt did not think the resolutions amounted to much. Diary of Theodore Roosevelt, Jr., Dec. 29, 1921, Roosevelt Papers.

[53] *C. L. A.*, 610, 690–712; Lodge and Root opposed prohibiting the arming of merchant ships. Diary of Chandler P. Anderson, Jan. 2, 1922, Anderson Papers; Roskill, *Naval Policy*, 326.

an arms conference since submarines were not reduced nor limited. It was also, without doubt, the best arrangement the American delegation believed it could make.[54] The treaty provisions on submarine commanders' being tried for an act of piracy if they did not follow the traditional rules of visit and search would probably have collapsed under wartime pressures; in fact, in 1926 the British Admiralty said that "if in a naval war we were forced to sink merchant ships as a reprisal we might have to suspend or abrogate this provision . . . ."[55] The French later refused to ratify, and the treaty died without a wartime test of its weak provisions.

Along with the defeat on submarines and closely connected to it came a setback on the limitation of auxiliary ships—cruisers and destroyers. The original American plan envisioned each nation's having a tonnage of auxiliaries in the same ratio as capital ships.[56] Faced with the French threat to build submarines, the British delegation said that under no circumstances could it agree to limit auxiliary ships—the main weapon against submarines; Lloyd George had sent instructions to Balfour on this point. If the French government insisted on 90,000 tons of submarines, which could only be aimed at England, the island empire reserved the right to build auxiliaries.[57]

Hughes and the American delegation long had recognized that French demands on submarines would lead to the abandonment of any limits on auxiliary ships; because quantitative limits were not possible Hughes proposed a limit of 10,000 tons and 8-inch guns.[58] The conference adopted the proposal with little debate, for they did not want nations building auxiliaries that

[54] Diary of Theodore Roosevelt, Jr., Jan. 4, 1922, Roosevelt Papers.
[55] As quoted in Roskill, *Naval Policy*, 328.
[56] *C. L. A.*, 66.
[57] Lloyd George to Balfour, Nov. 27, 1921, F. O. A8763/18/45. See also letter from Lloyd George to Balfour quoted by Winston Churchill, May 15, 1930, in the debate over the London Naval Conference. House of Commons, *Parliamentary Debates*, vol. 238, p. 2103; Roskill, *Naval Policy*, 324–26.
[58] Diary of Theodore Roosevelt, Jr., Dec. 19, 1921, Roosevelt Papers; diary of Henry Cabot Lodge, Dec. 20, 1921, Lodge Papers. Roskill, *Naval Policy*, 325, claims that the 10,000-ton figure came out of the British Naval Section at the conference.

were capital ships in everything but name.[59] Some naval experts have claimed that this decision had important strategic effects in World War II, but neither the American nor British experts gave the question great consideration at the time.[60]

How did that major naval weapon of World War II—the aircraft carrier—fare at the Washington Conference? The original American proposal[61] had suggested 80,000 tons for the United States and Britain, with 48,000 tons for Japan (quotas for the French and Italians were again left open). This was a cut in the figures of 100,000 tons and 60,000 tons recommended by the General Board in preconference planning.[62] The American proposal retained ships under construction but forbade new construction for seventeen years. No carrier could mount guns over 8 inches.[63]

The decision on aircraft carriers was put off until December 30, when Hughes restated the American proposal, adding 28,000 tons of carriers for Italy and France. He recommended a limit of 27,000 tons on individual carriers.[64] All governments expressed dissatisfaction with these quotas. Vice-Admiral Ferdinando Acton of Italy wanted another carrier (for a 54,000-ton total); in case his country's single carrier was damaged or sunk then another would still be left. Lord Lee desired five carriers (135,000 tons) for fleet action and antisubmarine warfare. According to de Bon, the French wished 60,000 tons of carriers. Admiral Kato asked for three carriers of the maximum size, totaling 81,000 tons. Hughes accepted all the modifications and noted that a 5—5—3 ratio would result if the United States took 135,000 tons and

[59] *C. L. A.*, 590–94, 666.

[60] Sprout and Sprout, *Toward A New Order*, 206–16; Roskill, *Naval Policy*, 326.

[61] *C.L.A.*, 88.

[62] The United States had 19,360 tons of aircraft carriers, built or building, in 1921, while Great Britain had 87,190 tons, Japan had 21,000 tons, France had 24,230 tons, and Italy had none. Report of the General Board, "Auxiliary Combatant Ships," Oct. 8, 1921, Washington Conference Papers.

[63] *C. L. A.*, 88–90.

[64] The proposal originated with Hughes and Roosevelt. Longhand draft, Dec. 30, 1921, Washington Conference Papers.

achieved parity with Britain. Also adopted were the 27,000-ton and 8-inch gun limits.[65] In this instance arms expansion, not arms limitation, was authorized by the conference.

For reasons of economy Admirals Pratt and Coontz had suggested that the Harding administration convert two of the uncompleted battle cruisers, listed for scrapping, into aircraft carriers of 33,000 tons apiece.[66] Conversion of the *Lexington* and *Saratoga* would not violate the 135,000-ton limit since the United States government would simply build its other carriers smaller. But conversion of the two battle cruisers would go over the 27,000-ton restriction. The Naval Advisers Subcommittee approved the American request, but it ran into a road block in the main Committee on the Limitation of Armament. The British, also for economy, wished to use some of their ships which were to be scrapped for naval training vessels, harbor boats, and other nonmilitary purposes. Hughes was sure that if the conference approved that proposal the public would regard the treaty as a sham which scrapped no ships. Balfour said that the same argument might apply if the Americans converted two battle cruisers into carriers. Hughes replied that if such were the belief he favored taking out the carrier conversion clause along with similar clauses. The Secretary "would not for the sake of ten or twenty million spoil this Treaty." [67] The meeting adjourned, but argument continued in the American delegation. Hughes favored cutting out the carrier conversion clause; Underwood and Root joined him. But Roosevelt argued that although Congress in the future might not vote funds to build two new carriers, money was probably available to convert the battle cruisers. There was thus a possibility that the United States might not have any carriers for the ten years of the agreement.[68] The American delegation finally

---

[65] *C. L. A.*, 672–82.

[66] Diary of Theodore Roosevelt, Jr., Jan. 3, 1922, Roosevelt Papers.

[67] Memorandum by Hankey, Jan. 11, 1922, *FR: 1922*, I, 188–200; Chatfield had thought before the conference that the *Lexington* would make a fine aircraft carrier. Roskill, *Naval Policy*, 310.

[68] Diary of Theodore Roosevelt, Jr., Jan. 11 and Jan. 12, 1922, Roosevelt Papers.

accepted the reasoning of Roosevelt, and the conversion feature, along with the British proposals, won approval of the conference.[69] The British were also given permission to convert two of their projected super *Hoods* to aircraft carriers but chose to convert two smaller vessels; here the Americans made the wise decision, for the *Lexington* and *Saratoga* were of great importance in the war in the western Pacific some twenty years later when their size and speed were a considerable advantage.[70]

When the conference delegates then turned to aircraft, they found that the opening American proposal had not mentioned the limitation of aircraft, for this subject like submarines seemed to fall under the agenda category "rules for control of new agencies of warfare." The phrase implied regulation rather than limitation. The General Board had recommended retention of aircraft as legitimate weapons of war and called only for regulation by international rules, thus classifying aircraft with submarines. And there was no practical measurement, such as tonnage for limiting ships, which the Board could recommend for planes.[71]

At the time of the conference the French possessed the largest air force.[72] After the French had refused to limit their army and threatened to build capital ships and submarines, the British concluded that the French were aiming their air force at the British Isles. The British wanted some restriction on aircraft in peacetime.[73] An expert subcommittee, composed of military aviation men from each nation, held twelve meetings and thoroughly discussed limiting aircraft. It was apparent that to find a practical method of limitation would take ingenuity. Mitchell suggested that the "only practicable limitation as to the numbers of aircraft for military purposes would be to abolish the use of aircraft for

[69] Memorandum by Hankey, Jan. 12, 1922, *FR: 1922*, I, 201–19.

[70] Roskill, *Naval Policy*, 324.

[71] Report of the General Board, "Aircraft," Nov. 9, 1921, Washington Conference Papers.

[72] The United States had 537 military planes, Great Britain had 1,048, France had 1,722, Italy had 494, and Japan had 537. Report of the Subcommittee on Aircraft, Dec. 30, 1921, *Subcommittees*, 270.

[73] *C. L. A.*, 412. The British were very upset about the threat of French airpower; see Balfour to Curzon, Dec. 1, 1921, F. O. A8616/18/45.

any purpose." [74] He knew this was a facetious proposal, but it reflected the feeling of the subcommittee that it could do nothing. The final report of the subcommittee was pessimistic. Commercial aviation offered the world a new method of transport and communication. To restrict its growth at an early stage might cripple it forever. Commercial aircraft easily could convert to military aircraft because the same factors which constituted high military performance—speed, range, capacity, altitude—were desirable in civilian craft. The subcommittee stated that it was impossible to restrict commercial aircraft with the single exception of lighter-than-air craft. With regard to military aircraft the subcommittee believed it could set no ratio among countries because of the different development of aircraft in each country, and that it was not feasible to limit the number or character of military aircraft. It did suggest that aircraft should operate only within rules that the nine nations should determine at a later conference. [75]

The chief delegates on January 9, 1922, quietly accepted the subcommittee's report unanimously. Schanzer believed it possible to limit aircraft by restricting the number of trained pilots for each country, but he gathered little support. Senator Underwood concurred that it was not practical to limit the numbers or character of aircraft. Hughes, however, read a resolution of the American Advisory Committee which condemned the bombing of unfortified towns and cities. Schanzer proposed that this practice be prohibited by international law, but de Bon rejoined that the Hague convention of 1907 covered it. After some debate a resolution set up a commission of jurists, to meet after the conference, to report on whether rules of international law covered the new methods of warfare. If not, it should recommend new rules. The conference also supported this resolution unanimously. [76]

[74] *Subcommittees*, 196.
[75] *Ibid.*, 252, 266, 268.
[76] *C. L. A.*, 792–816. The British did believe that it was possible to limit by numbers if a system of international inspection could be put through, which they felt was impossible. Memorandum by the British member of the aircraft subcommittee, General Board Papers, Naval History Division, Department of the Navy.

In the 1930's and thereafter, critics of the Washington Conference pointed out that few of the experts or diplomats at the grand meeting saw the importance of new weapons of war despite the depredations of the submarine in the recent world war. It is indeed a curious fact that the statesmen of 1921–1922 did not see how submarines, airplanes, and aircraft carriers would change the strategy of war by retiring capital ships. Later critics have underlined the blindness of naval theorists to the technological possibilities of the weapons and pointed out that here was a real failure of the conference—a failure of foresight. Still, naval experts and diplomats, like all human beings, cannot cover all possibilities. The revolutionary changes in naval technology in the years after the Washington Conference were far beyond the ken of men living at the time. General Mitchell saw dimly into the future. But the American Army court-martialed him when his apocalytic visions became too urgent and his methods too crudely dramatic.

Having considered arrangements for aircraft and aircraft carriers, the limitation committee had one remaining problem—a decision on poison gas. This proved to be an unusual problem for the American delegation, which had no proposal to make. The General Board of the Navy had advised that it would be sound policy to prohibit gas warfare in every form and against every objective. Knowing that the United States had the best industrial plant for this sort of warfare, the Board nevertheless condemned a practice which it felt caused too much human suffering.[77] The Board was sure it was expressing the opinion of the average American. Besides, poison gas could not sink battleships.

Findings by the American Advisory Committee also supported the view that gas should not be sanctioned at the conference by the American delegation. In a report signed by General Pershing the committee members said they "would not be doing their

---

[77] Report of the General Board, "Gas Warfare," Dec. 5, 1921, Washington Conference Papers.

duty in expressing the conscience of the American people were they to fail in insisting on the total abolition of chemical warfare." A resolution was sent to the conference calling for the prohibition of all gas warfare.[78]

Apparently the American delegates and advisers all had agreed on poison gas, but such was not the case. The War Department had concluded that "gas is an accepted weapon of warfare. Its use as a weapon of warfare should be continued . . . ." [79] It would, however, prohibit the use of gas against noncombatants. The American members of the Washington Conference's Subcommittee on Poison Gas, Professor Edgar F. Smith and General Amos Fries, agreed not with the General Board or Advisory Committee, but with the War Department. They attacked the Advisory Committee report that the American people favored the abolition of gas warfare. Where, Smith asked, did the Advisory Committee get this information? He had looked at the same clippings and newspapers and found no evidence. Smith contended that he could prove gas was a perfect weapon because it put men temporarily out of action but did not injure them permanently except in a few cases. Smith submitted a report that 24 per cent of all men hit by explosives died in the World War, as compared to only 2 per cent struck down by gas.[80]

The final report to the conference of the Subcommittee on Poison Gas said the only limit possible was to prohibit use of gas against cities or large groups of noncombatants. The report pointed out that it was impossible to stop research or even manufacture of gases, many of which were by-products of other industrial processes.[81]

If the report thus said nothing about prohibiting gas warfare, it did not wish to approve of gas. An additional memorandum of

[78] Advisory Committee Reports, "Report on New Agencies of Warfare," Dec. 1, 1921, Washington Conference Papers.

[79] Letter from Secretary of War John W. Weeks to Hughes, Nov. 2, 1921, State Department Index 500.A41a/124.

[80] Memorandum by Smith, "Report on the Findings of Advisory Committee on New Agencies of Warfare," Dec. 16, 1921, Washington Conference Papers.

[81] *Subcommittees*, 285–90.

the subcommittee, printed in the official conference record, omits the last three paragraphs appearing in the original manuscript document. According to this the American members of the subcommittee thought gas warfare more humane than any other method since it killed or injured a much smaller percentage of combatants. The principal British and French delegates proved unwilling to go on record to that effect.[82] When poison gas was discussed at the plenary meeting of the conference, Hughes read the subcommittee report—omitting the last three paragraphs—and also the reports of the General Board and Advisory Committee.[83] To the public he displayed a front united against gas warfare, even though he knew his subcommittee subordinates disagreed. To this day few people realize that immediately after the World War, American representatives at an international conference came out in favor of gas warfare. Hughes must have realized that if this fact became public the criticism might prove enormous.

Elihu Root formally presented a resolution calling for a prohibition of poison gas and suggested its acceptance as a binding rule of international law. Both Sarraut and Balfour duly explained that the Hague Conferences had passed resolutions of this kind, but there could be no harm, they said, in emphasizing the revulsion of the entire civilized world against gas. The Root resolution passed unanimously, and the limitation of armaments aspect of the conference came to an end.[84]

The failure to apply the capital ship ratio to auxiliary ships and submarines, as called for by the American proposal, was indeed a setback to the limitation of naval armament; the result was a naval race in auxiliary ships during the interwar period and an abortive attempt to limit them at a conference in Geneva in

[82] Memorandum by Fries, "Findings of Chemical Warfare Committee," Dec. 17, 1921, Washington Conference Papers; see also memorandum by Fries to J. Butler Wright, Dec. 17, 1921, Washington Conference Papers, in which Fries wrote that the American members would like to "proclaim chemical warfare as a proper method of waging war."

[83] *C. L. A.*, 728–36.

[84] *Ibid.*, 738–50.

1927. At the bottom of the dispute and failure was a European problem rather than a Far Eastern one: British-French antagonism. There was nothing, except an American guarantee of French security, that the United States could offer to break the deadlock between the two ancient European competitors. France played the role of spoiler at the conference, and the United States could have done very little to influence the French.

It is also of some interest that the developing weapons of war, those that were to play a key role in World War II—aircraft, aircraft carriers, and submarines—were either not curbed or only nominally restricted. The conference limited the chief offensive weapon of its day but left defensive and new weapons an almost unlimited latitude in which to develop. Battleship technology stagnated during the interwar period of limitation while the new weapons developed so highly that they were able to displace the battleship as the chief offensive weapon during World War II. The Washington Conference was the beginning of the end for the battleship.

IX. THE FOUR-POWER TREATY

IT WAS DIFFICULT TO DIVINE the political future of the Japanese nation in 1921. The recently ended world war had offered the Japanese a golden economic opportunity, and despite a postwar recession they had raised their national income to new heights. A large part of the increase, of course, was going into military expenditures. Among the Japanese there was some feeling that a more popular participation in government might solve remaining economic problems, for had not the democratic nations of Europe and the world won out against those nations less responsive to the popular will, and were not the victorious nations economically strong?

It was hard to be certain about Japan, a nation which in its recent past had shown distressingly bellicose feelings. But noticing the new democratic yearnings of Japanese city workers and civil servants, Western observers were fairly sanguine that a more democratic Japan would be peaceful and prove internationally an excellent neighbor; the Japanese might even become guardians of the Open Door in the Far East—selfless benefactors to the struggling people of China.

The American government hoped that the Japanese did indeed have peaceful intentions. American statesmen were eager to take every step to insure that the Japanese would not turn belligerent. Thus because American diplomats believed the Anglo-Japanese Alliance encouraged aggressive tendencies, they hoped to end it at the Washington Conference.

The Japanese, however, preferred to retain the alliance and come to a separate understanding with the United States about the Pacific and Far East. A top-secret memorandum by the Asian Bureau of the Foreign Ministry, dated July 28, 1921, discussed the alliance and recommended the avoidance of conflicts with the United States in order to establish friendly relations. The Bureau saw no difference between the Anglo-Japanese Alliance and previous understandings with the United States. The Japanese stressed the earlier Root-Takahira agreement which, with its broad emphasis on equal economic opportunity and respect of territories, was the type of arrangement—a vague gentlemen's agreement—they hoped to reaffirm at the forthcoming conference.[1]

But Secretary Hughes, as noted, had let Ambassador Geddes know that the Harding administration would oppose renewal. When Geddes had asked Hughes if the three nations could not cooperate, Hughes had replied that if Geddes were suggesting that the United States join an alliance, such a possibility was out of the question. The Secretary, Geddes reported, had demonstrated interest in a tripartite agreement on policies in East Asia.[2] The British Foreign Office had concluded, somewhat precipitously, that the task was to find a formula that would satisfy both nations and continue to protect British interests.[3] Lloyd George in a speech on August 18, 1921, gave an indication of what the British hoped for at the conference. He wished the Anglo-Japanese Alliance to become a "greater understanding" with the United States: "the surest way of making a success of the disarmament conference is first to have such an understanding." [4]

Within the Foreign Office two formulas became the basis of discussion. Neither included a military clause nor implied more than a declaration of policy. The first, by Geddes, was a broad proposal including a call for international economic development that was judged undesirable by some officials. The second,

---

[1] Memorandum by the Asian Bureau, July 28, 1921, reel MT 306, pp. 1–129.

[2] Memorandum of a conversation between Hughes and Geddes, June 23, 1921, *FR: 1921*, II, 314–16.

[3] Telegram from Geddes to Curzon, Sept. 21, 1921, F. O. A6915/18/45.

[4] New York *Times*, Aug. 19, 1921. Hughes noted this himself in Hughes to Henry Brown, Sept. 17, 1921, Hughes Papers.

by Sir John Jordan, mutually pledged to respect territorial possessions in the Pacific and East Asia, support China's independence, and provide equal economic opportunity in China; in event of a threat to those principles the three powers would decide on action. The Foreign Secretary agreed with these proposals but was not happy about exchanging general principles for the tangible assets of the Anglo-Japanese Alliance. "I regard the loss of these advantages," Curzon wrote, "with no small apprehension and am not at all sure that they will be compensated for by a temporary conquest of the *beaux yeux* of America." [5]

Some desultory conversations followed. Two days before the conference opened, the Canadian member of the British delegation, Borden, told Lodge that the Australians blocked the way of abandoning the Anglo-Japanese Alliance. Fearful of Japanese aggression, the Australians found protection in the agreement. Lodge told Borden that the alliance, fears or not, was unpopular in the United States, a "background for warlike preparations and for an unreasonable attitude toward the United States." Borden, Lodge reported, agreed. [6] Next day the head of the British delegation explained to Hughes that the Japanese were looking for him, Balfour, and that it was essential to have some policy on the Anglo-Japanese Alliance. Balfour gave Hughes a draft of a tripartite treaty which he had drawn up on his own responsibility, he said. This proposal dealt with preservation of peace and the territorial status quo in "regions of Eastern Asia . . . the islands of the Pacific and the territories bordering thereon." If a threat arose to territorial rights of a signatory, two of the nations could conclude a defensive military alliance. Balfour thus had left the door open for a defensive alliance with Japan. Included was a provision canceling previous agreements but not explicitly naming the Anglo-Japanese Alliance. Hughes told Balfour he did not

[5] Memorandum on tripartite agreement, Oct. 17, 1921, F. O. A3930/2905/10.
[6] Diary of Henry Cabot Lodge, Nov. 10, 1921, Lodge Papers. Lodge wrote to Lord Godfrey Charnwood in London that difficulties about the alliance would be met "if we can offer an alternative which will give Australia an equal or better protection than she has from the treaty with Japan alone." Nov. 18, 1921, Lodge Papers.

want to call any agreement an alliance. He believed any new "arrangement" would have to be large, to take the place of the Anglo-Japanese Alliance, the Root-Takahira, and Lansing-Ishii agreements.[7] Hughes decided that Balfour's draft was unsatisfactory, for the British could recreate the old alliance, and nowhere did the draft say the alliance would end. The Secretary's main objection was that the treaty was tripartite; the Japanese and British might gang up on the Americans.[8]

The British meanwhile conferred with the Japanese. Sir Maurice Hankey, head of the British Conference Secretariat, approached Saburi Sado of the Japanese delegation in the first of several candid conferences. They were old friends, both having acted as secretary-general for their delegations at the Paris Peace Conference. Saburi said that the Japanese government wanted renewal of the alliance but recognized that modifications were in order. Hankey wondered whether it might be possible to include some formula to reconstitute the alliance "in case the old circumstances should recur." [9] Balfour and Kato came to much the same conclusion on November 23. Neither was eager to give up an alliance that had benefited both, but they recognized the interest of the United States.[10]

There was no action on the American side until November 20, when Chandler P. Anderson met with Lodge and Root at the latter's apartment. Lodge there told Anderson that the two men desired him to draw a draft treaty dealing with the security of the Pacific islands and Australia; he was to use the old alliance as a basis but delete all reference to forcible measures. The two dele-

[7] Memorandum by Hughes of a conversation with Balfour, Nov. 11, 1921, *FR: 1922*, I, 1–2. Ambassador Harvey a week before had said in Liverpool that the entrance of the United States into a permanent alliance with France or Great Britain was an impossibility. New York *Times*, Nov. 4, 1921.

[8] Beerits memorandum, "The Four-Power Treaty," Hughes Papers; a good general description of the Four-Power evolution can be found in John Chalmers Vinson, "The Drafting of the Four-Power Treaty of the Washington Conference," *The Journal of Modern History*, XXV (March 1953), 40–47.

[9] Memorandum of Nov. 18, 1921, meeting between Hankey and Saburi as enclosure in Balfour to Lloyd George, Nov. 24, 1921, F. O. F4563/2905/23.

[10] Balfour to Lloyd George, Nov. 24, 1921, *ibid.*

gates hoped to invent a general international agreement, acceptable to all parties, which would recognize the territorial integrity and sovereignty of the powers in their Pacific possessions.[11] Anderson drew such a treaty and submitted it to Lodge. The draft called for preservation of the peace and respect for territorial rights by signatories in their "insular and territorial possessions or dominions in the Pacific and Indian oceans." When peace was in jeopardy the nations were to consult. The draft prohibited future agreements of the same type but said nothing about past treaties. Lodge approved and it was later shown to Balfour. But Hughes rejected Anderson's proposal, for it did not end the Anglo-Japanese Alliance and did not say which powers were to be signatories.[12]

The next move came from Baron Shidehara, in charge of the Japanese delegates on these negotiations, who presented Hughes with a proposed tripartite arrangement based on the Balfour draft. This essay provided that if "territorial rights or vital interests"

11 Diary of Chandler P. Anderson, Nov. 20, 1921, Anderson Papers.

12 "With a view to the preservation of the general peace and the maintenance of their rights with respect to the Pacific and Indian Oceans, the signatory powers make the following declaration:

"(1) Each of the Signatory Powers declares that it will respect the rights and the aforesaid possessions and dominions belonging to each of the other signatory powers in those regions.

"(2) Each of the Signatory Powers declares that whenever the general peace seems to be in jeopardy or any of the rights or posssions above mentioned are threatened, it will communicate with the other powers signatories to this declaration, freely and frankly in order to arrive at an understanding as to what measures should be taken to preserve the general peace and safeguard said rights and possessions.

"(3) Each of the Signatory Powers declares that it will not enter into any separate arrangement with any power or powers, signatories to this declaration or not, prejudicial to the general peace or to the rights of any of the other powers signatories hereto, or to the integrity of their possessions or dominions in those regions." Four-Power Treaty draft by Chandler P. Anderson, Nov. 21, 1921, Department of State 500.A4a/162; diary of Chandler P. Anderson, Nov. 21, 1921, Anderson Papers.

Lodge did suggest that the words "and territorial" along with "and Indian" be crossed out in the preamble. In paragraph two he added "or possessions" twice and added a fourth paragraph stating, "This arrangement shall supersede any treaty of earlier date dealing with the defence of territorial rights in the regions to which this agreement refers." Washington Conference Box, Lodge Papers; Beerits memorandum, "The Four-Power Treaty," Hughes Papers.

of a signatory were threatened by an outside power in the regions of the "Pacific Ocean and of the Far East," the three nations were to consult. Or if two signatories should have a controversy, they could invite the third to a conference. Shidehara's draft abrogated the Anglo-Japanese Alliance, and he cabled Tokyo that the alliance had to be nullified. This draft said nothing about respecting each other's rights.[13]

Maneuverings went on, for, as everyone recognized, a great deal was at stake. Hughes and Balfour recognized that the danger of the Japanese proposition lay in the phrase "vital interests," which could have covered almost any Japanese interest in the Pacific.[14] The Anglo-Americans were wary. Shidehara's draft, unlike that of Anderson, was not discarded and served as a basis for negotiation. Lodge and Root told Balfour that they approved the Japanese draft but felt they could not take it up until the Shantung controversy was settled; Balfour and Root relayed this news to the Japanese.[15]

There now occurred a strange personal indiscretion. In a private talk on December 5, a record of which does not appear in the American archives, Root told Kato that the United States

[13] Memorandum by Hughes of a conversation with Saburi, counselor of the Japanese Embassy, Nov. 26, 1921, *FR: 1922,* I, 3–4.

A corrected Japanese draft by Balfour read:

"I. In regard to the territorial rights of the High Contracting parties in the Pacific Ocean and Far East, it is agreed that if these are threatened by the aggressive action of any third Power, the High Contracting parties shall communicate with one another fully and frankly, in order to arrive at an understanding as to the most efficient measures to be taken, jointly or separately, to meet the exigencies of the particular situation.

"II. The High Contracting parties further engage to respect these rights as between themselves and if there should develop between any two of them controversies on any matter in the aforesaid regions which is likely to affect the relations of harmonious accord now happily subsisting between them, they agree to invite the other contending party to a joint conference, to which the whole subject matter will be referred for consideration and adjustment.

"III. The present agreement shall supersede the agreement of alliance hitherto in force between Japan and Great Britain." Washington Conference Box, Lodge Papers.

[14] Memorandum by Hughes on Elihu Root's draft treaty to include the Netherlands in the Four-Power Treaty, n.d., Department of State 500.A4a/162.

[15] Telegram from Balfour to Curzon, Nov. 28, 1921, F. O. F4372/2905/23.

government was primarily interested in naval limitation and not Far Eastern issues. The implication was plain that the Japanese government had nothing to fear from Root. He went on to assure Kato of his assistance—proven, he said, by his activities at the time of the Russo-Japanese War and the Korean annexation. Overplaying his role, he advised Kato, in utmost secrecy, that despite public pressures the American delegation was not going to permit the question of the Twenty-One Demands to appear on the agenda. Believing, apparently, that this proved his friendship, he chided Kato for dispatch of Japanese troops to the continent and advised that it should have been done more "neatly." [16]

Hughes at this time was insisting on the inclusion of the French in any agreement, a quadruple treaty. This move had several advantages. In the event of a dispute the two former allies could not outvote the Americans at a conference (assuming France supported the United States; if France did not, it made no difference). Second, it smoothed the feathers of the French delegation at a crucial time and may have influenced Briand to agree to the capital-ship quota. It also would make the entire conference arrangement more acceptable to the Senate. [17]

Hughes then presented his own draft, approved by Root and Lodge, the most noticeable change of which, in what is basically a restatement of previous drafts, was reduction in the area to which the treaty would apply. While other proposals had included parts of Asia, Hughes's draft applied only to "insular possessions and dominions in the Pacific Ocean." Hughes also asked each party to pledge respect for the other's rights. In the event of a controversy a conference of the four powers would adjust the

[16] Telegram from the delegation to Uchida, Dec. 5, 1921, reel MT 317, pp. 716-19. Hughes had made an agreement with the Chinese that the Twenty-One Demands would not be discussed until the Shantung problem was settled. *C. L. A.*, 1212.

[17] Minutes of the American delegation, Dec. 1, 1921, Washington Conference Papers. Balfour later wrote that "it was Hughes' idea to bring in the French in order to soothe their somewhat ruffled pride." Balfour to Sir Charles Eliot as quoted in Blanche E. C. Dugdale, *Arthur James Balfour* (2 vols.; New York, 1937), II, 243.

issue. Should an outside power threaten, the signatories would decide for joint or separate action. Hughes suggested that the treaty run for ten years, after which the parties could end it on six months' notice.[18]

Before presenting his draft to the French delegates, Hughes conferred with the British and Japanese. Back in London, Curzon was not at all pleased with the addition of France but had instructed Balfour to consent to accommodate the United States; Kato, acting without orders, also assented.[19] The Secretary made a few changes: a conference of the four powers, in the event of a dispute between two of them, would not occur without an attempt to settle the controversy through diplomatic channels; at the suggestion of Balfour he increased the period of notification from six to twelve months.[20]

Hughes then presented the corrected draft to the chief French delegate, Viviani, at the Secretary's house, explained what had taken place, and asked if the French government would join. Viviani, delighted, proceeded to kiss the startled Secretary.[21]

This Gallic salutation does not seem to have turned Hughes's mind from essentials. All four governments were to meet the next afternoon to discuss the draft, but before that meeting Hughes had a conference with Balfour in which he claimed that certain rights had accrued to the United States with respect to the Pacific mandates because of the American status as an Associated Power in the recent war. Negotiations between the United States and Japan were then taking place regarding mandates north of the equator. Balfour said an exchange of notes between the governments of the United States and Britain would suffice to reserve American rights in mandates controlled by Britain south of the equator. Hughes wanted it clear that the proposed quadruple

---

[18] Beerits memorandum, "The Four-Power Treaty," Hughes Papers; draft by Hughes of the Four-Power Treaty, n.d., *FR: 1922*, I, 7.

[19] Telegram from Curzon to Balfour, Dec. 7, 1921, F. O. F4484/2905/23; delegation to Uchida, Dec. 9, 1921, reel MT 317, p. 893.

[20] Four-Power Treaty draft, n.d., Lodge Papers. See also Beerits memorandum, "The Four-Power Treaty," Hughes Papers.

[21] *Ibid.*

treaty would not affect American rights in the mandates. Anticipating early assent from the Japanese and French, Hughes and Balfour agreed on a public statement about the Four-Power Treaty as soon as possible, to quiet rumors of an alliance. Hughes did have qualms about announcing the agreement before the Japanese withdrew their demand for a 10:7 naval ratio. He finally decided that the Four-Power Treaty would destroy any reason for a higher ratio and also might encourage the Japanese to retreat.[22]

When the chief delegates of the four nations met, Baron Shidehara presented a second Japanese proposal, a draft sent by Uchida from Tokyo. It introduced a clause which called for a "free and peaceful development of trade" in the Pacific area; this was designed to apply the Open Door and provide easier access for Japanese traders to the islands. Uchida instructed the delegation that the clause was desirable but not mandatory. There also was a provision that in the event of a dispute two of the powers could "invite the other contracting parties to a joint conference." Shidehara had used that same phrase in his first draft. Hughes again opposed its inclusion. It was far too vague; in time of stress it might recreate the Anglo-Japanese Alliance.

After Hughes excluded the Chinese mainland from the agreement, Shidehara asked if the term "insular possessions" included mandates. Prepared, Hughes replied that it did and made American acceptance of the Four-Power Treaty conditional on a mandate arrangement between the United States and Japan.[23]

[22] Memorandum of a conversation between Hughes and Balfour, Dec. 8, 1921, *FR: 1922*, I, 11–12.

[23] Memorandum of a conversation between Hughes, Balfour, Viviani, and Shidehara, *ibid.*, 13–22. Baron Shidehara's draft read:

"The United States of America, the British Empire, France and Japan, with a view to the maintenance of their insular possessions and dominions in the Pacific Ocean, and to the preservation of their mutual relations of friendship, agree as follows:

"Article 1—The High Contracting Parties engage mutually to respect their rights respecting their insular possessions and dominions in the Pacific Ocean.

"Article 2—If there should develop between any two of the High Contracting Parties controversies on any matter in the above mentioned region which is likely to affect the relations of harmonious accord now happily subsisting between

Shidehara raised the point of whether the phrase included the Japanese main islands. Hughes interpreted the treaty to include the main islands, although he did not appear to care one way or the other.[24] To everyone's surprise, Shidehara asked for exclusion of Japan proper on orders from Uchida, who was worried that the other signatories might use the treaty to justify their interfering in the internal affairs of Japan, whereas the United States would be taking no such risk because her mainland would clearly not be included. However, Balfour said it might prove embarrassing if the agreement included Australia and New Zealand and not Japan. The British legal adviser, Malkin, suggested a clause which would exempt any matter that by international law fell within domestic jurisdiction. The delegates finally decided to sleep on the problem.[25] Next day Shidehara withdrew his proposal for exclusion of the main islands.[26] This decision, made on his initiative, was to cause him grief when he informed Uchida. What appeared to be a point of minor importance turned out to be a question of national honor and prestige—but all that was in the future.

There was one last change. During this discussion before the public announcement of the treaty, Hughes broadened the scope of the treaty. He suggested that it cover not only disputes involving the Pacific islands but also controversies "arising out of any Pacific question." He was eager to provide settlement for dis-

---

them, such contracting parties shall, in mutual agreement with each other, invite the other contracting parties to a joint conference to which the whole subject will be referred for consideration and adjustment.

"Article 3—If the rights mentioned in Article 1 of this agreement are threatened by the aggressive action of any third power, the High Contracting Parties shall communicate with one another fully and frankly in order to arrive at an understanding as to the most efficient measures to be taken, jointly or separately, to meet the exigencies of the particular situation.

"Articles 4 and 5 (same as articles 3 and 4 of the American draft)." Department of State 500.A4a/162.

24 Hughes told Theodore Roosevelt, Jr., that it was impossible to imagine a war which would affect the Japanese mainland without affecting the islands. Diary of Theodore Roosevelt, Jr., Dec. 29, 1921, Roosevelt Papers.

25 Memorandum of a conversation between Hughes, Balfour, Viviani, and Shidehara, Dec. 8, 1921, *FR: 1922*, I, 22.

26 Dec. 9, 1921, *ibid.*, 23.

putes arising out of the islands and for controversies which, while not related to Pacific possessions, might affect the security of the possessions. Balfour agreed that this proposal would give the treaty a broader effect upon world peace. He and the other delegates approved.[27]

The delegates duly met in the fourth open session of the conference on Saturday morning, December 10, 1921, and Hughes opened the session on a business-like note by reading resolutions on China discussed in the Far Eastern committee. The conference then voted to adopt the resolutions. The Secretary, with what was becoming a well-developed sense of dramatic timing, asked Senator Lodge to make known a matter not on the agenda. Lodge followed by reading the Four-Power Treaty.

The American delegate launched into a literary sidetrip describing the romantic attributes of the Pacific islands. Aided and abetted by Robert Louis Stevenson, Robert Browning, and Herman Melville, the scholar in politics concluded with the hope that the treaty, "which rests only upon the will and honor of those who sign it," would preserve the charms of the area by maintaining peace in the Pacific.[28]

Although it was wise of Hughes to have Lodge present the treaty, showing the old warrior's approval, even Lodge's literary skill could not whitewash it. Negotiations had been secret, and the result was being sprung on the conference. Nor was the treaty as clear as Lodge claimed.

Criticism came from several sources. In the Senate some of the same men who had opposed American entry into the League spoke out. James A. Reed said the treaty was "treacherous, treasonable, and damnable" and predicted a hot fight.[29] He later called the treaty a gold brick "finished one night at 11:00 o'clock in secret session and handed the American people the next morning evidently with the idea that at that time it could be sold quickly

---

[27] *Ibid.*, 24.
[28] *C. L. A.*, 146–66; Roosevelt called it an "excellent speech of the early English university school type." Diary of Theodore Roosevelt, Jr., Dec. 10, 1921.
[29] Washington *Post*, Dec. 11, 1921.

to an unsuspecting public." [30] After careful study, Borah concluded it was an alliance more subtle than the Versailles Treaty but no less dangerous. It would make Japanese power supreme in the Pacific.[31] Outside the Senate chamber, former Secretary of State Lansing thought Article 2 of the treaty a "close blood relation of Article X" of the Covenant. There was the same moral obligation to employ force; Balfour, a proponent of the League of Nations, must have drafted the article. To Lansing the treaty guaranteed the status quo in the Pacific much as Article X had done for Europe.[32] The Four-Power Treaty also caused grumbling among American legal advisers, who could not understand why Hughes had not consulted them. It was, of course, natural that the advisers brought up such a question. The main function of a legal adviser is to prevent another nation from hoodwinking his own delegates. At the request of a delegate a legal expert may draft an entire treaty which a conference adopts word-for-word. Seldom does he receive credit. The spokesman for the legal advisers, Anderson, told Root that his colleagues objected. Anderson believed the treaty authorized the four nations to settle a controversy by majority vote. The treaty should make clear that the powers would decide action in "mutual agreement"—in plain language, by unanimous assent. Anderson pointed out that the French seemed to think the treaty implicitly bound the signatories to take joint measures against aggressors. He also thought there should be a provision for another conference before the termination date.[33]

The Secretary of State seemed to have a guilty conscience when he all but apologized to Neilsen, one of the legal advisers, for not having consulted him.[34]

[30] *Congressional Record*, Dec. 16, 1921, p. 436.
[31] Borah to Arthur H. Vandenberg, Dec. 19, 1921, and Borah to Mrs. Uriah S. Vincent, Dec. 16, 1921, Borah Papers.
[32] Memorandum by Robert Lansing, "Article Two of the Four-Power Treaty," Dec. 15, 1921, Lansing Papers.
[33] Diary of Chandler P. Anderson, Dec. 12, 1921, Anderson Papers. Along with Anderson the chief legal advisers were George S. Wilson, James Brown Scott, and F. K. Neilsen.
[34] *Ibid.*, Dec. 21, 1921.

Then happened perhaps the most famous misunderstanding of the Washington Conference. At one of the President's regular news conferences a reporter asked Harding if the treaty covered the Japanese main islands. Harding said it did not. The President's statement appeared in headlines.[35] At best, this was a misunderstanding. At worst, the President was in the dark about the "plain and simple" Four-Power Treaty. Hughes, Lodge reported, did not know what to do and asked Lodge to see Harding. Accompanied by Underwood, the senators caught Harding right after his golf game and straightened the matter out.[36] This left the problem of what to do. Underwood favored changing the treaty to exclude Japan while Root did not.[37] Hughes went to the White House and reminded Harding that he, Hughes, had explained the situation to him as negotiations progressed. Harding confessed that he should have kept quiet and referred the question to the American delegation. "Hughes," he said, "I didn't want to appear to be a dub." After having a good laugh the two Republican leaders prepared a press statement stating that the President had no objection to including the main islands.[38]

As mentioned, Shidehara's inclusion of the main islands set off a dispute with Uchida. Shidehara reported that he had given in because the United States, Britain, and France would not approve exclusion of Japan, and that Japanese delegates had understood that the Imperial government had not meant to insist on exclusion. The Anglo-Japanese Alliance had included the Japanese mainland. But Uchida ordered Shidehara to reopen negotiations. National honor, he said, was at stake. He preferred to exclude Australia and New Zealand, if possible, but certainly the Japanese main islands. Shidehara replied that there were some senators who were arguing that inclusion was a privilege only Japan received and they considered this unfair.[39] Shidehara asked Hughes if it

[35] New York *Times*, Dec. 21, 1921.
[36] Diary of Henry Cabot Lodge, Dec. 20, 1921, Lodge Papers.
[37] *Ibid.*, Dec. 23, 1921.
[38] Beerits memorandum, "The Four-Power Treaty," Hughes Papers.
[39] Telegram from delegation to Uchida, Dec. 11, 1921, reel MT 314, pp. 147–

were true that some senators objected to the Four-Power Treaty because it included the main islands. He feared that the Senate might make a reservation insulting to the Japanese. The Secretary thought that the reports were inaccurate and that the Senate would not stop ratification of the treaty. Shidehara suggested it might be best to exclude the main islands. Hughes promised to speak to Lodge and Underwood.[40] A luncheon on December 25 between Lodge and Balfour indicated that a change was possible.[41] Japanese worries continued. General Tanaka reported to Tokyo that Japan had gained nothing out of the treaty. He believed it cut off Japan's advancement to the south; "this," he lamented, "is truly a sad situation." [42] Uchida warned the delegation that a special committee from the Kenseikai party had visited the Foreign Ministry and expressed concern over inclusion. He had, he said, gone so far as to tell the American Ambassador that the Privy Council might not ratify the treaty.[43] Finally, on December 30, as a result of a Cabinet decision, Uchida ordered the delegation to insist on exclusion.[44]

At a conference with Hughes the Japanese Ambassador produced a proposed supplementary agreement excluding the Japanese islands, which Hughes rejected since it would give the impression that the treaty was ambiguous; Hughes would provide that the treaty not apply to the islands, rather than attempt to interpret the treaty. He suggested that Shidehara write a letter specifying the islands of Japan to which the treaty would apply.[45] After consultation with Uchida, Shidehara on February 6 sent a

---

95; *ibid.,* Dec. 13, 1921, reel MT 317, pp. 1030–50; telegram from Uchida to the delegation, Dec. 1, 1921, reel MT 313, pp. 511–16.

[40] Memorandum by Hughes of a conversation with Shidehara, Dec. 19, 1921, *FR: 1922,* I, 37–38.

[41] Diary of Henry Cabot Lodge, Dec. 24, 1921, Lodge Papers.

[42] Telegram to the Army Minister, Dec. 29, 1921, Army and Navy Archives, reel 131, pp. 49482–83.

[43] Telegram from Uchida to delegation, Dec. 27, 1921, reel MT 313, pp. 603–605.

[44] Telegram from Uchida to the delegation, Dec. 30, 1921, reel MT 313, pp. 655–61.

[45] Memorandum of a Hughes conversation with Shidehara, Jan. 14, 1922, *FR: 1922,* I, 42.

draft which stated that the treaty covered only Karafuto (Southern Sakhalin), Formosa, the Pescadores, and the Japanese mandates. Hughes accepted the agreement, which became part of the Four-Power Treaty.[46]

This arrangement settled the issue of the Japanese main islands and left the problem of whether to admit other nations to the pact. The requests of Italy and Siam were easily refused since these countries did not have possessions in the Pacific—although Italy characteristically protested that she might some day acquire land there.[47] The application of the Netherlands was another matter. To meet the objections of the Netherlands, Elihu Root drafted a treaty which included all powers at the conference except China in an entirely new version of the Four-Power Treaty. Each nation pledged to respect the territorial rights of the others in the "region of the Pacific Ocean." Root's draft also mentioned the future Nine-Power Treaty on China and by implication linked the two. The draft did not mention settlement of disputes or length of the agreement, nor did it void the Anglo-Japanese Alliance. On the Department's copy of this draft, in Hughes's handwriting, are the words "Impossible for many reasons—CEH."[48] The four countries eventually presented the Netherlands government with identical notes that they would "respect the right of the Netherlands in relation to their insular possessions in the region of the Pacific Ocean."[49]

Anyone who attempts to analyze the Four-Power Treaty must consider the connected question of the Japanese-mandated Pacific islands. The islands were former German possessions north of the equator, placed under a Japanese mandate by the Supreme Allied War Council on May 7, 1919, and included the Carolines,

---

[46] Letter from Shidehara to Hughes, Feb. 6, 1922, Department of State 500.A4a/3; Hughes to Shidehara, Feb. 6, 1922, *FR: 1922*, I, 45–46.

[47] *FR: 1922*, I, 5, 39, 41, 45.

[48] Root's draft of Dec. 28, 1921, can be found in the State Department Index 500.A4a/162; memorandum by Hughes on Root's draft, *ibid.*

[49] Telegram from Hughes to William Phillips, American Minister at The Hague, Feb. 3, 1921, *FR: 1922*, I, 45.

Marianas, Marshalls, and Bismarck Archipelago.[50] A controversy had developed between Americans and Japanese over the small island of Yap, in the western part of the Caroline group nine degrees north of the equator in longitude 138°E; 1,200 miles from Manila and 500 from Guam, Yap was a cable center from which messages went to Guam, Menado, Shanghai, and indirectly to the Philippines. In a secret pact of 1917 the Japanese and British had agreed to split German possessions in the Pacific at the equator, with Japan gaining those to the north and Britain those to the south. The Paris Peace Conference accepted this agreement by so assigning mandates. The Wilson administration contended that it had made protests at the conference against inclusion of Yap in the mandates agreement. It did not believe one country should control this center. Lansing and Wilson had informally asked the Council to reserve Yap. But the mandate was conferred on Japan and an agreement drawn in December 1920. The Department refused to recognize it. Its position was that Germany under Article 119 of the Versailles Treaty had turned over all territories to the Allied and Associated Powers, which in turn had granted mandates to member nations of the League. As one of the Allied and Associated Powers the American government contended that it had not given its permission.

The Japanese Foreign Ministry, however, replied that President Wilson had made no reservation of record on May 7, 1919, nor was any included in the terms of the mandate. The League ducked the issue by pointing out that the American dispute was not with it but with the Allied and Associated Powers, who had conferred the mandate.[51]

Before the Washington Conference, Shidehara asked if an agreement internationalizing the island for cable purposes would satisfy the American government. Hughes suggested that Shide-

---

[50] In the notes of the Supreme War Council of May 7, 1919, attended by Wilson, the following appears: "German islands North of the Equator. The Mandate shall be held by Japan." *FR: 1919, Paris Peace Conference*, V, 508.

[51] The best summary can be found in Samuel Flagg Bemis, "Yap Island Controversy," *Pacific Review*, II (Sept. 1921), 308–28. See also *FR: 1921*, II, 263ff.

hara prepare a proposal. Shidehara presented two treaty drafts dealing with Yap. The first would give the United States equal cable rights with Japan. The second divided ownership of the three cables among the United States (Yap to Guam), Japan (Yap to Naba to Shanghai), and the Netherlands (Yap to Menado), and arranged for their operation. Hughes countered with a list of rights which he believed the United States would require regarding Yap. He stated that the second agreement would have to be among the Allied and Associated Powers.[52]

Negotiations continued at the Washington Conference even though the subject was not on the agenda. The Japanese finally agreed to apply all commercial treaties between the United States and Japan to mandated islands north of the equator. They agreed to give American vessels the usual comities in visiting Yap island and to send to Washington a duplicate report of the annual one sent the League. All these agreements were lumped together in a treaty signed on February 11, 1922. The Yap agreement was a compromise since the United States won full operational rights on the island but did recognize Japan's control of mandates north of the equator.[53]

The Four-Power Treaty, one may say in conclusion, achieved the main hope of the American government—abrogation of the Anglo-Japanese Alliance. Whether the alliance had been a threat to the United States is a moot point. General feeling at the time was that there was little chance the British would fight the Americans in the event the latter should clash with the Japanese. As Hughes and the American government realized, the danger was that the Japanese would continue to use the alliance to further their interests on the Chinese mainland and in the Pacific. Acquisition of former German possessions during the World War seemed

---

[52] Memoranda of conversations between Hughes and Shidehara, June 18, 1921, and Aug. 19, 1921, *FR: 1921*, II, 290–95.

[53] Japanese Embassy in Washington to the Department of State, *ca.* Dec. 2, 1921, *ibid.*, 304–305, and Hughes to Shidehara, Dec. 5, 1921, *ibid.*, 305–306; Shidehara to Hughes, Dec. 12, 1921, *ibid.*, 306–307; statement issued to the press by the Department of State, Dec. 12, 1921, *FR: 1922*, I, 31–37; convention between the United States and Japan, signed at Washington, Feb. 11, 1922, *FR: 1922*, II, 600–604.

to demonstrate Japanese expansive tendencies that were furthered by the existence of the alliance.

The American delegation believed it was fortunate in bringing about the replacement of a two-power defensive alliance calling for the use of force with a broader four-power agreement in which the United States did not assume heavy obligations. This was in keeping with the American rejection of the League of Nations. The only responsibility was a promise to attempt to settle any dispute arising in the Pacific by diplomacy or conference—both methods long used in American foreign relations.

While the powers agreed to respect the status quo, they did not provide enforcement either by military power or economic sanctions. The American government assumed that the Japanese would honor the agreement. All treaties rely on the good will of their signatories. If the United States was unwilling to support its diplomacy in the Pacific with a large navy, the alternative was acceptance at face value of the Japanese pledge to respect American possessions. There was probably about as much reason to be hopeful or distrustful of Japanese intentions in 1921 as to adopt the same sentiments toward the Soviet Union during World War II. In both cases the gamble of accommodation appeared preferable to the alternatives. The Japanese did not, in fact, break the treaty during the subsequent ten years.

X. CHINA: NINE-POWER TREATY

IN THE FIRST HALF of the twentieth century the chief locus of disagreement between the American and Japanese governments was, to be sure, China. After World War I the affection of the United States government for China tended to prevent closer relations with the Japanese. In the years before the war the Japanese had involved themselves in China, mostly in Manchuria but throughout the Chinese subcontinent, and these involvements threatened the American Open Door policy. By 1921 it was clear that disagreement over China could lead to serious complications for statesmen in Washington and Tokyo.[1]

At the base of the conflict over China was the idea of the Open Door, proclaimed by Secretary of State John Milton Hay in notes to the leading powers in 1899 and 1900. The first note was an attempt to line up the powers behind the traditional American policy of free competition for the trade of China. It did not envision the destruction of spheres of influence nor express any concern about China's welfare. It was a simple statement, with which Hay hoped the powers would agree. During the Boxer Rebellion of 1900 Hay sent the second Open Door note, which was a stronger proposition. The Secretary stated that American policy would attempt to seek a solution that would "preserve Chinese territorial and administrative entity" and safeguard commercial equality in "all parts" of the Chinese empire. It was a move against the parti-

[1] John Van Antwerp MacMurray advised Hughes that Japan by herself was not a menace, "but Japan in control of the mineral resources of China, with outside contact cut off, and with unimpeded access on her own part to the mainland, would be in a position to cause serious trouble to almost any power." MacMurray to Hughes, Oct. 20, 1921, Department of State 500.A41a/169.

145

tion of China, a long step away from the first Open Door note, and a most ambitious proposal by the United States government.[2] Its principles were often piously and publicly worshiped by other nations, but the backsliders in the congregation were always more numerous than were the faithful few.

American violations of the spirit of the note were also conspicuous in the Samsah Bay incident of 1900 and the Lansing-Ishii agreement of 1917. The author of the Open Door, in the year of its announcement, asked the Japanese if they would consent to American occupation of a naval base at Samsah Bay opposite Formosa, but the Japanese carefully reminded him of his Open Door principles.[3] Then the agreement between Secretary Lansing and the Japanese envoy Ishii, reached under some duress (the United States had entered the World War) on November 2, 1917, was a classic example of diplomatic mumbo jumbo. It stated that the United States and Japan "recognize that territorial propinquity creates special relations between countries, and consequently the government of the United States recognizes that Japan has special interests in China, particularly in the part to which her possessions are contiguous. The territorial sovereignty of China, nevertheless, remains unimpaired." [4] The sides interpreted the agreement differently. The Japanese saw it as a recognition of the existing paramount (i.e., superior) influence of Japan in China and therefore as a reversal of the Open Door policy.[5] Lansing claimed the agreement covered only economic interests created by geo-

2 A complete set of documents on the first Open Door note is printed in House Document 547, 56 Cong., 1 Sess.; the circular telegram from Hay can be found in *FR: 1900*, July 3, 1900, p. 299. Te-kong Tong, in *United States Diplomacy in China, 1844–60* (Seattle, 1964), demonstrates that the ideas of the second Open Door note date back to a much earlier period.

3 Copy of a telegram from the Japanese Foreign Office to the Japanese Embassy in Washington, D. C., handed to Secretary of State Hay on December 11, 1900. In *FR: 1915*, 115.

4 Notes exchanged between Secretary of State Robert Lansing and the special Japanese ambassador, Ishii Kikujiro, Nov, 2, 1917, *FR: 1917*, 264–65.

5 Memorandum by Nelson Trusler Johnson, "Japanese Interpretation of the Lansing-Ishii Agreement," n.d., Washington Conference Papers.

graphical propinquity.[6] A blunder? Perhaps not, but a mistake in need of correction.

It is understandable that on the eve of the Washington Conference there was official confusion over the Open Door. General Pershing asked for a definite Far Eastern policy since the "Open Door policy is a mere dream." [7] A Far Eastern expert in the Department of State, Stanley K. Hornbeck, concluded, in an understatement, that "some nations have either failed to understand the letter and spirit of the open door policy or have deliberately chosen to disregard both." [8] The recent commander of the Asiatic fleet, Rear Admiral William L. Rodgers, believed the door would stay open if China had an honest governing class capable of working with controlled foreign financial consortiums.[9] Herbert Hoover wanted more than Open Door principles: a $250 million loan to China, "conditional upon the elimination of the Communists and the creation of a much stiffer internal administration." He advised Hughes to follow such a policy rather than a "hands off" attitude.[10]

It was a special counselor of the Department of State, J. Reuben Clark, who presented the most realistic advice on the Far East; in 1928 he was to give some equally careful views on Latin America. The conference, he believed, should not attempt to expose wrongs of the past. It should assess existing evils and try to prevent their repetition. American security was foremost. The United States government should attempt to prevent the rise of any single great Asiatic power or the growth of pan-Asianism. On the latter problem he warned: "Give the Christian world, therefore—which

[6] Memorandum by Lansing, "The Lansing-Ishii Agreement," 1921, Lansing Papers.

[7] Comments by John J. Pershing on American Far Eastern policy, Aug. 1921, Pershing Papers.

[8] Memorandum by Hornbeck, "The Open Door Policy in China," n.d., Washington Conference Papers.

[9] General Board Report, "Stabilization of China," Nov. 3, 1921, *ibid.*

[10] Herbert Hoover, *Memoirs*, 180. For details of the consortium, established in 1921 before this proposal, see the Carnegie Endowment for International Peace, *The Consortium* (Washington, D. C., 1921).

means the white race—one more great world war of extermina-
tion and it will lie at the feet of the hordes of the Orient." To forestall the rise of the Japanese to Asian dominance he believed the
Chinese must secure independence; Clark was proposing a balance
of power rather than the Open Door (although the two were not
necessarily in opposition). He cautioned that the United States
government must recognize that the Japanese did have a special
relation with China. While building a railroad was just another
commercial venture for Americans, it might be economic survival
for the Japanese; the United States could afford to lose its small
trade with China (Clark believed American commerce with China
would never be great), but the Japanese could not. The Department should distinguish between positive (occupation of Shantung and negative (building railways) spheres and work to abolish the former.[11]

The Japanese Foreign Ministry in a departmental memorandum
of July 28 carefully surveyed the Japanese approach to China, the
Open Door, and the United States. If at all possible they wanted
to keep Chinese topics off the Washington agenda (here they
failed) and talk about principles rather than solutions to problems.
Should the conference decide to concentrate on Japanese activities
in China, the Japanese delegates should counterattack by bringing
up immigration into the United States, Western economic restrictions against Japanese trade, and racial discrimination. Such a tactic had worked at Paris.

If the Western powers gave up some of their privileges, the
Japanese might have to do the same. This appealed to them, on
one condition. Throughout the Japanese archives are scattered
references to the "closed door" which, the Japanese argued, was
the policy of the Chinese government in placing restrictions on
Japanese economic activities in China. The Chinese government
should not only grease the hinges of the Open Door but act as a
willing butler graciously serving up the riches of China.

[11] Memorandum by Clark to Hughes, "Some Basic Elements of the Far Eastern Problem," Sept. 29, 1921, Washington Conference Papers.

Finally, the Japanese memorandum concentrated on the Root-Takahira and Lansing-Ishii agreements as keys to the American attitude. The Japanese believed both of these documents were recognitions of Japanese special interests on the Chinese mainland. Any tripartite treaty replacing the Anglo-Japanese Alliance would apply to China. They hoped for another recognition of the special Japanese position. In strengthening ties with Britain with such an agreement "we can expect the Empire's position in the Orient to be secured." With British support and an understanding with the Americans, the future could be bright. The Japanese did not expect the Lansing-Ishii agreement to end since the American government was "always" attempting to "maintain present conditions and to have equal opportunity." [12]

Nor was British support of the Open Door unqualified. Foreign Officer adviser Ashton-Gwatkin wrote of the "fixed policy of the Japanese government to create an exclusive sphere in South Manchuria to an extent which, in spirit if not in letter, is a deliberate violation of the Open Door policy." British interests, according to Ashton-Gwatkin, were "essentially financial and non-political." He suggested a renewal of the Anglo-Japanese Alliance so that Japan's "special position in South Manchuria might be more clearly recognized." "Japan in Manchuria," he wrote, "has to a certain extent played the part of Great Britain in Egypt." He would thus oppose Japanese ambitions in Shantung, which, after all, could infringe on British interests, but would give "sympathetic consideration" to Japan's role in Manchuria.[13] Sir John Jordan offered perhaps wiser advice: that there was no easy solution to the China problem, that "China must in the main work out her own salvation and, given time, those who know her believe she can do it." Despite the best of intentions, foreign intervention and financial control would probably lead to chaos. The greatest service the Washington Conference could perform was to keep Chi-

[12] Memorandum by Japanese Foreign Ministry, July 28, 1921, reel MT 306, pp. 1–128.
[13] Memorandum by Ashton-Gwatkin on "Japan and the Open Door," Oct. 10, 1921, F. O. F4212/223/23.

na in one piece and accord "benevolent sympathy and reasonable time for putting her house in some sort of order." [14]

Reporters speculated that Hughes might suggest a plan on China much as he had presented naval limitation. The American delegation, however, had not worked out such a plan and deliberately left Chinese issues until last for three reasons. First, the naval arrangement and understanding with Japan regarding Pacific possessions that directly threatened American security seemed more important. By the time Chinese issues came before the conference, the Japanese, unwilling to jeopardize the Five- and Four-Power Treaties, discussed issues in a spirit of conciliation.

Second, Hughes recognized that vital American interests were not at stake in China when he said "this country would never go to war over any aggression on the part of Japan in China." [15] According to the diary of Chandler Anderson, Root said the American delegation began with the proposition that the United States government "would not be sufficiently interested in the open door or the preservation of Chinese integrity to go to war about them and that Japan realized this better than the average American." [16] The delegation would seek public support for the Open Door with virtuous example and moral exhortation, but no force.

Third, a group within the Japanese government seemed to desire a more peaceful path. A display of American faith in Japan, Americans reasoned, might encourage the group. Root said the United States must "show friendliness to Japan in order to give strength to the party in Japan which wanted to establish better foreign relations." [17]

During the Hughes-Geddes conversations in June of 1921 about renewal of the Anglo-Japanese Alliance, the Ambassador suggested that if a tripartite alliance were impossible then a dec-

---

[14] Memorandum by Jordan, Oct. 17, 1921, F. O. F3820/2635/10.
[15] Minutes of the American delegation, Dec. 17, 1921, Washington Conference Papers.
[16] Entry of Nov. 26, 1921, Anderson Papers.
[17] *Ibid.*

laration of common policies toward the Far East might serve.[18] Hughes appeared receptive, but the subject did not come up until November 11 when Balfour offered the draft of a five-power (Britain, China, Japan, France, the United States) treaty for peace in East Asia and preservation of Chinese integrity. Balfour could not have been too surprised to find Hughes unreceptive, for the draft called for periodic meetings and collective use of force, provisos which smacked of the League.[19]

Meanwhile, the isolated Chinese decided to present proposals. At the first meeting of the Committee on Pacific and Far Eastern Questions the chief Chinese delegate, Sao-ke Alfred Sze, present-ed ten principles. He asked the powers to respect his country's independence and territorial integrity. Sze explained that China was in full accord with the Open Door and wished to remove all limits on economic and political rights held by the powers.[20]

The Chinese secured wide publicity, but the three great powers paid little attention. At the next meeting of the committee each delegate pledged support for the Open Door. Root, who had been Secretary of War in McKinley's Cabinet when Hay had proposed the Open Door, said he was delighted to hear such endorsements. He offered to present a resolution which he hoped the nations would apply in their relations with China.[21] That same afternoon, November 19, 1921, the American delegation produced a propo-sition with the assistance of MacMurray and E. T. Williams, De-partment of State Far Eastern advisers; the advice of the Chinese was neither desired nor sought.[22] As modified and adopted by the conference, with almost no debate, the nine powers pledged, in what became famous phrases:

[18] Memorandum of a conversation between Hughes and Geddes, June 23, 1921, Department of State 741.9411/140½.

[19] Draft of a treaty presented to Hughes by Balfour in a conversation on Nov. 11, 1921, *FR: 1922*, I, 271–72.

[20] *C. L. A.*, Nov. 16, 1921, p. 866.

[21] *Ibid.*, 874–82.

[22] Minutes of the American delegation, Nov. 19, 1921, Washington Conference Papers.

To respect the sovereignty, the independence, and the territorial and administrative integrity of China;

(2) To provide the fullest and most unembarrassed opportunity to China to develop and maintain for herself an effective and stable government;

(3) To use their influence for the purpose of effectually establishing and maintaining the principle of equal opportunity for the commerce and industry of all nations throughout the territory of China;

(4) To refrain from taking advantage of the present conditions in order to seek special rights or privileges which would abridge the rights of the subjects or citizens of friendly states and from countenancing action inimical to the security of such states.[23]

Here were the so-called Root resolutions. The first three were restatements of policies toward China expressed by the powers on many occasions; Roosevelt commented in his diary that "these have been enunciated a thousand times before. There is nothing new in them." [24] But the first part of the fourth clause was a quotation from the secret protocol of the Lansing-Ishii agreement. Hughes, according to his own later description, had taken the opportunity to insert this clause, which limited American recognition of Japanese interests. It was an attempt to rectify the damage of Lansing's agreement.[25]

An article by the scholar Sadao Asada, based on his study of the Japanese archives, claims that Root in a serious indiscretion added to the fourth clause the phrase "from countenancing action inimical to the security of such states." Japanese diplomats in 1918–1920 had tried to exclude areas of Manchuria and Mongolia from consortium arrangements by arguing that the security of Japan closely related to those areas. The Japanese had claimed that an American note of March 16, 1920, which used the phrase "refuse their countenance to any operation inimical to the vital interests of Japan" had recognized the Japanese position. They concluded

23 *C. L. A.*, Nov. 21, 1921, p. 900.
24 Entry of Jan. 13, 1921, Roosevelt Papers.
25 Beerits memorandum, Far Eastern Questions, Hughes Papers.

that Root, who had told Hanihara he supported Japan's position in East Asia, was now affirming the interests of the Japanese government in Manchuria and Inner Mongolia; those areas, they believed, were now excluded from the Open Door.[26]

It was an important issue. If the Japanese interpretation were correct, what the first part of the fourth clause of the Root resolutions gave, the second part took away. Root did believe the United States government would never go to war for China, was less suspicious of the Japanese than were his colleagues, and was sure the American government did not have vital interests and the Japanese did.[27] But there is no indication in the American archives that this sort of understanding was reached with the Japanese. If so, such an agreement went undetected and unsupported by the rest of the American delegation or the conference record; moreover, it conflicts with other clauses.

In the absence of evidence from the American or British archives, or further support from the Japanese archives, this author finds little support for the Asada thesis; if the agreement existed at all, it existed in the minds of the Japanese and not the Americans, and even that is questionable. For reports by Major General Tanaka back to the Army and his general report to the Regent (not mentioned by Asada) do not support the allegation that the Japanese received such a recognition. On February 5, 1922, Tanaka argued that the purpose of the United States government "is to chase the Japanese out of Manchuria," but the Americans did not actively pursue that goal because of a similar position by the British in Kowloon.[28] In the report to the Regent he said that "Japan gave up all that she had in China." [29] Tanaka, who represented the mil-

---

[26] Sadao Asada, "Japan's Special Interests and the Washington Conference, 1921–22," *American Historical Review*, LXVII (Oct. 1961), 62–70.

[27] Memorandum of a visit by Henry L. Stimson on Nov. 16, 1921, with Elihu Root, Stimson Papers (Yale University).

[28] Telegram from Tanaka to the Army Minister, Feb. 5, 1922, Army and Navy Archives, reel 131, pp. 49496–49503. There is of course the fact that the Japanese and Americans seemed able to agree only by formulating statements which each could interpret in his own way; the evidence is still weak.

[29] Report on the Washington Conference by General Tanaka to the Regent,

itary group which had received a setback in the conference treaties, was unhappy; his comments, however, do raise the question of why he did not mention the last clause of the fourth part of the Root resolutions as a recognition of the Japanese position in Manchuria and Inner Mongolia, for he certainly would have regarded this as an advancement of Japanese interests.

Hughes later was to argue that the Root resolutions (incorporated into the Nine-Power Treaty) ended the Lansing-Ishii agreement, but to the amazement of Hughes the Japanese replied that they did not feel the two agreements conflicted. In the ensuing debate the Japanese Foreign Ministry never mentioned the Root additional phrase. When they finally agreed to cancellation of the Lansing-Ishii agreement in 1923, the Japanese did so with the understanding that such action "was not to be taken as an indication of a change in the position of Japan relating to China." [30]

There was criticism of the Root resolutions, and in a letter to the New York *Herald* an opponent protested: "They are vague and general and in the light of history are bound to be looked upon by the parties in interest as meaningless." [31] Root indignantly told Anderson that the well-oiled British propaganda machine was producing these attacks. He suspected the British delegation opposed the resolutions, for they might interfere with British economic interests.[32] But the powers at the conference including Britain supported Root by passing an additional resolve prohibiting treaties or agreements that would impair the Root resolutions.[33]

Hughes, who wanted a more definite statement of the Open Door, presented a resolution on January 16, 1922, which forbade economic practices such as monopolies; the next day Hughes presented an extended, revised draft prepared by Sir Llewellyn Smith and MacMurray. The only important addition was an internation-

---

March 18, 1922, Army and Navy Archives, reel 131, pp. 48982–49023. Tanaka may have been referring only to China proper.

[30] Correspondence relating to the cancellation of the Lansing-Ishii agreement can be found in *FR: 1922*, II, 591–99.

[31] New York *Herald*, Nov. 23, 1921.

[32] Diary of Chandler P. Anderson, Nov. 24, 1921, Anderson Papers.

[33] *C. L. A.*, Dec. 8, 1921, p. 1124.

al board to which nations could refer disagreements about the Open Door. Both the American and British delegations had discussed this idea. Because of possible senatorial opposition over decisions by an international group, Hughes withdrew American support just before adoption of the Open Door resolution. The conference did provide that the board plan should be reconsidered at a future conference on the Chinese tariff.[34]

Coupled with the Open Door resolution was another resolve sponsored by the American delegation, that none of the powers would make any agreements which "create spheres of influence or . . . provide for the enjoyment of mutually exclusive opportunities in designated parts of Chinese territory." [35] This was certainly in line with traditional American foreign policy.

Hughes realized, as did Root, that all the resolutions would not have the force of a treaty, and Root now suggested that the most important resolutions should go into a treaty.[36] At first the American draft included almost all the resolutions pertaining to China adopted by the conference. Hughes limited the Nine-Power Treaty to the Root resolutions (and the agreement not to make treaties in conflict with them), the Open Door resolution, the spheres-of-influence prohibition, a promise by China not to discriminate on its railroads, a pledge by the powers to respect China's neutral rights in the event of a war, and a promise by the nine nations to communicate if a dispute arose.[37] In this form the conference approved the Nine-Power Treaty on February 3, 1922.[38]

The Nine-Power Treaty proved to be the weakest link in the Washington treaty chain. The Open Door had a fine sound to American ears; preserving Chinese territorial and administrative integrity sounded important, if not essential. Behind the words,

[34] *Ibid.*, 1214, 1224–26; diary of Chandler P. Anderson, Jan. 30, 1922, Anderson Papers; *C. L. A.*, 284.

[35] *C. L. A.*, 1366.

[36] Diary of Chandler P. Anderson, Dec. 11, 1921, Anderson Papers.

[37] *Ibid.*, Jan. 14, 1922.

[38] *C. L. A.*, 1526. Roosevelt again commented to his diary that "as far as I can see there is nothing objectionable . . . . I think it will be treated as of very little interest." Diary of Theodore Roosevelt, Jr., Jan. 14, 1922, Roosevelt Papers.

however, there was no power, nor even the desire to use power. The broad, unlimited goal of the Open Door had not been defined in terms narrow enough to be in accord with the available, limited extent of American military and political power. China possessed a vast area far from the United States, a huge population, and a complex politics difficult, if not impossible, for a foreign nation to influence by ordinary political, economic, or military means. China was not united, and all the President's ships and all the President's sailors could not have put China back together again. Yet, within the United States the Open Door was widely regarded as having prevented the partition of China by virtue of the American "guarantee" of its territorial integrity; this was not true since the balance of power was primarily responsible. Despite the fact that the image did not accord with reality, domestically the Open Door was popular. American statesmen were guilty of not pointing out the limitations of the Open Door to the American people and found it impossible to abandon the Open Door for a more realistic policy. Continued support of the Open Door, by formally writing it into treaty form without explaining its weaknesses to the American public, was a mistake on the part of the American delegation. What was needed was an American statesman with the foresight and courage to forget about the Open Door and to apply a more carefully defined metaphor to American China policy that conformed with reality.

XI. CHINA: SHANTUNG AND SOVEREIGNTY

TWO OTHER ASPECTS of the China problem, the Sino-Japanese dispute over Shantung and the Chinese attempt to regain sovereign control over their internal affairs, concerned the conference delegates. Japanese occupation of the rich and hugely populous peninsula of Shantung had caused much wrangling before the conference. Hughes and Balfour were to make a large effort to persuade the two Asian countries to agree. The Chinese delegates also were interested in dissolving the restrictions on their government's political and economic sovereignty. Such problems, more directly touching treaty rights and foreign interests than the Nine-Power Treaty, proved hard to solve. Agreement in principle with the Open Door was one thing, application another.

The most important special problem in regard to China at the Washington Conference was how to get the Japanese out of the province of Shantung. Directly west of Korea, the province juts out into the Eastern Sea and contains deposits of iron, gold, coal, and sulphur. Wellington Koo at Paris had called it "the Holy Land of the Chinese, the Home of Confucius." Hughes and Balfour realized that a successful disposition of the Shantung question would go far to allay Chinese fears about its future, and thus generally produce a more peaceful atmosphere in East Asia.

The Japanese had moved into Shantung as a result of the development of a situation that appeared to favor Japanese interests. The Chinese in 1898 had granted the German government a ninety-year lease of a naval base at Kiaochow Bay along with an economic influence in the area within the peninsula later served by the Shantung Railway. (In that same year the British forced the

Chinese to hand over a lease for a naval base at Weihaiwei, also in the area, to maintain a power balance.) Later, in August 1914, the Japanese government, acting as an ally of Britain under the Anglo-Japanese Alliance, declared war on Germany and proceeded to occupy the German concession in Shantung. The Japanese Foreign Ministry, in an attempt to further solidify its position, made secret agreements with the French, Russian, and British governments in which the Western powers promised to support a Japanese claim to Shantung at the forthcoming peace conference. By that date Japanese troops had extended their control into the interior along the entire Shantung Railway and had what amounted to almost complete political control.[1]

Although Japanese actions in Shantung exceeded the conditions of the German lease, the Japanese government found some justification in the Shantung clauses of the Twenty-One Demands of 1915. Unwillingly the Chinese government had signed away its future claims by agreeing to recognize any arrangement that might be made between the Japanese and German governments regarding the latter's interests in Shantung. The Japanese Foreign Ministry in principle agreed to return the leased territory to China, but only after Japanese economic interests had received a preferred position in the province; a September 1918 agreement spelled out the very special economic rights the Japanese would retain when retrocession occurred.[2]

The Versailles Treaty clauses on Shantung, according to which Germany gave to Japan "rights, title, and privileges . . . and other arrangements relative to the province," gave formal international recognition to the Japanese position.[3] Having entered the war on the side of the Allies against Germany in hope of regaining Shantung as a reward for its efforts, the Chinese government, bitterly disappointed and under strong domestic pressures, did not sign

[1] Russell H. Fifield, *Woodrow Wilson and the Far East: The Diplomacy of the Shantung Question* (New York, 1952), reviews the background. See also Carnegie Endowment for International Peace, *Shantung: Treaties and Agreements* (Washington, D. C., 1921), 1–9, 65–66, 82–84.

[2] Carnegie Endowment, *Shantung*, 84–88, 91–93.

[3] *Ibid.*, 98.

the treaty.[4] The Japanese came to regard the Versailles Treaty as final. They did offer to negotiate with the Chinese, but the Peking government, fearful of losing face, refused.

The Shantung situation had proved embarrassing to the United States government. In principle it did not favor concessions and spheres in China; Hay's second Open Door note was a protest against such practices. In addition, Secretary Bryan in 1915 had refused to recognize any treaty flowing from the Twenty-One Demands.[5] A reversal took place at Paris when President Wilson, to assure the membership of Japan in the projected League, agreed to the allocation of Germany's interests in Shantung to the Japanese government. The Shantung provisions had then become one of the chief arguments of the anti-League group in the Senate debate as they accused Wilson of selling the Chinese down the proverbial river.[6]

The Shantung controversy dragged on into the summer of 1921. The Chinese refused to negotiate on an issue based on treaties they did not recognize. Shidehara, in July 1921, told Hughes that despite the poor legal position of the Chinese, the Japanese government was willing to enter negotiations to settle the problem before the conference met. This idea appealed to Hughes, who said he would suggest to the Chinese that negotiations start, but only if Japanese terms were reasonable.[7] A short time later Sze told Hughes that his government was reluctant to negotiate without the Department of State as mediator. Hughes stated that the Department would not accept the role of formal mediator, but he would inquire about the Japanese proposals. Hughes was very careful, for he did not wish to raise obstacles between Japan and

[4] Payson J. Treat, "The Shantung Question," *The Pacific Review*, II (Sept. 1921), 298–308, is a good contemporary review of the situation on the eve of the conference. Russell H. Fifield, "Secretary Hughes and the Shantung Question," *Pacific Historical Review*, XXIII (Nov. 1954), 373–85, covers the conference.

[5] Telegram from Secretary of State William Jennings Bryan to the American Ambassador in Tokyo, George W. Guthrie, May 11, 1915, *FR: 1915*, 146.

[6] For criticism by Senator Warren G. Harding of Wilson and Shantung, see New York *Times*, Sept. 22, 1920.

[7] Memorandum by Hughes of a conversation with Shidehara, July 21, 1921, *FR: 1921*, I, 613–15.

the United States that might interfere with more important issues at the conference.[8]

Within a month Shidehara presented the Japanese proposals, and although they were not final demands the Chinese assumed that they were and rejected them. The Department's Far Eastern advisers, MacMurray, Hornbeck, and Williams, concluded that the Shantung Railway was the key. The Japanese wanted control. The experts felt the Japanese should give up the railway, and if they did not the Department should dissociate itself from the proposals.[9]

The Chinese delegation wanted to bring up Shantung at the conference, and although Hughes was sympathetic he advised against it. He pointed out that since seven of the powers at the conference had signed the Versailles Treaty, it would be difficult for them to agree to a change. There was also the possibility that in public discussion the Japanese position might harden. Hughes, it must be noted, was well aware of the political significance of the Shantung question, for the conference treaties themselves might run into opposition in the Senate, much as the Versailles Treaty had, if the Japanese continued to retain Shantung; thus for domestic, as well as international reasons, a Far Eastern settlement was impossible without a satisfactory disposition of Shantung. Bilateral negotiation between the two Asian nations appeared to offer the best chance for a settlement.[10]

Even the British demonstrated some interest. Foreign Office adviser Miles Lampson had written, shortly before the conference, that the British government had made the 1917 agreement with the Japanese under the pressure of the World War and should now rectify that mistake, for the British had "unwittingly been a party to a great injustice to China" and should not renew the Anglo-Japanese Alliance without attempting to redress the wrong. Even

[8] Memorandum by Hughes of a conversation with Sze, Aug. 11, 1921, *ibid.,* 615.
[9] Memorandum by MacMurray, Hornbeck, and Williams, "Japan's Shantung Proposals," Sept. 15, 1921, Department of State 793.94/1284.
[10] Telegram from Hughes to Schurman, Oct. 29, 1921, *FR: 1921,* I, 628.

if such an attempt were unsuccessful, it would at the least win the British some friends in China.[11]

Shortly after the conference opened, Hughes and Balfour, working together, separately approached both the chief Japanese delegate, Kato, and the Chinese representative, Sze. They suggested negotiation under their good offices. Hughes cabled the American minister in Peking to impress on the Chinese the desirability of taking part in such conversations.[12]

Kato carefully reported to Uchida that he had told Hughes and Balfour that the Japanese government wanted to solve the Shantung issue without bringing it up to the conference. He asked for an immediate Cabinet meeting to approve the acceptance of the American and British mediation. Because the Chinese were afraid to approach the Japanese, Kato gave his approval to the mediation as the best possible solution. He saw one drawback: the mediators might attempt to advise on the disposition of the railway. By return wire Uchida gave permission.[13]

The Shantung conversations began on December 1 and continued on and off for two months. After the first meeting Hughes and Balfour did not attend, and MacMurray and Counselor Edward Bell observed for the United States, with Lampson for Britain. In all there were thirty-six meetings.[14] By December 20 the Chinese, led by Koo, and the Japanese, headed by Shidehara, had reached a preliminary agreement on almost everything except the 290-mile-long Tsingtao-Tsinanfu Railroad. The Chinese delegates would not agree to the Japanese proposal for a joint enter-

[11] Memorandum by Miles Lampson, Dec. 1, 1920, F. O. F3062/33/10.

[12] Telegram from Hughes to Schurman, Nov. 25, 1921, *FR: 1922,* I, 934–35.

[13] Telegram from the Japanese delegation to Uchida, Nov. 26, 1920, reel MT 317, pp. 450–53; telegram from Uchida to the delegation, Nov. 29, 1921, reel MT 313, pp. 216–17.

[14] The two main printed sources on the conversations are *Conversations between the Chinese and Japanese Representatives in regard to the Shantung Question: Minutes prepared by the Japanese Delegation* (Washington, D. C., 1922) and *Conversations between the Chinese and Japanese Representatives in regard to the Shantung Question: Prepared by the Chinese Delegation* (Washington, D. C., 1923). The Japanese account is a fuller, more detailed account. The Chinese version is more of a summary prepared by W. W. Willoughby for the Chinese delegation.

prise. Shidehara then proposed that the Japanese return the road to Chinese control, but that the Chinese government—to pay for the railway secured from the Germans—accept from Japanese financiers a fifteen-year long-term loan. Technical experts would remain on the road until the loan was paid. The Chinese delegates wanted to pay cash immediately or Chinese treasury notes, but the Japanese were not willing to gamble on the value of Chinese currency or immediate Chinese control. Privately the American delegation favored the cash settlement but did not indicate this fact to representatives of the two nations.[15] From all indications Shidehara in backing off from the proposal of joint ownership was acting on his own, but his timing on Shantung was wrong, for at the end of December orders came from Tokyo; under attack in Japanese newspapers, the Japanese position hardened and they would move no further than the offer of a long-term loan.[16]

Negotiations had lapsed when the Japanese had referred the controversy to Tokyo for instructions. They resumed on January 4, 1922, when Shidehara repeated his offer of a long-term loan of from five to fifteen years. China's delegates again proposed an immediate cash payment or deferred payment of Chinese treasury notes. The Chinese suggested that the two nations avail themselves of the good offices of Hughes and Balfour. Shidehara replied that his instructions were so explicit that he could not agree to invite the mediators. Again the meeting broke off, and the first serious threat to the negotiation had arisen, as anticipated, over the crucial question of the railway.[17]

Hughes and Balfour moved indirectly; by way of the American and British observers they proposed four avenues of compromise.[18] Conversation resumed on January 11 on all unsettled questions except the railroad. Meanwhile, Hughes and Balfour had

---

[15] Minutes of the American delegation, Dec. 16, 1921, Washington Conference Papers.

[16] Conversation of Lampson with Matsudaira, Dec. 31, 1921, Cabinet Office 30, 27/1.

[17] *Minutes Prepared by the Japanese Delegation*, 91–93. See also RCS to Lansing, Jan. 9, 1922, Lansing Papers.

[18] Hughes to Schurman, Feb. 15, 1922, *FR: 1922*, I, 960–67.

informal talks with the delegates in which, with difficulty, they persuaded the Japanese and Chinese to accept the fourth American proposal as a basis of discussion, payment based in Chinese treasury notes over a fifteen-year period.[19] Lodge confided to his diary that the Chinese, who wanted control of the railway immediately, "are very difficult . . . . We shall have to take a very strong ground with them." [20]

Within the American advisory group there was some opposition to pressing the Chinese. In separate memoranda Hornbeck and Williams advised Hughes to press the Japanese. Williams felt it "better to leave the question unsettled than to be put in a position of aiding Japanese aggression." [21] In a blistering reply Hughes wrote, "I have the responsibility of dealing with this matter and am dealing with it because I am convinced that if China does not accept this settlement she will lose Shantung, and I am trying to save it for her." [22]

At the same time Hanihara reported he had discussed Shantung with Root in another unofficial talk. Root told Hanihara there were pro- and anti-Japanese groups among the American advisers and that the anti-Japanese group was urging the delegates to help China. Confidentially he told Hanihara that the American delegation was not listening.[23] This could only have encouraged the Japanese. If the Americans were reading intercepted Japanese telegrams, the Japanese were reading Root.

Hughes took Sze to see Harding on the Shantung question, and the President told the Chinese that they would be making a colossal blunder if they did not seize the opportunity to settle the problem. He warned of the likelihood of losing the province for-

[19] Minutes by Hankey on the meetings of Jan. 18, 19, and 22, in Department of State 793.94/1300a; memorandum of a Hughes-Balfour talk, Jan. 18, 1922, F. O. F480/69/10.

[20] Entry of Jan. 18, 1922, Lodge Papers.

[21] Memorandum from Hornbeck to Hughes, Jan. 23, 1922, and memorandum from Williams to Hughes, Jan. 23, 1922, Department of State 793.94/1309.

[22] Hughes to MacMurray (to be relayed to Hornbeck and Williams), Jan. 26, 1922, Department of State 793.94/1265.

[23] Telegram from Hanihara to Uchida, Jan. 24, 1922, reel MT 319, pp. 2603-607.

ever.[24] Clearly, the problem was of great importance to the American delegation, and even the Japanese delegates recognized the danger to the other conference treaties when they reported that Senator Thomas J. Walsh had requested a report on American actions with regard to Shantung. The Senator then stated that the Senate should not consent to the Four-Power Treaty until Shantung was settled.[25]

Using the American proposal as a basis, the Japanese finally agreed to accept Chinese treasury notes, backed by revenues of the road, over a fifteen-year period (the Chinese government to have an option of paying off after five years), and the Chinese agreed to the employment of two Japanese technical experts. Hughes proudly announced completion of the Shantung negotiations on January 31, 1922, at the fifth plenary session of the conference.[26]

Each country looked at the settlement in its own way. Roosevelt concluded it was "much more than I think anyone had a right to expect . . . . I can't see how anyone, even the wildest-eyed, can point a finger of scorn in this matter." [27] Balfour regarded it as a "principal achievement." [28] The Japanese delegation reported failure, but argued that its concessions had given the other nations a good impression of Japanese intentions.[29]

Balfour now promised to return to the Chinese the concession at Weihaiwei.[30] With support of the delegation he had wanted to use such a retrocession during the Shantung negotiation, but Curzon initially had refused. Balfour had moved on, despite Curzon's

[24] Hughes to Schurman, Feb. 15, 1922, *FR: 1922*, I, 1963.

[25] Telegram from the delegation to Uchida, Jan. 26, 1922, reel MT 319, pp. 2686–88.

[26] Treaty between Japan and China for the settlement of outstanding questions relative to Shantung, Feb. 4, 1922, *FR: 1922*, I, 948–60; *C. L. A.*, 200. See also telegram from the delegation to Uchida, Jan. 29, 1922, reel MT 319, pp. 3099–116.

[27] Diary of Theodore Roosevelt, Jr., Feb. 1, 1922, Roosevelt Papers.

[28] Balfour to Lloyd George, Feb. 4, 1922, F. O. F716/69/10.

[29] Telegram from the delegation to Uchida, Feb. 6, 1922, reel MT 319, pp. 3441–43.

[30] *C. L. A.*, 226.

continued reluctance, and made the offer.[31] It was not restored to China, however, until October 1930.

When one considers that the Japanese by treaty were in possession of the province and could not be evicted by the Chinese, the return of Shantung was quite an achievement for China. By the end of 1922, Japanese troops had left Tsingtao. The Chinese Republic received political control, and interest payments were made, but no amortization took place until June 1937, when war canceled the indebtedness. Part of the credit belonged to Hughes and Balfour. Insisting upon separate negotiations, they gave the Chinese an opportunity to regain Shantung and made certain the Japanese would not suffer humiliation; if the Chinese had brought the question before the conference, it is doubtful if they could have had any favorable settlement. But it was the conciliatory attitude of the Japanese that made the outcome possible.

One should add a note about another Japanese withdrawal promised at the conference: Japan's removal of her troops from Siberia. The Japanese had intervened there in 1918 during the Russian revolution; American troops had left in 1920, but the Japanese had remained. The Japanese government claimed it had to protect citizens in the area and afford security to Korea against Bolshevist activities. The United States government had refused to recognize Japanese claims in the area.[32] Hughes had included Siberia on the Washington agenda in order to call attention to the Japanese presence. When that portion of the agenda came up for discussion, Shidehara referred to Japanese negotiations with a provisional Russian government of Chita at Dairen; when satisfactory arrangements were made, he said, Japanese troops would with-

---

[31] Telegram from Balfour to Curzon, Dec. 19, 1921, F. O. F4749/833/10; telegram from Curzon to Balfour, Dec. 23, 1921, F. O. F4749/833/10; telegram from Curzon to Balfour, Jan. 30, 1922, F. O. F421/138/10; Balfour to Lloyd George, Feb. 4, 1922, F. O. F823/138/10.

[32] For Japanese-American correspondence on this point see *FR: 1921*, II, 701–20; an excellent description can be found in Betty Miller Unterberger, *America's Siberian Expedition: 1918–1920: A Study of National Policy* (Durham, N. C., 1956).

draw, and from Northern Sakhalin as well.[33] Hughes implied in his reply that Shidehara's offer pertained to economic as well as military withdrawal, but the Japanese delegates reported to Tokyo that they did not believe themselves so bound.[34] Roosevelt believed Shidehara's pronouncement would "satisfy our people, and it is all we can get, but I do not for a moment think she will live up to it, nor do I think that we will attempt to make her live up to it." [35] To the amazement of skeptics, shortly after the conference, but only after further American prodding, the Japanese withdrew.[36]

Matters of domestic jurisdiction are not generally the concern of international conferences, but the Chinese during the last decades of the Manchu dynasty had given economic and political concessions to foreign nations which the Republic after 1911 was eager to regain, but China in the 1920's was a nation torn by civil war. Competing nationalistic groups, while primarily fighting for power and position, also hoped to create a strong, modern country that could meet foreign nations on an equal basis. Whether looking to the Confucian past, communist Russia, or the Western democracies for aid and ideology, all agreed that rights and privileges held by foreigners in China had to end. The elaborate "unequal treaty" system, dating from the Treaty of Nanking in 1842, was under concerted attack, clearly in danger of destruction. All civil wars temporarily bring dislocation and problems to international relations, but in China these were magnified and intensified by the Chinese effort to change the treaty system. The Peking government in 1921 was not powerful enough to unilaterally abrogate the commitments but did hope that nations holding concessions might voluntarily surrender all or part of them.

[33] *C. L. A.*, 354–56, 1394–1402.
[34] Telegram from the delegation to Uchida, Feb. 9, 1922, reel MT 319, pp. 3575–76.
[35] Diary of Theodore Roosevelt, Jr., Jan. 23, 1922, Roosevelt Papers.
[36] For correspondence between the United States and Japan about the final

There were two drawbacks to the Chinese plan, the chief of which, of course, was the weakness of the Peking government. A competing government at Canton questioned its legitimacy, and local warlords held much power. The civil wars devastated the country and impoverished the national treasury. Although the Peking government in good faith might contend that it had eliminated the political conditions that had forced the powers to demand special rights, this obviously was not the case. A second drawback to the Chinese plan was that even if a united Chinese state appeared there was no easy method by which the government could purchase or end foreign economic interests short of expropriation. Could the Chinese develop their industries without assistance? China's government had defaulted on a foreign loan on the eve of the Washington Conference. It was doubtful if the Chinese could purchase the concessions or operate them at a profit to pay off foreign stockholders.

American delegates favored abolition of foreign territorial and economic concessions; any abrogation was a step toward the Open Door since spheres of influence probably meant restrictions on American goods, and territorial control certainly did. Here again the concessions came from treaties, and the Americans could not easily force a nation to give up a treaty right. And could, or should, the American government place itself at an economic disadvantage in China by surrendering privileges which the other powers did not relinquish?

The extraterritorial problem in China was not an easy one. The principle of administrative integrity so often voiced by Americans as part of the Open Door policy had led the Chinese to ask for a loosening of extraterritorial rights and abolition within the foreseeable future.[37] At the conference the American government supported a resolution that a committee study China's extraterritorial as well as judicial system. Each nation was "free to accept

---

withdrawal of Japanese troops, which took place in October 1922, see *FR: 1922*, II, 840–67.

[37] *C. L. A.*, 932–36.

or to reject all or any portion of the recommendations of the commission." [38] It did put off a decision, and without doubt did reflect a suspicion among the powers, including the United States, that China's judicial structure was not in such order that foreign nations could hope for fair treatment of nationals. The conference was held in 1925, but it was not until during World War II that the leading Western nations gave up their extraterritorial rights (the United States government not acting until 1943) although several governments, including the American, were favorably disposed toward doing so in the 1920's.[39]

The Chinese delegates did win a slight improvement in the tariff. The Peking government wished autonomy, but if that were unobtainable it desired a raise in rates. China had treaties with many of the powers setting the rate at 5 per cent ad valorem; by treaties the Chinese government had pledged part of the revenue to foreign bankers to pay off loans. There had been attempts to raise the rate, none successful, and it was not surprising when the conference did not raise the rate. A proposal to raise the tariff to 7½ per cent met Japanese opposition. The only result was a provision calling for a conference to make the rate an effective 5 per cent (this conference was to meet in Shanghai in 1922, but it was not until 1925 that effective negotiations began) and another which allowed a 2½ per cent surtax.[40] France did not ratify the

---

[38] *Ibid.*, 150–54.

[39] In a memorandum to Hughes, E. T. Williams described the working of the extraterritorial system. "In 1902 two Americans, one Englishman, a Dane and two Chinese were all concerned in the robbery of a pawnshop at Tungchou and the killing of the proprietor. All were arrested on the day following . . . . The two Chinese were executed within 48 hours; the two Americans a few weeks later were sentenced to four years in a federal penitentiary; the Englishman waited in jail six months for trial, by which time the witnesses had lost interest and did not appear against him, so that he was acquited; and Denmark not having a consular official at hand, the Dane was released." Memorandum by Williams, "Extraterritoriality in China," n.d., Washington Conference Papers. See also Wesley R. Fishel, *The End of Extraterritoriality in China* (Berkeley, Cal., 1952).

[40] *C. L. A.*, 920–24, 294–306; *Subcommittees*, 560; minutes of the American delegation, Nov. 30, 1921, Washington Conference Papers. Curzon instructed Balfour that he should stick to general principles and leave details on the tariff to

treaty until 1925, and it was not until 1930 that the Chinese gained tariff autonomy.

Senator Underwood revealed that the United States government wanted complete tariff autonomy for China but did not believe that it would be possible until the Chinese had established a stable government. It was feared that the increased revenues would simply be used by the Peking government to increase its armaments and lead to a continuation of the civil war and chaos in China.[41] The United States played a leading role in the movement toward tariff autonomy in China during the 1920's, but the American delegation might have taken a stronger stand at the Washington Conference without endangering its interests.

American delegates did support a move by the Chinese to abolish foreign post offices in China. Out of the diplomatic courier system of delivering dispatches these establishments had developed into a full-scale postal system in competition with the regular Chinese organization. As the Chinese correctly pointed out, the foreign postal trade was the lucrative part, the carriage trade of all Chinese mails. The Chinese delegation promised an efficient postal system and a foreign postal director. The Japanese reluctantly agreed and the Chinese won their point.[42]

Chinese attempts to reassert their sovereignty over their country continued. The Chinese government was eager for the withdrawal of foreign troops in China "without the authority of any treaty or agreement." This largely involved the Japanese, who had troops in China under the guise of protecting Japanese citizens and concessions from bandits. The Japanese perhaps would have been willing to pull out some troops, but the conference not only seemingly condoned the practice of foreign troops but

---

the legation at Peking and "British traders in China." Telegram from Curzon to Balfour, Dec. 17, 1921, F. O. F4637/61/10. The Japanese were instructed to hold back from putting the revised taxation into practice in Uchida to delegation, Nov. 28, 1921, reel MT 313, pp. 181–83.

[41] *C. L. A.*, 292.

[42] *Ibid.*, 940–78. Telegram from Uchida to the delegation, Dec. 4, 1921, reel MT 313, pp. 246–48.

passed a resolution that the Chinese reduce the numbers of their own soldiers. Delegates from the United States kept silent on the issue, again asking investigation by a committee.[43]

The conference tried to settle the problem of the Chinese Eastern Railway, the main line of Manchuria which afforded the Russians a shortcut to Vladivostok. Although the road was in Chinese territory, the Russians had furnished the funds, directed its construction, and operated the road. For nearly twenty years the railway had belonged to the Russian government although the Chinese retained reversionary rights. The Bolshevist revolution in Russia upset this arrangement and brought an inter-Allied agreement in 1919 which placed the Siberian and Chinese Eastern under a sort of trusteeship; upon establishment of a stable government in Russia the railroad would revert to the old arrangement.[44] The technical subcommittee at the Washington Conference recommended some changes in the agreement of 1919, such as a new commission to handle the problems of finance, operation, and protection. The Chinese insisted they could handle these problems.[45] John F. Stevens, the American expert in charge of the inter-Allied commission, commented that the Chinese proposed "to take the railway from Russia without paying for it, which [they are] not entitled to do under the treaty until the end of 81 years." [46] Two resolutions concerning the Chinese Eastern passed the conference: one asked for better protection, service, and use of funds and recommended negotiation. The second, not signed by the Chinese, insisted that the Chinese government shoulder the obligations of the railroad. To the last the Chinese delegates contended they were running the railroad in absence of a recognized Russian government.[47]

The American delegates did sponsor a resolution calling on

[43] *C.L.A.*, 184–86, 192.

[44] Carnegie Endowment for International Peace, *Manchuria: Treaties and Agreements* (Washington, D. C., 1921), 13–17, 32–34.

[45] *C. L. A.*, 376–78, 1378–80.

[46] Memorandum by Stevens to Hughes, Dec. 3, 1921, Washington Conference Papers.

[47] *C. L. A.*, 1658, 320–24.

each nation to submit a list of contracts (government and individual), conventions, and treaties with China. Unsure of their international obligations, the Chinese thought such a listing would help, and the conference concurred.[48]

Glancing from the Chinese viewpoint at the results of the Washington Conference, one could say that China gained little; but a more careful look would reveal progress, not an affirmation of the status quo. The conference marked the beginning of a new day. With the exception of Shantung, foreign treaty rights remained, but no new restrictions tied the Chinese; they were safe from depredations and had only to gather strength and confidence to rid themselves of the past.

For the American government the result was more tangible and encouraging as it observed one of the rare spectacles of the interwar period: a voluntary check to Japanese expansion. The withdrawal of Japan from Shantung and Siberia was an achievement. It is true, however, that the position and dominance of Japan in Manchuria, the key area as far as the Japanese were concerned, was basically untouched. Again, as in the case of the Nine-Power Treaty, it was a question of whether the United States wanted to attack the Japanese position and, if so, how to do it most effectively. The gamble of accommodation with the Japanese appeared a more realistic choice, in view of the small degree of the American interest, than military competition. China in the long run, and perhaps even in the short run, would determine its own destiny and the United States recognized that fact.

[48] *Ibid.*, 194–96, 1290.

XII. THE SENATE AND THE TREATIES

THE WASHINGTON CONFERENCE ended on February 6, 1922, in the same way in which it had begun nearly three months before—with an address by Harding. It was the same sort of speech. The President declared that the Washington agreements marked "the beginning of a new and better epoch in human affairs." Any one of the treaties, he believed, was justification for the conference, and in an obvious contrast to those instruments drawn up at Paris in 1919 he was sure that no treaty contained the seed of future conflict. Harding remarked, "How simple it all has been." [1]

Few senators dared attack the popular naval treaty or the agreements pertaining to China. It was apparent that the main battle—if there were one—would come on the more controversial Four-Power Treaty.

From the President on down, the administration supported the treaties by praising them at every opportunity, even with some exaggeration. Hughes said that the Five-Power Naval Treaty "ends, absolutely ends, the race in competition in naval armament." The report to the President by the American delegation stated that "probably no more significant treaty was ever made." Vice-President Calvin Coolidge thought that the Washington agreements "promised to be one of the achievements of history." [2]

[1] C. L. A., 396–404.
[2] Secretary of the Interior Albert B. Fall refused to speak for the Four-Power Treaty because the cabinet had not been consulted or informed about its negotiation. Diary of Theodore Roosevelt, Jr., Jan. 30, 1922, Roosevelt Papers; C. L. A., 248; report of the American delegation, Feb. 9, 1922, FR: 1922, I, 328; Congressional Record, March 26, 1922, p. 4723.

Newspapers urged ratification by a nine-to-one ratio in a poll taken by the *Literary Digest* which concluded, "Reports of opposition are so negligible as to make it clear to us that the people are more significantly united on the proposals of the conference than they have been on any similar issue." [3]

Only the Hearst press was in opposition. Hearst allowed, encouraged, and ordered his employees to print large the idea of an Englishman or Japanese behind every tree waiting to pounce on unwary Americans. Hearst's favorite paper, the San Francisco *Examiner*, editorialized that the whole conference was a plot to reduce the American navy so that the Japanese and British navies could crush the United States. One cartoon depicted two pigs, "Rich and Natural Resources" and "Vast Wealth," running past a pack of wolves labeled "Hate," "Jealousy," "Envy," "Treachery"; fortunately, Uncle Sam was guarding the pigs with a gun called "A Mighty Navy." Hearst's chief columnist, Arthur Brisbane, wrote of the Four-Power Treaty that Europe and Asia had decided "what we shall be forbidden to do with our own territory. And we, like mild sheep, do not for a moment dream of telling them what to do with their land. It is too preposterous, too profoundly asinine for belief." A headline quoted Pershing as saying "Disarmament Now Unwise," although in the following news story Pershing said he favored a disarmament conference.[4]

The Friends of Irish Freedom were so vocal that Senator John Sharp Williams attacked them on the floor of the Senate. He pointed out their anti-British bias, suggesting they were sometimes more Irish than American.[5] Shortly before the conference Admiral Sims had said of this Irish group, "They are like zebras, either black horses with white stripes, or white horses with black stripes. But we know they are not horses—they are asses, but

[3] Of 803 papers polled, 723 were for ratification and 66 were against it, with 14 uncommitted. "The Treaty Triumph in the Senate," *Literary Digest*, LXXIII (April 8, 1922), 12–13.
[4] Hoag, *Preface to Preparedness*, 152, 153–54, 159.
[5] *Congressional Record*, March 15, 1922, p. 3907.

each of these asses has a vote, and there are lots of them . . . . One inconvenience of a republic is that these jackass votes must be catered to." [6]

Supporters were well organized. A Committee for Treaty Ratification included men like George W. Wickersham, Stephen P. Duggan, John Foster Dulles, John H. Finley, and A. Lawrence Lowell. After canvassing the United States to ascertain popular feeling toward the treaties, the committee reported to Congress that church forces, civic organizations, educational institutions, women's groups, and labor organizations supported the treaties.[7]

The support of churches of America helped the administration, for the conference and its treaties were in part an atonement for support of the World War. No organization was more active than the Federal Council of Churches. Such groups as the Church Peace Union, the Unitarian Layman's League, the Central Conference of American Rabbis, and the Quakers were also hard at work.[8] The American Advisory Committee estimated that of 13,878,671 letters received by January 15, 1922, a total of 10,092,-736 had some religious connotation.[9]

Even steel manufacturers indicated approval of the American program. Charles M. Schwab, head of Bethlehem Steel, said he "would gladly see the war-making machinery" of his company "sink to the bottom of the ocean." The companies competed to prove that they were not dependent on war.[10] Reduction of federal taxes was perhaps one motive behind this stand, but it is more likely they were attempting to erase the bad reputation acquired during the World War.

Civic, educational, and pacifist groups joined in an ad hoc National Council for the Limitation of Armaments. It included rep-

[6] New York *Times*, June 8, 1921.

[7] *Congressional Record*, March 22, 1922, pp. 4226–27.

[8] Copies of petitions, pamphlets, and other materials of these groups can be found in the Washington Conference Papers.

[9] Report of the American Advisory Committee, Jan. 15, 1922, Washington Conference Papers. Hughes wrote and thanked the Federal Council for its support in Hughes to Federal Council, April 1922, Hughes Papers.

[10] Hoag, *Preface to Preparedness*, 143–44.

resentatives from forty-three organizations and claimed that it spoke for over six million people. It had worked during the conference and promised later to campaign for the treaties.[11]

Labor had come out for the treaties although it was careful to point out that it did not support pacifism. Samuel Gompers had served on the Advisory Committee. He had organized a General Committee on the Limitation of Armament.[12] But Gompers was shocked when over 10,000 navy yard workers found themselves out of work because of the cutback in naval construction. An appeal to Secretary Denby brought the retort that the government could not continue to pay men for needless employment.[13]

The Washington Conference did arouse some opposition from American naval experts, but most officers were hesitant about criticizing the Five-Power Naval Treaty for a good reason—denunciation was criticism of both the Navy Department and the Commander-in-Chief, Harding. There was little open complaint. As Admiral Hilary P. Jones noted, the naval agreement was so popular that it was impossible to advance counterarguments.[14] As 1922 went by, attacks on the treaty became more frequent, but then it was too late.

Comment by citizens and senators indicated the popularity of the treaties. Chief Justice William H. Taft thought the results

[11] Among the member organizations were the National Grange, American Farm Bureau Federation, National Milk Producer's Federation, International Association of Machinists, National Women's Trade Union League, National League of Women Voters, Women's Committee for World Disarmament, National Congress of Mothers and Parents-Teachers Associations, Women's International League for Peace and Freedom, Association to Abolish War, American School Citizenship League, Fellowship of Reconciliation, Friends Disarmament Council, Foreign Policy Association, American Union Against Militarism, International Lyceum and Chautauqua Association, World Friendship Bureau, and the Society to Eliminate Economic Causes of War. Membership list in 500.A4P81/20 index of Washington Conference Papers. The papers of this group are in the Peace Collection at Swarthmore College.

[12] An almost complete record of organized labor's role can be found in the papers of Samuel Gompers, item 214 (American Federation of Labor Library, Washington, D. C.,). Hereinafter cited as Gompers Papers.

[13] Gompers to Denby, Feb. 15, 1922, and Denby to Gompers, Feb. 22, 1922, Gompers Papers.

[14] Admiral Jones to Vice-Admiral John Daniel McDonald, March 10, 1922, Papers of the Naval Historical Foundation (Library of Congress).

were substantial and was glad public opinion was so "strong in favor." [15] Robert Lansing believed that China had gained, and regretted the lack of provision for another Far Eastern conference.[16] Senator Atlee Pomerene said a vote against the treaties would not coincide with what he conceived to be the "well-defined sentiment of the country." [17] Joining him was Senator Lawrence Phipps, who said, "Our citizens are in earnest regarding this pact." [18]

The foregoing is a sample of the overwhelming support for the treaties on the eve of ratification.[19] Hughes had captured the American imagination.

Henry Cabot Lodge escorted the treaties through the Senate. The wisdom of appointing the senior Senator from Massachusetts to the delegation was never more apparent than in the debates. Lodge had a majority, and the problem was to gain the necessary two-thirds.[20] He tried to put the treaties through while they were on the crest of popular support. There were no long committee meetings to read the treaties aloud, no long debate, and no complex charges to try public patience. As a newspaper commented, "One great difference between the Four-Power Treaty and the League Covenant is that one was of Republican origin and the other of Democratic origin." [21]

To open the Senate battle the administration brought out its chief asset, President Harding. On February 10, the President boasted he was submitting the "complete minutes of both plenary sessions and committee meetings," along with a report by the American delegation. Open diplomacy. He noted that the treaties

[15] Carbon of Taft to Willie Blake, Feb. 6, 1922, Taft Papers.

[16] Memorandum by Lansing, "The Washington Conference and the Future," Feb. 1922, Lansing Papers.

[17] *Congressional Record*, March 22, 1922, p. 4250.

[18] *Ibid.*, March 23, 1922, p. 4322.

[19] Hoag, *Preface to Preparedness*, gives a more detailed, extended treatment of this subject.

[20] There were fifty-nine Republicans, thirty-six Democrats, and one Progressive (Johnson) in the Senate.

[21] The Brooklyn *Eagle* as quoted in Thomas A. Bailey, *The Man in the Street* (New York, 1948), 93.

attempted to solve problems without a sacrifice of national pride —"There were no punishments to inflict, no rewards to bestow." The President said he knew the sentiment against European entanglement. He pledged that the Four-Power Treaty was "no commitment to armed force, no alliance, no written or moral obligation to join in defense, no expressed or implied commitment to arrive at any agreement except in accordance with our constitutional methods." He believed that the treaty would give a strong moral warning that aggression was a "hazardous enterprise." The President voiced his appeal in Wilsonian terms. If the Senate did not approve the treaties, "we shall discredit the influence of the Republic, render future efforts futile or unlikely, and write discouragement where to-day the world is ready to acclaim new hope." He invited the Senate to approve all the treaties since each depended upon another.[22]

It did not take the senators long to realize that the "complete record" did not include the Four-Power negotiations nor the minutes of subcommittees.[23] The Senate on November 8, 1921, had passed a resolution asking the American delegates to admit representatives of the press to the conference and to preserve a complete record.[24] Harding and Hughes had apparently not understood that request. The Senate passed another resolution on February 16 requesting records, minutes, arguments, debates, and conversations relating to the Four-Power Treaty.[25]

Hughes drafted a tactful refusal which Harding sent to the Senate. In this message the President replied that many of the intimate conversations were unrecorded. Even if such memoranda had existed, he did not think it "compatible with public interest or consistent with the amenities of international negotiation" to reveal such information. He concluded that there were "no concealed understanding, and no secret exchanges of notes, and . . .

[22] Message of the President, Feb. 10, 1922, *FR: 1922*, I, 298–306.
[23] The documents submitted to the Senate are printed in Senate Document 126, 67 Cong., 2 Sess.
[24] *Congressional Record*, Nov. 8, 1921, p. 7537.
[25] *Ibid.*, Feb. 16, 1922, p. 2640.

no commitments whatever" regarding the Four-Power Treaty.[26]

In the Senate the Yap Treaty came first, widely regarded as a test for the more important treaties. Johnson, Robinson, France, and Pittman led the opposition, contending that the treaty represented a victory for the Japanese, who gained title to the Pacific mandates. Lodge replied that American acquiescence in the League decision did not mean the islands would remain Japanese. Underwood even felt the United States, having refused to join the League, had no rights over Yap; it was up to Japan to give the United States concessions.[27] After some attempts to amend the treaty, the final vote came on March 11—67 in favor, 22 against, 7 abstentions.[28]

The Four-Power Treaty might run into difficulties. Of 60 Republican senators (counting the Progressive senator, Hiram Johnson) 57 had voted, with 54 favoring the Yap Treaty.[29] Of 36 Democratic senators 32 had voted, with 19 against, 13 in favor. A shift of four or five votes, even with the addition of the absent seven senators (four Democrats and three Republicans, one of whom, La Follette, had spoken against the treaty), could mean the defeat of the Four-Power Treaty.

The Republican-controlled Committee on Foreign Relations decided to resolve the difficulty by adding the Brandegee reservation on February 27: "no commitment to armed force, no alliance, no obligation to join in any defense." Harding had felt that any reservation was useless but if a "becoming reservation" would reassure some senator he had no objection. He would have preferred to thresh out the question with the Senate. He believed it was time to settle whether an executive could negotiate treaties without fear of senatorial repudiation.[30]

26 Harding to Hughes, Feb. 18, 1922, and Hughes to Harding, Feb. 19, 1922, Department of State 500.A4a/1; copy of Harding letter to Senate, Feb. 20, 1922, Department of State 500.A4a/17½.
27 *Congressional Record*, Feb. 22, 1922, p. 2881, and March 1, 1922, p. 3183.
28 *Ibid.*, March 1, 1922, p. 3193.
29 The three Republicans voting against the treaty were Borah, Joseph Irvin France, and Hiram Johnson; absent were William Evans Crow, Thomas Coleman Dupont, and Robert M. La Follette.
30 Harding himself drafted a reservation which duplicated the no-alliance

When debate started, foes of the Four-Power Treaty expressed disbelief that Japan and Britain could give up the advantages of the Anglo-Japanese Alliance for the quadruple agreement. There was more to the treaty than met the eye: the United States must have promised something. Lodge's literary presentation had aroused suspicion. Senator Reed said it reminded him of a "mother's blandishments when she is about to administer a dose of castor oil." [31] Harding's press conference blunder of not including the Japanese islands, and his reversal, brought comment by the Missouri senator, who told of a blacksmith and wheelwright deciding on a sign for their partnership which read, "All kinds of twisting and turning done here." [32] There was further suspicion when Harding refused to submit any conference records on the treaty.

Johnson believed the Harding administration had misled people by calling a disarmament conference intended to find a replacement for the Anglo-Japanese Alliance.[33] And Borah wrote that he favored the naval treaty but that the Four-Power Treaty was another alliance. He declared that "even if every man, woman, and child in the United States were in favor of it, I should unhesitatingly defeat it if I could." [34]

Lodge pointed out that a question of war would not come before a conference; "if the fleet of Japan were to attack the Hawaiian islands, . . . an act of war," there was no need to confer. The only obligation was to consult if an outside power committed aggression against a treaty power. Moreover, any decision would take a unanimous vote. The most important point was the termination of the Anglo-Japanese Alliance.[35]

Secretary Hughes discussed defense of the treaty with Chandler P. Anderson, who wished some arguments to relay to Fred Kent in preparation for a speech before the United States Cham-

statement of his February 10 speech. A longhand draft is in the Lodge Papers; New York *Times,* Feb. 26, 1922; Harding to Lodge, Feb. 23, 1922, Lodge Papers.

[31] *Congressional Record,* Dec. 16, 1922, p. 438.

[32] *Ibid.,* Dec. 21, 1921, p. 629.

[33] *Ibid.,* March 13, 1922, p. 3777.

[34] Borah to James Barton, March 6, 1922, Borah Papers.

[35] *Congressional Record,* March 8, 1922, pp. 3547–54.

ber of Commerce. Hughes stressed that the treaty obligated the United States to do nothing except to confer. Hughes told Anderson that the American delegation felt fortunate in accomplishing so much by assuming so little. Anderson reported to Kent that the treaty's friends should stress the abolition of the Anglo-Japanese Alliance.[36]

Anderson's visit to Hughes caused the Secretary to write Senator Underwood, who then read the letter to his colleagues, prefaced by a remark that the treaty was a "model regional agreement" which destroyed any reason for war between the four sea powers of the Pacific. Hughes regretted implications that the American delegates were taken in by the Japanese and British. The American delegation, he said, had negotiated with the understanding that the United States would join no alliances or obligations pertaining to the use of force. The treaty was short, clear, and required no commentary. The Secretary admitted he had prepared the draft which was the basis of the final agreement. He warned that "its failure would be nothing short of a national calamity." [37]

The first vote came on March 14 when an amendment offered by Senator Joseph T. Robinson requiring the four nations to refrain from aggression met defeat by a vote of 30 to 55, eleven members not voting. Two other attempts to amend the treaty were beaten down, and on March 15 a unanimous consent agreement passed which cut off voting until March 24 when the final treaty vote would come.[38] During this breather Senator Thomas E. Watson mounted a scathing attack on the treaty and Elihu Root. Behind the treaty, he said, was the money trust represented by Root, who was the lawyer of predatory corporations, Boss Tweed, the Ryans, and Belmonts. The Senator charged Root

[36] Diary of Chandler P. Anderson, March 10, 1922, Anderson Papers; copy of letter from Chandler P. Anderson to Fred Kent, March 12, 1922, Hughes Papers.

[37] Diary of Chandler P. Anderson, March 14, 1922, Anderson Papers; *Congressional Record*, March 11, 1922, p. 3711; Hughes to Underwood, March 11, 1922, *FR: 1922*, I, 48–50.

[38] *Congressional Record*, March 14, 1922, pp. 3854, 3859; March 15, 1922, pp. 3893, 3915.

with selling Korea to Japan in 1905 by refusing to heed a Korean appeal. He declared that if the United States ratified the treaty it would surrender independence. "What sort of speeches," he asked, "will orators make on the Fourth of July hereafter? Spread eagleism will be out of date. You will have caged your eagle. He will not have the freedom to look into the eyes of the sun and beat the heavens with perfectly free wings. Ah, no." [39]

Then came an incident capitalized on by the treaty's senatorial opponents. New York lawyer Paul D. Cravath, seemingly in touch with the Harding administration, had made a speech before the Council on Foreign Relations that the most important achievement of the Washington Conference did not appear in the written record or in any treaty: it was an "understanding" between the United States and Great Britain concerning the Far East. His view, he said, was in agreement with "every member of the American delegation," who had told him that because of this understanding each nation could count on the other for "closest cooperation" in an emergency.[40] Borah read a stenographic report of the speech into the record and charged an alliance had been made. Underwood and Lodge denied they had made such a statement, and the latter became furious with those attacking the motives of the American delegates. A strong denial from Cravath which Lodge presented next day did not seem to convince anyone that he had been misquoted.[41]

Hughes again came to the defense of the treaty by writing an open letter to Lodge in which he denied an understanding with Britain. "Any such statement," he declared, "is absolutely false." The Secretary hoped that the American delegates would not listen to "further aspersions upon their veracity and honor." [42]

[39] *Ibid.*, March 17, 1922, pp. 4013–16.

[40] *Ibid.*, March 20, 1922, p. 4119.

[41] Root was the only American delegate who never denied talking to Cravath; *Congressional Record*, March 20, 1922, pp. 4120, 4123; March 21, 1922, p. 4157; the Secretary of State wrote Cravath, "Of course I did not believe that you had said anything of the sort reported." Hughes to Cravath, March 22, 1922, Hughes Papers.

[42] Hughes to Lodge, March 21, 1922, as printed in the *Congressional Record*, March 21, 1922, p. 4158.

March 24 and the vote on the treaty approached, and on the basis of the Yap Treaty and the Robinson amendment it looked as if the Harding administration had the votes. As long as Underwood would swing Democratic votes, the treaty would pass. Underwood called at the White House on the evening of March 21 and promised the President the treaty would pass by at least three votes.[43]

Voting on the Four-Power Treaty advanced article-by-article on March 24. Acceptance of Article 1 came by a vote of 74 to 15, seven members not voting. This was not the controversial section of the treaty. Opposition centered on Article 2 which seemed to make the quadruple agreement an alliance: "If the said rights are threatened by the aggressive action of any other Power, the High Contracting Powers shall communicate with one another fully and frankly in order to arrive at an understanding as to the most effective measure to be taken, jointly or separately, to meet the exigencies of the situation." Was this clause like Article X of the League? Hours went by as senators looked up the term "alliance" in dictionaries, encyclopedias, international law texts, even history books. Six attempts to amend the article failed. By vote of 66 to 28, with two abstentions, the article passed.[44] Articles 3 and 4 passed by 67 to 26 and 73 to 8.[45]

This left the Brandegee reservation and the final treaty vote. There were sixteen attempts by Senators Walsh, Robinson, Pittman, La Follette, Johnson, Reed, and Pomerene to broaden the reservation. All failed, with thirty-six votes the highest number in favor of any proposal.[46]

Lodge then offered the Brandegee reservation which passed by 91 to 2.[47]

The Four-Power Treaty passed by a vote of 67 to 27, with 2

---

[43] New York *Times,* March 22, 1922.
[44] *Congressional Record,* March 24, 1922, p. 4487.
[45] *Ibid.,* 4490.
[46] *Ibid.,* 4491–96.
[47] *Ibid.,* 4496. Selden Spencer (R–Mo.) and John Sharp Williams (D–Miss.) voted against the reservation.

abstentions.[48] Fifty-five Republicans and twelve Democrats supported the treaty, while twenty-three Democrats and four Republicans did not.

One cannot help but reflect on the League controversy and Wilson's refusal to accept reservations. Wilson's stubbornness had prevented American entrance into the League, but Lodge in a similar situation was willing to compromise. Lodge did have the cooperation of Underwood, undoubtedly important. Still, the old Senator from Massachusetts had proved more practical, more successful, than the former President he so disliked.

Three days later the Senate adopted the supplementary Four-Power Treaty, which defined the islands included in the agreement. Pittman had offered an amendment giving the United States the right to decide when a controversy in the islands fell within domestic jurisdiction. He claimed this proposal was the same reservation Lodge had offered during the League debate. This move lost by a vote of 21 in favor to 49 against, and Lodge voted against it with no apparent embarrassment.[49]

Resistance thereupon collapsed.[50] There were only two big speeches against the Five-Power Naval Treaty. Reed believed that in the event of war the Philippines would fall in three days and Guam in twenty-four hours. He quoted two unnamed naval experts who advised that tonnage figures in the naval treaty were all wrong.[51] Joseph France, senator for Maryland, a shipbuilding state, outlined his reason for a vote against the naval treaty. He

[48] *Ibid.*, 4497. The Republicans who voted against the treaty were Borah (Idaho), France (Maryland), Johnson (California), and La Follette (Wisconsin). The Democrats who voted for the treaty were Edwin S. Broussard (Louisiana), Nathaniel B. Dial (South Carolina), Duncan U. Fletcher (Florida), John B. Kendrick (Wyoming), Kenneth D. McKellar (Tennessee), Henry L. Myers (Montana), Robert Owen (Oklahoma), Atlee Pomerene (Ohio), Joseph Ransdell (Louisiana), Park Trammell (Florida), Oscar W. Underwood (Alabama), and John Sharp Williams (Mississippi).

[49] *Ibid.*, 4621. The vote was 73 in the affirmative, 0 against, and 23 not voting; *ibid.*, 4620.

[50] Hughes wrote Lodge on April 1, 1922, and congratulated him on the passage of the Four-Power Treaty which, Hughes believed, destroyed the opposition. Lodge Papers.

[51] *Congressional Record*, March 16, 1922, pp. 3944–57.

realized he was in a minority (he was to cast the only vote against the Five-Power Treaty), but he believed people did not want to reduce the navy. The treaty thereupon was adopted, 74 to 1.[52]

The Nine-Power Treaty and the Poison Gas and Submarine Treaty passed without recorded opposition, while one vote was cast against the Chinese Customs Treaty by Senator William H. King of Utah, who thought the customs treaty an infringement on China's integrity.[53]

The Washington treaties went through the Senate with little difficulty. With enormous pride Lodge wrote George Harvey, "I not only got two-thirds of the Senate, but I had thirteen to spare on the vote on the Four-Power Treaty where the fight centered, and all the other treaties passed unanimously, with single exception of one vote by France against the naval treaty. I must say, speaking without regard to imputations of vanity, that it was on the whole pretty well done." [54]

Thus the Harding administration had succeeded in securing the assent of the Senate. In a conversation with H. H. Kohlsaat, the President had stated, " 'The success or failure of this administration depends on the ratification of these treaties. . . . If these treaties are ratified by the Senate, then this administration's name is secure in history.' " [55] Strong popular support for the limitation of armaments (aroused and mobilized by Hughes's opening speech) coupled with astute parliamentary tactics had secured ratification. And the pontifical, prophetic pronouncement of the President on the attainment of a place in history for his administration proved to be precise.

---

[52] *Ibid.*, March 29, 1922, pp. 4708, 4718–19. Senator James A. Reed did not vote.
[53] The Nine-Power vote was 66 to 0 with 30 not voting; *ibid.*, March 30, 1922, p. 4784. The Gas and Submarine vote was 72 to 0 with 24 not voting; *ibid.*, March 29, 1922, p. 4730. The Chinese Customs vote was 58 in favor, 1 opposed, with 37 not voting; *ibid.*, March 30, 1922, p. 4791.
[54] Lodge to Harvey, April 15, 1922, Lodge Papers.
[55] As quoted in Francis Russell, *The Shadow of Blooming Grove: Warren G. Harding in His Times* (New York, 1968), 485.

XIII. IN CONCLUSION

SECRETARY OF STATE HUGHES believed that "foreign policies [were] not based upon abstractions" but were the "result of practical considerations of national interest." The American delegation at the Washington Conference sought limited goals. There were no attempts to make the world over in the American image, no proposals for universal disarmament, no promises of peace for all time. There was instead an attempt to achieve attainable ends through practical negotiation. With the achievement of limited objectives the American delegation took a necessary first step toward a Pacific and Far Eastern policy based on a realistic assessment of American interests.

Elimination of a naval race in capital ships that could threaten American interests in the Pacific was the first goal of the United States. Great Britain and Japan, America's two main competitors for trade and influence in the Pacific and Far East, were building capital ships. In 1921, it must not be forgotten, the two nations were bound together in a military pact that had survived, despite some strains, a major war in 1905 (Russo-Japanese), the presentation of the Twenty-One Demands to China in 1915, a world war, and the Paris Peace Conference. Neither power had displayed any inclination to abrogate the alliance and all signs pointed toward the continuation of some kind of agreement between the two powers after the expiration date in 1921, for it had served to protect both British possessions and interests and to further Japanese ambitions. The military threat of the alliance to the United States was admittedly a moot one. There were firm believers in Anglo-American amity who thought that Great Britain would never join the Japanese, directly or indirectly, in a struggle against the United States; but international relationships are not immutable. The friend of one day was often the enemy of another and no prudent American statesman, aware of the advice of George Washington that each nation has its own vital interests, could help but be aware of that fact. And American-British relations had not been noticeably smooth after 1914. The American government had to meet the threat of the naval race, not on the basis of traditional friendships or enmities, but by deciding whether its interests in the Pacific and Far East—protection of the Pacific possessions, the Open Door in China, penetration of Far Eastern markets, and general political influence within the area—were worth the cost of preparing for and perhaps fighting a war, or by deciding, on the other hand, that those interests were not vital and were open to negotiation. The Harding administration, consciously or unconsciously, chose the latter.

In making the choice that American interests in the Pacific and Far East were not of sufficient consequence to rank as vital interests, the American delegation was influenced by the existing situation, not by what it wished the situation were, but by what it actually was. Pacific possessions were far from the United States, vulnerable to attack by the Japanese, and Congress in the past had decided that it was easy not to spend money on them. Under those circumstances it appeared the islands could be better protected by diplomatic means than by military ones. To defend the Open Door in China by military force was such an obvious impossibility that not even William Jennings Bryan had suggested it. Again a diplomatic agreement whereby the competing powers would agree to support the principles of the Open Door seemed much more feasible. Trade with China had never been large despite great hopes placed in its potential; indeed, the Japanese were better customers. The United States, in its new status as a leading creditor nation, was confident of its ability to compete economically anywhere with anyone; the dollar could conquer where bullets could not. And finally, America's political ambitions in the

Far East—primarily an often expressed hope for a peaceful, democratic China—were not amenable to military, that is, naval power. There thus appeared to be no vital interest at stake that called for a continuation of the naval race or was worth fighting a war for. It was simply not an area susceptible to available or even potential military force; American goals could be better achieved by diplomatic means.

Faced with the challenge of the British and Japanese building programs, the Harding administration had to make a choice that would relate its military power to the attainment of its political goals: it could either gamble on increased public and congressional support for a building program, hope to "win" the race, and thus increase its naval influence (and perhaps economic and political) in the Pacific and Far East, or it could attempt to halt the race at a position favorable to the national interests of the United States. With his dramatic presentation at the opening session, Secretary Hughes took the second route and succeeded in gaining the support of the British and Japanese for the Five-Power Treaty. This arrangement did not sacrifice the interests of the United States. The American government did not give up actual naval superiority—only potential, if even that—and it did not weaken its Pacific bases, for it is doubtful if Congress would have appropriated funds to complete the fleet or to construct adequate fortifications on Guam or the Philippines. Why not trade uncompleted ships and bases and an uncertain future in the Pacific for a limit to the offensive power of its competitors? The American government achieved a better position in relation to its competitors in the Pacific by a limitation of arms than it might have gained by arming; therein lay the wisdom of the American proposal.

With the Four-Power Treaty and end of the Anglo-Japanese Alliance the American government achieved a second practical goal. The Department of State had regarded the alliance uneasily, not so much from fear of conflict as from the knowledge that the Japanese often acquired interests under the umbrella of Great Britain. Bringing the alliance to an end was a negative achievement but an important one, for the British were to become, if not immediate opponents, at least not silent partners of Japanese imperialism. The American delegation felt fortunate in replacing a military alliance with a treaty in which the United States government had to assume no obligation for or against the actions of other powers. This was in keeping not only with the rejection of the League of Nations, and any Washington Conference treaty would have to be ratified by that same Senate, but was also a recognition that the United States wanted to retain its freedom of action in an area of the world that was in considerable flux. There was no obligation to do anything for the next ten years except confer, and if and when an incident occurred the United States government could then decide what action, if any, it wanted to take; this, incidentally, is exactly how members of the League of Nations, despite the stronger words and obligations of the Covenant, acted when a dispute came before the League. The actual situation at that moment was what counted and all the words and obligations, legal, moral, or otherwise, could not make a government act if it chose not to do so. In the face of an uncertain and changing situation there was no compelling reason for the United States to sign a treaty pledging it to military action if the status quo in the Pacific were upset.

The American delegation achieved a cherished objective when the Japanese, British, and delegates from other nations agreed to the Open Door policy of the United States government as the principle basic to their relations with China. For the first time this policy was formally accepted by the powers. Diplomats cannot hope to do more than influence other countries to accept their policies. In climbing to that pinnacle of success, however, the American delegation had overreached, for behind the words was neither the intent nor the power. The Japanese recognized this. In effect, but not in words, the American delegates had relegated the China problem to second place because defense of China's territorial and administrative integrity was not within reach of American power; they did not, however, have the political courage to abandon the policy formally and adopt a more realistic formulation. Continued support of the Open Door, even in words, was to take the American government along the road to war twenty years later. It is ironic that as a result of that war the Open Door disappeared, as the Chinese Communists emerged from the following civil war and closed their country's portals to Americans in a manner that the Japanese never conceived or achieved.

American policy toward China involved more than just the Open Door. After World War I had revealed the inability of the Western powers to control the Far Eastern situation, it was apparent that there was a power vacuum in China. The Japanese wanted to fill that vacuum, but it is often forgotten that there was another aspirant—China. It is true that she was torn by a civil war and that no claimant to the ancient ruling mandate was manifestly superior to any other, but each was stimulated by a growing sense of nationalism to throw off the unequal treaties and regain China's sovereign rights. The American government sympathized with those goals, as its policies in the 1920's were to further demonstrate, and the Washington Conference took the first step toward the achievement of them. What China needed most was the unfettered opportunity to gather her strength, settle her own problems, and choose her own government without outside interference. By not shackling China with further burdens and indeed by lifting some of those weights—such as the Japanese retrocession of Shantung—and looking to the abolition of others—such as the tariff and extraterritoriality—the Washington Conference took some most important steps. In the last analysis only China was going to determine her own future and American policy at the Washington Conference recognized that fact.

At the Washington Conference the limitation of armaments and political agreements were deliberately tied together; the Five-Power Naval Treaty on armaments was closely tied to the Four-Power Treaty on the Pacific. The American delegation would not have signed the one without the other. It was a clear recognition of the connection between political tensions and the arms race. To have dealt only with disarmament would have been to deal only with the surface and not to go beneath it to the antagonisms that had caused the nations to build capital ships. To have dealt with the former and not the latter would have jeopardized the security of all concerned. The experience of the Washington Conference suggests that those who believe that world peace can be secured through disarmament alone, without making political arrangements concurrently, are ignoring reality.

The Washington treaties did not in themselves fail; rather, weakness resided in the failure to follow up the auspicious detente of pragmatic advantage and reciprocity drawn up in 1921 at Washington. The reduction of naval armaments, which were, after all the manifestation of deeper conflicts, and the reduction of military tensions purchased breathing space, but no one took advantage of it to solve other areas of conflict. With the advent of the Great Depression time ran out. It was foolish to hope that any temporary settlement, designed to be only the first step, would in itself prove to be permanent. Never adequately reinforced, in time the Washington settlement creaked, cracked, and crumbled at its weakest point—the Nine-Power Treaty—and for this failure, American governments in the interwar period bear a heavy responsibility.

BIBLIOGRAPHICAL ESSAY

BIBLIOGRAPHICAL AIDS

The most useful aids to finding books on recent American diplomacy are those sponsored by the Council on Foreign Relations: William L. Langer and Hamilton Fish Armstrong, eds., *Foreign Affairs Bibliography: 1919–1932* (New York, 1933); Robert Gale Woolbert, ed., *Foreign Affairs Bibliography: 1932–1942* (New York, 1945); and Henry L. Roberts, ed., *Foreign Affairs Bibliography: 1942–1952* (New York, 1955) and *Foreign Affairs Bibliography: 1952–1962* (New York, 1964). Oscar Handlin, *et al.*, *Harvard Guide to American History* (Cambridge, Mass., 1954), contains unannotated listings. For books and articles published since 1954 one must search laboriously through the *Journal of American History* (formerly *Mississippi Valley Historical Review*), quarterly and annual lists of the *American Historical Review*, the *Far Eastern Quarterly* (now the *Journal of Asian Studies*), the *Journal of Modern History*, and *Foreign Affairs*. Diplomatic history is in need of a special guide to articles in the periodical press on foreign relations. Eric H. Boehm, ed., *Historical Abstracts: 1775–1945* (Santa Barbara, Cal., 1955–) and *America: History and Life* (Santa Barbara, Cal., 1964–) partly fill the periodical gap.

Philip M. Hamer, ed., *A Guide to Archives and Manuscripts in the United States* (New Haven, Conn., 1961), is indispensable assistance for research in manuscripts. One can supplement this compilation with the fuller volumes of the Library of Congress, *National Union Catalog of Manuscript Collections* (1962–).

GENERAL WORKS

Life in the United States is colorfully treated in Frederick Lewis Allen's *Only Yesterday* (New York, 1931) and Mark Sullivan's *Our Times: The Twenties* (New York, 1935). A careful reader can find in Henry M. Robinson's *Fantastic Interim* (New York, 1943) and Karl Schriftgiesser's *This Was Normalcy* (Boston, 1948) much less than meets the eye.

A good introduction to American foreign policy in the twentieth century is Samuel Flagg Bemis, "The Shifting Strategy of American Defense and Diplomacy," in Dwight E. Lee and George McReynolds, eds., *Essays in History and International Relations in Honor of George Hubbard Blakeslee* (Worcester, Mass., 1949), 1–14. There is also an interpretive treatment by George Kennan in *American Diplomacy: 1900–1950* (Chicago, 1951).

Frank H. Simonds, a leading journalist of the era, disagrees with Republican policies in the 1920's in *American Foreign Policy in the Post-War Years* (Baltimore, 1935). A broad survey is in Allan Nevins, *The United States in a Chaotic World: A Chronicle of International Affairs, 1918–1933* (New Haven, Conn., 1950). Selig Adler sets out *The Isolationist Impulse* (New York, 1957) in a suggestive manner; a later interpretation by the same author is *The Uncertain Giant* (New York, 1965).

Two general surveys of American Far Eastern policy by Foster Rhea Dulles are *Forty Years of American-Japanese Relations* (New York, 1937) and *China and America: The Story of Their Relations Since 1784* (Princeton, N.J., 1946). Much greater insight is shown by Edwin O. Reischauer in *The United States and Japan* (3rd ed.; New York, 1965) and by John King Fairbank in *The United States and China* (rev. ed.; New York, 1962). The classic approach to twentieth-century American diplomacy in Asia is A. Whitney Griswold's *Far Eastern Policy of the United States* (New York, 1938), now unfortunately in need of revision. Highly interpretive and extremely interesting is the recent work by Akira Iriye, *Across the Pacific: An Inner History of*

American-East Asian Relations (New York, 1967). Tien-yi Li in *Woodrow Wilson's China Policy: 1913–1917* (New York, 1952) and Roy W. Curry in *Woodrow Wilson and Far Eastern Policy: 1913–1921* (New York, 1957) carefully describe American policies in the years before the Washington Conference. George H. Blakeslee's *The Recent Foreign Policy of the United States* (New York, 1925) takes a favorable view of American Far Eastern policy which he, as a Department of State adviser, helped make. A more critical view can be found in Dorothy Borg's *American Policy and the Chinese Revolution: 1925–1928* (New York, 1947).

General works on the powers and their policies are numerous. Robert T. Pollard treats China's foreign relations in the 1920's in *China's Foreign Relations: 1917–1931* (New York, 1933). Useful is S. Tatsuji Takeuchi's *War and Diplomacy in the Japanese Empire* (Chicago, 1935). More recent is Hikomatsu Kamikawa, ed., *Japan-American Diplomatic Relations in the Meiji-Taisho Era* (Tokyo, 1958). Also of some interest is Morinosuke Kajima's *The Emergence of Japan as a World Power* (Rutland, Vt., 1968). Akira Iriye, *After Imperialism: The Search for a New Order in the Far East, 1921–1931* (Cambridge, Mass., 1965), has little on the conference itself, but much on other aspects of American and Japanese policy after the conference; it is an excellent work. *The Twenty Years' Crisis, 1919–1939* (New York, 1939) by Edward Hallett Carr is an interpretive treatment that describes European policies in the interwar period.

SPECIAL WORKS

Monographs

Limitation of armaments was the main topic at the Washington Conference, and Henry W. Harris briefly describes general naval limitation during the interwar period in his *Naval Disarmament* (London, 1930); Benjamin H. Williams' *The United States and Disarmament* (New York, 1931) and Merze Tate's *The United*

States and Armaments (Cambridge, Mass., 1948) are standard treatments. Miss Tate is critical of disarmament conferences and believes the United States can best guard its security with strong military forces.

On the status of the American navy before the conference, a contemporary book by Hector C. Bywater, *Sea-Power in the Pacific: A Study of the American-Japanese Naval Problem* (New York, 1921), concluded that the United States would fight Japan at a disadvantage in any naval war in the western Pacific. Dudley W. Knox's *The Eclipse of American Sea Power* (New York, 1922) attacks the Five-Power Treaty. Harold and Margaret Sprout's *The Rise of American Naval Power: 1776–1918* (Princeton, N.J., 1939) and George T. Davis' *A Navy Second to None* (New York, 1940) set out the growth of the American navy. A recent able work is Gerald E. Wheeler's *Prelude to Pearl Harbor: The United States Navy and the Far East, 1921–1931* (Columbia, Mo., 1936). A brief interpretation is Ernest Andrade's "The United States Navy and the Washington Conference," *Historian*, XXXI (March 1969), 345–63. On the British side one can profit from Stephen Roskill's *Naval Policy Between the Wars: The Period of Anglo-American Antagonism, 1919–1929* (London, 1968); his assessments of American policy, however, are not always precise.

Of importance equal to limitation of armaments at the Washington Conference was the problem of the Anglo-Japanese Alliance. A strong anti-Japanese view is in Alfred L. P. Dennis' *The Anglo-Japanese Alliance* (Berkeley, Cal., 1923). Prepared for the American delegation at the conference, it gives a dark picture of the threat of the alliance to the United States. Chung-fu Chang's *The Anglo-Japanese Alliance* (Baltimore, 1931) is more reasoned. The British problem in 1921 of whether to renew the alliance can best be approached through J. B. Brebner, "Canada, the Anglo-Japanese Alliance, and the Washington Conference," *Political Science Quarterly*, L (1935), 45–48, and Charles N. Spinks, "The Termination of the Anglo-Japanese Alliance,"

Pacific Historical Review, VI (1937), 321–40. J. Chalmers Vinson discusses imperial pressures in "The Imperial Conference of 1921 and the Anglo-Japanese Alliance," *Pacific Historical Review* XXXI (1962), 257–66. A major contribution is M. G. Fry's "The North Atlantic Triangle and the Abrogation of the Anglo-Japanese Alliance," *Journal of Modern History*, XXXIX (March 1967), 46–64.

Several works appeared by journalists who attended the Washington talks. Raymond Leslie Buell's *The Washington Conference* (New York, 1922) was written almost immediately after the events, but it is still considered the standard work on the whole conference. It of course suffers from a lack of materials. Mark Sullivan in *The Great Adventure at Washington* (New York, 1922) aptly recreated the atmosphere of the gathering. Three books—Kiyoshi Karl Kawakami, *Japan's Pacific Policy, Especially in Relation to China, the Far East, and the Washington Conference* (New York, 1922); Ida M. Tarbell, *Peacemakers, Blessed and Otherwise: Observations, Reflections, and Irritations at an International Conference* (New York, 1922); H. G. Wells, *Washington and the Riddle of Peace* (New York, 1922)—are collections of reprints of daily articles written at the conference. Together they illustrate reporting based on rumor, inaccurate information, and bias of a sort which some American newspapers still offer.

Among the books on the Washington Conference two are outstanding. On the Five-Power Treaty, Harold and Margaret Sprout have much to contribute with *Toward A New Order of Sea Power* (Princeton, N. J., 1943). The Sprouts did not have access to the conference records, but for the naval negotiations were able to use selections from the unpublished diary of Theodore Roosevelt, Jr. J. Chalmers Vinson was the first scholar to use the official papers of the conference in *The Parchment Peace: The United States Senate and the Washington Conference, 1921–1922* (Athens, Ga., 1955). Vinson concentrates on the Senate and the Four-Power Treaty.

Special treatments of the conference include Westel W. Willoughby, *China at the Conference* (Baltimore, 1922), and Wunsz King, *China at the Washington Conference: 1921–1922* (New York, 1963). A good study is Stanley J. Granat, "Chinese Participation at the Washington Conference, 1921–1922" (doctoral dissertation, Indiana University, 1969). Leon Archimbaud in *La Conference de Washington* (Paris, 1923) presents French arguments for submarines and land forces. Yamato Ichihashi, Baron Kato's interpreter and later a Stanford professor, writes with tongue in cheek in *The Washington Conference and After* (Stanford, Cal., 1928). He must have known far more than he put in print. Then there is an unusual book by Herbert Osborn Yardley, *The American Black Chamber* (Indianapolis, 1931). Yardley headed a group of Army intelligence workers who cracked the Japanese code during the conference and read the telegrams to and from Japan. Several of the telegrams are reprinted in the book; the decoded, translated messages have disappeared from the American records. Ladislas Fargo describes the sensational aspects of the Yardley story in *The Broken Seal* (Boston, 1967), and David Kahn's *The Code-breakers* (New York, 1967) is a definitive study. Charles L. Hoag discusses public opinion forces in *Preface to Preparedness: The Washington Conference and Public Opinion* (Washington, D.C., 1941).

Biographies and Autobiographies

The first solidly researched histories of the Harding administration are now appearing after the opening of the Harding papers in 1964. Francis Russell's *The Shadow of Blooming Grove: Warren G. Harding in His Times* (New York, 1968) presents a provocative interpretation. Samuel Hopkins Adams in *Incredible Era: The Life and Times of Warren Gamaliel Harding* (Boston, 1929) colorfully captures the spirit of the erstwhile editor from Ohio. The sketch by Charles Cheney Hyde of the leading Cabinet member, "Charles Evans Hughes," in Samuel Flagg Bemis, ed., *The American Secretaries of State and Their Diplomacy* (10 vols.; New York, 1927–29), X, suffers from a lack of perspective. Merlo Pusey treats the Secretary in his Pulitzer prize-winning *Charles Evans Hughes* (2 vols.; New York, 1951). His book came almost entirely from the Hughes papers at the Library of Congress; he did not use the Department of State archives. Although this technique speaks well for the Hughes papers, it speaks poorly for Pusey, who spends some two hundred pages on Hughes as Secretary of State. Dexter Perkins offers an introduction in *Charles Evans Hughes and American Democratic Statesmanship* (Boston, 1956). The shortest essay on Hughes is by J. Chalmers Vinson in Norman Graebner, ed., *An Uncertain Tradition: American Secretaries of State in the Twentieth Century* (New York, 1961). Vinson criticizes Hughes with faint praise, as does Betty Glad in *Charles Evans Hughes and the Illusions of Innocence* (Urbana, Ill., 1966).

In addition to Hughes, Henry Cabot Lodge, Elihu Root, and Oscar Underwood served as American delegates to the Washington Conference. Karl Schriftgiesser's *The Gentleman from Massachusetts: Henry Cabot Lodge* (Boston, 1944) is an example of a book in which the author let antagonisms about a subject get out of hand. John A. Garraty has written a first-rate biography, *Henry Cabot Lodge* (New York, 1953), and was the first scholar to use the Lodge papers. Philip C. Jessup in *Elihu Root* (2 vols.; New York, 1938) has written an excellent biography. Root gave Jessup unrestricted access to his papers while he was alive and gave the author an opportunity to question him on any and all events in his life; Jessup, with his critical faculties, made the most of a unique opportunity. Richard W. Leopold's *Elihu Root and the Conservative Tradition* (Boston, 1954) contains careful interpretation. No one has yet published a biography of Democratic Senator Oscar W. Underwood; a major figure in the Wilson administration, Underwood deserves one.

Other biographies or autobiographies of interest are Calvin Coolidge's candid *Autobiography* (New York, 1929); as Vice-President at the time, Coolidge had little to do with the Washington Conference. William Allen White is at his best in *A Puri-*

tan in Babylon: Calvin Coolidge (New York, 1938), but the book by Claude M. Fuess, *Calvin Coolidge: The Man from Vermont* (Boston, 1940), is much more reliable. Harding's Secretary of Commerce, Herbert Hoover, has a straightforward account in *The Memoirs of Herbert Hoover: The Cabinet and the Presidency 1920–1933* (New York, 1952). Indiana Senator James E. Watson defends his crony Harding in *As I Knew Them* (Indianapolis, 1936). Willis Fletcher Johnson is uncritical in *George Harvey: A Passionate Patriot* (Boston, 1929). Claudius Osborne Johnson did not take full advantage of the voluminous Borah papers in his *Borah of Idaho* (New York, 1936). A more solid study is Marion C. McKenna's *Borah* (Ann Arbor, Mich., 1961). Two British observers at the conference kept diaries: Colonel Charles A'Court Repington wrote *After the War: A Diary* (Boston, 1922); *Lord Riddell's Intimate Diary of the Peace Conference and After, 1918–1923* (New York, 1934) was by the British press agent at the conference who let the French demands for capital ships slip out to the newspapers.

NEWSPAPERS AND PERIODICALS

The New York *Times* has long printed more columns of news and speeches than any other American newspaper. Little wonder that the historian of modern American history most often turns to it; the *Times*, of course, has an admirable index. Another good source is the Washington *Post*. For other newspapers I have relied on Hoag's *Preface to Preparedness*, cited under monographs. Also useful was the *Literary Digest*, which conducted polls of newspapers on important questions.

PRINTED SOURCES

For background materials John Van Antwerp MacMurray, ed., *Treaties and Agreements With and Concerning China: 1849–1919* (New York, 1921), is a useful collection. The Carnegie Endowment for International Peace also published a series of documents pertaining to the Far East and disarmament in their pamphlet series of the Division of International Law in 1921–1922.

Congressional publications are of some importance. The *Congressional Record* of 1920–1922 includes congressional debate over the Borah resolution, the naval bills, the Washington Conference, and the ratification struggle. Minutes of House and Senate hearings have material on the subject of disarmament. *Report of the Conference*, Senate Document 126 (67 Cong., 2 Sess.) contains papers submitted by Harding to the Senate.

The Department of State published the *Conference on the Limitation of Armament* (Washington, D. C., 1922), which is the record of plenary and committee meetings; a companion volume is *Conference on the Limitation of Armament: Subcommittees* (Washington, D. C., 1922). One should remember that each delegation edited and approved all minutes, and that a speaker was directly quoted in the published record only at his request. The Shantung conversations can be followed in the *Minutes Prepared by the Japanese Delegation* (Washington, D. C., 1922) and *Minutes Prepared by the Chinese Delegation* (Washington, D. C., 1923).

There is perhaps no publication in the world that compares with the Department of State publication *Foreign Relations of the United States*. Only the United States government prints its diplomatic papers so fully, so accurately, and so quickly after events. The 1921 volumes of *Foreign Relations* (2 vols.; Washington, D. C., 1936) cover preconference activities while the 1922 volumes (2 vols.; Washington, D. C., 1938) include documents not printed in the official record of the conference along with copies of the treaties.

Documentary publications by other countries on the Washington Conference are slim indeed. Rohan O. Butler, J. P. T. Bury, and M. E. Lambert, editors of *Documents on British Foreign Policy: 1919–1939* (London, 1948–), include discussions with Japan on the renewal of the Anglo-Japanese Alliance in Volume XIII (London, 1963) in the First Series. Volume XIV (London, 1966) includes most, but not all, of the important papers on the Washington Conference. The French are laggard and have published little in their series, *Documents diplomatique français*.

MANUSCRIPT SOURCES

Archives

One of the major reasons for the present study has been that in recent years many collections of public and private manuscript materials bearing on the conference have become available. There is notably the availability of the Washington Conference Papers of the Department of State deposited in the National Archives. The manuscripts have no index and one can approach them only through a guide compiled by H. Stephen Helton, *Preliminary Inventory of the Records of United States Participation in International Conferences, Commissions, and Expositions* (Washington, D. C., 1955). Even this compilation is only a rough guide. Included in the Washington Conference Papers are original stenographic reports of plenary, committee, and subcommittee meetings (some have been destroyed); conference documents; press releases; correspondence; memoranda on all subjects before the conference; reports on national and foreign press comments; and records of the American delegation. One Department of State official commented to the author that the department could not possibly take the time to prepare a similar amount of material for a present-day conference.

The Navy Department has retained many papers on the Washington Conference which are not in the National Archives but are open to scholars through the Navy Department. Most important are the reports of the General Board and the Department on Naval Limitation. Also in the records of Naval Historical Division are papers of the Naval Advisory Committee headed by Theodore Roosevelt, Jr.

French archival materials on the Washington Conference are not yet available, but Japanese documents from the Ministry of Foreign Affairs and the Army and Navy Ministries were microfilmed during the occupation of Japan by the Library of Congress. These materials can be located through Edwin G. Beal and Cecil H. Uyehara, comps., *Checklist of Archives in the Japanese Ministry of Foreign Affairs, Tokyo, Japan, 1868–1945: Microfilmed for the Library of Congress, 1949–1951* (Washington, D. C., 1959). The following reels were used: MT 306, 312, 313, 314, 315, 316, 317, 318, 319: UD 29–30; and 131. The documents include preconference departmental memoranda, conference memoranda, conference minutes and reports, and most important, telegrams and dispatches to and from Tokyo to Washington. The latter group is an especially full one since the Japanese delegates reported everything, and orders from Tokyo reflected the same attention to detail. These valuable primary materials are in Japanese and were translated for me by Michio D. Kano.

The British government, under considerable pressure from the British historical profession (disturbed that the history of recent British foreign policy is being written largely from American and German records rather than British), backed away from its fifty-year rule in the spring of 1966. The archives are now open to 1924, and there is reason to hope that others will be opened. The documentary materials on the Washington Conference can be approached through the *Guide to the Contents of the Public Record Office* (2 vols.; London, 1963). The present study used the manuscripts of the Foreign Office—preconference departmental memoranda on the fate of the Anglo-Japanese Alliance, position papers on various subjects to come up at the conference, and telegrams to and from the British delegation at Washington; those of the Cabinet Office—minutes of the British Empire Delegation at the Conference, notes of conversations with other delegations, and the minutes of the Committee of Imperial Defence; and those of the Admiralty—the Washington Conference Papers. These papers, of course, are deposited in the Public Record Office in London.

Personal Papers: Manuscript Collections

Warren G. Harding MSS. Ohio Historical Society, Columbus. This fine collection of materials deposited in 1964 should bring forth several good biographies of the Ohio President. Harding wrote many letters and had an active correspondence with many Republican leaders. His papers cast a great deal of light on both his own character and that of the era.

Charles Evans Hughes MSS. Library of Congress. The papers of Secretary Hughes are a large collection, extremely well indexed. Among the papers are memoranda on the Washington Conference dictated by Hughes to his secretary, Henry C. Beerits; although the dictation took place in 1932, the memoranda are highly accurate. Hughes in that same year sent a great deal of material to the Department of State.

Elihu Root MSS. Library of Congress. From the time the conference started until it ended, there is a hiatus in the Root papers. Either the papers were withdrawn or the materials existing are those in the American delegation section of the Washington Conference papers at the National Archives; if the latter is true, it would suggest Root did not play an important role at the conference. Root, however, was careful about what he put down on paper.

Henry Cabot Lodge MSS. Massachusetts Historical Society, Boston. Lodge's papers are not well indexed and are difficult to work in. His correspondence concentrates largely on domestic political problems. The Senator was much more interested in press clippings of the conference than documents of historical significance. His diary (see below), however, is of great value.

Oscar W. Underwood MSS. Alabama State Archives, Montgomery. I have not seen these papers, but a careful check by the Alabama archivist revealed nothing of importance on the conference. There are apparently enough papers for a full-scale biography of Underwood.

Chandler P. Anderson MSS. Library of Congress. Anderson was one of the American legal advisers and a close friend of Elihu

Root, with whom he had worked on the North Atlantic fisheries arbitration. He was an articulate, forceful writer with a great deal of insight into the treaty-drafting process.

William E. Borah MSS. Library of Congress. This is a vast collection; indeed, it is a pleasure to read the papers of a man who put almost all his thoughts down on paper. Borah was forthright in his correspondence and for that virtue one must admire him. He apparently saved a copy of every letter he wrote.

Mrs. Charles S. Bird MSS. East Walpole, Mass. Mrs. Bird was a member of the American Advisory Committee and a long-time Republican party worker. These family papers are most valuable for her impressions of the delegates and workings of the Advisory Committee.

Calvin Coolidge MSS. Library of Congress. That the Vice-President was not a noted conversationalist or letter writer is reflected in his correspondence. He did not play a large part in the Washington Conference, nor is there any great evidence that he was especially interested in foreign affairs.

James J. Davis MSS. Library of Congress. Davis was Harding's Secretary of Labor. He favored disarmament and in his travels found a great deal of support for the administration's foreign policies. He did not take part in any diplomatic activities.

Edwin Denby MSS. Detroit Public Library. These are the papers of Harding's Secretary of the Navy. Denby found it difficult to defend his department's interests in the preconference planning. Hughes and the Department of State, not Denby and the Navy Department, remained in firm control of the situation at all times. A more forceful Secretary of the Navy might have changed that situation.

Robert Borden MSS. Public Archives of Canada, Ottawa, Ont. Borden, a member of the British Empire Delegation, kept a diary in addition to retaining a set of delegation minutes in his papers. Borden was very much in favor of the American plan and was obviously eager to have a close friendship with the United States.

Samuel Gompers MSS. American Federation of Labor Library,

Washington, D. C. These provide a full record of Gompers' activities as a member of the American Advisory Committee and as a leader in the limitation of armaments movement. Gompers put the interests of the nation above those of organized labor, displaying a high degree of statesmanship.

Leland Harrison MSS. Library of Congress. Harrison, a communications adviser on the American technical commission, was far removed from important happenings.

Nelson T. Johnson MSS. Library of Congress. As a Far Eastern expert in the Department of State, Johnson had opportunity to learn a great deal. He later became American Ambassador to China and held that position at the time of the Manchurian crisis in 1931.

Philander C. Knox MSS. Library of Congress. Knox, a former Secretary of State, was one of Harding's advisers and in 1920 was mentioned as a candidate for another term as Secretary. He died shortly before the conference.

Robert Lansing MSS. Library of Congress. At the conference the former Secretary of State was an adviser to the Peking government. For his advice the Chinese government later decorated him.

William Mitchell MSS. Library of Congress. The well-known advocate of air power kept few records of importance, but he ably defended air power at the conference.

John J. Pershing MSS. Library of Congress. Pershing corresponded little and his papers show small interest in the conference. A carefully typed diary concentrates on the sound and color rather than on substantive issues. Had the Army been the subject of arms limitation discussions, his interest might have increased.

William H. Taft MSS. Library of Congress. The former President had wide contacts and a large correspondence. His letters are delightful and display much shrewdness. Taft at the time was conducting a quiet campaign for appointment as Chief Justice of the Supreme Court, a post which Harding later awarded him.

Stanley Washburn MSS. Library of Congress. Washburn was a member of the conference secretariat and was a close friend of Elihu Root.

Hilary P. Jones MSS, Dudley W. Knox MSS, and *William F. Fullam MSS*. Library of Congress (Naval Historical Foundation Collection). These three admirals were critics of the Washington agreements, but they were much more vocal after the conference than before or during.

Woodrow Wilson MSS. Library of Congress. There is little material on the Washington Conference in the former President's papers. The manuscripts that do reflect on the conference indicate that Wilson did not agree with all aspects of the treaties, but he certainly did not lead a campaign against ratification of the treaties.

Personal Papers: Diaries

Henry Cabot Lodge Diary. Massachusetts Historical Society, Boston. Lodge did not make entries in his diary with any great regularity; nevertheless, the diary is of some importance on many of the negotiations. Lodge did not think that Great Britain would accept the American naval proposal.

Chandler P. Anderson Diary. Library of Congress. This diary is almost the only source of information on Far Eastern aspects of the conference and probably overemphasizes the role of Anderson and Root. Anderson's personality shows clearly in the diary entries; he was always careful to distinguish between his treaty drafts and those of the other legal advisers.

Theodore Roosevelt, Jr., Diary. Library of Congress. This diary is delightfully informative. It casts much light on naval proceedings and conference personalities.

INDEX

Acton, Ferdinando, 119

Agenda: initial American proposals, 38; Japanese suggestions, 38–39, 41; Chinese suggestions, 39–40; announced, 40; British reaction to, 40

Aircraft carriers: in American proposal, 119; General Board on, 119; limits on, 119–20; tonnage increased, 119–20. *See also Lexington; Saratoga*

Airplanes: outmode battleships, 13; on agenda, 40; General Board on, 121; proposal to abolish, 121–22; problems of limitation, 122; subcommittee report, 122; committee report, 122; resolution passed on, 122

Alaska: excluded from nonfortifications agreement, 101

Albertini, Luigi, 68

Aleutians: fortifications agreement, 102

American Advisory Committee: selection of, 47; reports on submarines, 115–16; report on airplanes, 122; report on poison gas, 123; disagreement with poison gas report, 124; report on religious support, 174

American-Canadian border: demilitarization of, 4

American-Japanese war: threat of in Pacific, 28, 75–82

American Peace Society: Wilson, former member of, 5; James L. Hayden, former president of, 6

Anderson, Chandler P.: meeting with Kent, 85; drafts Four-Power Treaty, 130; protests to Root, 138; Four-Power Treaty discussion with Hughes, 179–80

Anglo-Japanese Alliance: 1902–1921, 26; Canadian position on, 27; American

Anglo-Japanese Alliance (*cont.*)
position on, 27–28; British attempts to exclude U. S., 29; arbitration clause of 1911, 29; British-Japanese discussions in 1921, 30; Curzon on, 31; in Imperial Conference, 31; Hughes's position on, 32; Japanese opinion of, 37; General Board opposition to, 49–50; in General Board modified plan, 52; Japanese support of, 76; encouraged Japanese imperialism, 127; Japanese view of, 128; Lloyd George proposal to broaden, 128; Curzon on loss of, 129; Hughes-Balfour discussion of, 129; Hughes calls for end of, 130; ended in tripartite pact draft, 132; re-creation in Japanese draft, 135; included Japanese main islands, 139; in Senate debate, 179. *See also* Four-Power Treaty; Tripartite pact

Armed merchant ship: definition of, 117

Asada, Sadao: argument on American recognition, 152–54

Ashton-Gwatkin, F.: dangers of Japanese-American war, 28; on China, 149

Association of Nations: in Republican platform of 1920, 10; in Harding's inaugural speech, 14; special message to Congress by Harding, 15

Australia: British interests, 26

Auxiliary ships: General Board first proposal, 51; Briand's instructions on, 112; discussion of, 118–19; restrictions placed on, 118–19

Balfour, Arthur: 1917 mission to U. S., 21; head of British delegation, 66;

Balfour, Arthur (*cont.*)
response to Hughes's speech, 82; on
Kato 10:7 demand, 85; approves naval
holiday, 88; on fortifications, 94; opposes Hughes on fortifications, 94;
discusssion with Kato on fortifications, 94; negotiations with Hughes
and Kato on fortifications, 96; in
preliminary fortifications agreement,
97; opposes Kato on fortifications, 99;
proposes parallelogram, 99; on Amer-
ican-French relations, 105; opposes
French demands, 109; instructions on
French quota, 109; orders on auxiliary ships, 118; on use of scrapped
ships, 120; on Anglo-Japanese Alliance, 129; drafts tripartite pact, 129;
discussion with Kato on tripartite
pact, 130; uses Japanese tripartite
pact draft, 131; Shantung-tripartite
link, 132; inclusion of Japanese main
islands in Four-Power Treaty, 136;
agrees with Hughes on broadened
Four-Power Treaty, 137; offers draft
of treaty on China, 151; on Shantung
mediation, 162; approves Shantung
settlement, 164; offers return of Weihaiwei, 164–65
Bar Harbor: suggested site, 36
Battleships. *See* Capital ships
Beatty, David: British naval delegate,
64; response to American proposal,
72; opposes naval holiday, 87; appeals
to Lloyd George, 88; opposes French
tonnage demands, 109
Belgium, 42
Bell, Edward: Japan would accept, 38;
in Shantung conversations, 161
Benson, William S.: threatens British,
22
Berthelot, Philippe, 66
Blakeslee, George H.: memorandums
on Pacific islands, 92
Bliss, Robert Woods, 64
Bliss, Tasker H., 12–13
de Bon, Ferdinand: French naval delegate, 64; on French tonnage, 108; opposes American tonnage figures, 110–
11; on aircraft rules, 122
Bonin Islands: acquired by Japanese,
90; Japanese proposal on partial abolition, 94; Japanese proposal on forti-

Bonin Islands (*cont.*)
fications, 94; in Japanese records, 94;
not in British records, 94; British ask
for inclusion of in fortifications, 98;
Japanese delegation's private opinion
on, 99. *See also* Fortifications
Borah, William E.: supports 1916 naval
program, 6; offers disarmament
resolution, 11; offers resolution on
modern navy, 13; objects to Edge
amendment, 14; scuttles Naval Act,
14; possible delegate, 44; on Hughes's
speech, 74; against Four-Power
Treaty, 138, 179; attacks Cravath
speech, 181; votes against Four-
Power Treaty, 183n
Borah resolution: offered, 11; public
support of, 12; House hearings, 12;
Root letter against, 13; Senate Foreign Relations Committee amends,
13; considered, 14; opposed by Harding, 16; similar proposals offered, 16;
does not pass House, 17; passes Senate, 17; Harding strategy on, 17;
Harding support of, 18; versus Porter
resolution, 18; opposition withdrawn,
18; passes Congress, 18; Geddes' criticism of, 26
Borden, Robert: Canadian delegate, 64;
supports naval holiday, 87; on Anglo-
Japanese Alliance, 129
Brandegee reservation: offered, 178;
passed, 182
Brandeis, Louis D., 69
Briand, Aristide: head of French delegation, 64; description of, 65; at table
of honor, 70; response to American
naval proposal, 82; on Hughes, 105;
on American domestic politics, 105;
pleads French case, 105; British re-
actions to speech, 105; cable from
Hughes, 111–12; reply to Hughes,
112; on auxiliary ships, 112; differing
interpretations of Briand's cable,
112–13. *See also* Five-Power Treaty
Brisbane, Arthur: attacks Four- and
Five-Power treaties, 173
Bryan, William Jennings: "cooling-
off" treaties, 6, 29; U.S.-British treaty
of 1911, 29; not selected as delegate,
46; at opening session, 69
De Bunsen, Maurice, 22

Butler, Thomas S., 12
Bywater, Hector C., 77

Cable and radio communication, 38
Canada: Panama Canal tolls bill, 41
Canton (China): government wants to attend conference, 43; not invited, 43
Capital ships: in 1916 program, 6, 7; in 1918 program, 7; outmoded by new weapons, 13; American proposal to buy British ships, 21; projected ratios, 23; in 1921, 23; building programs in 1921, 24; British desire more, 25; General Board first proposal, 51; General Board modified proposal, 52; in American Special Naval Advisory Board proposals, 53; in plan two, 53; in "stop-now" proposal, 55; already scrapped, 57; British proposal to limit by number, 60; in opening session proposal, 71–72; in scrapping proposals, 82; effect of *Mutsu*, 87; British want increased tonnage, 88; French tonnage, 107–13; Italian tonnage, 107–13; Hughes presents French-Italian tonnages, 109; ratio advantage to France, 110; French proposal on, 110; British gesture on, 111; Hughes cables Briand on, 111–12; Briand's instructions on, 112. *See also* Five-Power Treaty
Caroline Islands: acquired by Japan, 90
Castle, William R.: analyzes French position, 111
Central Conference of American Rabbis, 174
Chicherin, George, 43
China: British interests in, 26; American proposal to Great Britain on, 30; British propose Pacific conference on, 32; invited to the conference, 33; accepts invitation, 36; U. S. proposals on the agenda, 38; fearful of Japan, 39; agenda discussions, 39; topics on the agenda, 40; delegation, 67–68; source of tension, 75; at conference, 145–71; Clark suggestions on, 147; Hoover loan to proposed, 147; British position on, 149–50; treaty suggested by Geddes, 150; advice not sought by U. S., 151; presents ten

China (*cont.*)
principles, 151; refuses to sign Versailles Treaty, 158; desire to end unequal treaties, 166; extraterritoriality, 167; central government weakness, 167; extraterritorial commission provided for, 168; American position on extraterritorial rights, 167–68; tariff, 168–69; tariff treaty, 169; foreign troops resolution, 169; post offices, 169; treaty list, 170; results of conference for, 171; Lansing's opinion on results on treaties, 176; Senate vote on tariff treaty, 184. *See also* Nine-Power Treaty; Shantung
Chinese Eastern Railroad: on agenda, 40; problem of, 170; resolution passed, 170
Church Peace Union, 174
Churchill, Winston: opposes American 1916 program, 24; paper fleet suggestion, 61; on replacement tonnage, 87
Clark, J. Reuben: on General Board first proposal, 51; Navy Department proposal, 51; advice on China, 147–48
Cockran, Bourke, 16
Committee for Treaty Ratification, 174
Committee on Imperial Defence: pre-conference advice, 60–61; on naval holiday, 87; on French and Italian navies, 109
Committee on Pacific and Far Eastern Questions, 151
Congress. *See* United States
Continental Hall, 69
Coolidge, Calvin: attends opening session, 69; on achievements of conference, 172
Coontz, Robert E.: member of General Board, 49; on Special Naval Advisory Board, 52, 52n; suggests conversion of cruisers to aircraft carriers, 120
Cox, James M.: on League in 1920 election, 9; not selected as delegate, 46
Cravath, Paul, 181
Crowe, Eyre, 26
Crowley, James B., 79–80
Cruisers, 118–19. *See also* Capital ships
Curzon, Earl: on Japanese sphere in Manchuria, 27; on Anglo-Japanese Alliance, 30; discussion with Harvey

Curzon, Earl (*cont.*)
on Anglo-Japanese Alliance, 31; proposes Pacific conference, 32; suggests preliminary conference, 35; on non-attendance, 36; accepts arms conference, 36; on Panama Canal tolls, 41–42; reply to Briand charges, 105; on loss of Anglo-Japanese Alliance, 129; accepts France in Four-Power Treaty, 134; reluctant on Weihaiwei, 164–65

Daniels, Josephus: supports 1916 Naval Act, 6; suggests naval holiday, 6; submits 1918 program, 7; resubmits 1918 program, 8; testifies on Borah resolution, 12–13
David, Norman: refuses League proposal, 9; testifies on Borah resolution, 12
Davis, Calvin, 4
Denby, Edwin: not selected as delegate, 47; on Navy Department plans, 49; rejects General Board proposal, 51; on "stop-now" proposal, 55; reply to Gompers on layoffs in navy yards, 175
Destroyers, 7. *See also* Auxiliary ships
Disarmament: in American history, 3–4; duality of American policy, 4; Hensley resolution of 1916, 6; Wilson's Paris program, 7; League proposes commission on, 9; entangled in 1920 election, 9; Harding position on, 10–11; support for grows in 1921, 12; influence of women on, 12; Harding's qualified support of, 16; in Porter resolution, 17; Harding's negotiations on, 18. *See also* Borah resolution
Duggan, Stephen P., 174
Dulles, John Foster, 174

Edge, Walter: offers amendment, 14
Edge amendment: offered, 14; passes Senate, 14
Election of 1920: League of Nations issue, 9; disarmament issue, 10
Emigration: U. S. against having on agenda, 38
Existing strength: basis of U. S. naval proposal, 54
Extraterritoriality, 167–68

Fall, Albert, 69
Federal Council of Churches, 174
Five-Power Treaty: background of, 75; 10:6 ratio, 82–86; terms of, 89; linked to fortifications issue, 95; Article 19, 102; French problems on capital ships, 107–12; proposal to leave out France, 112; Japanese unwilling to jeopardize, 150; ends naval race, 172; great popularity of, 175; Senate debate on, 183–84; Senate vote on, 184
Fletcher, Henry P., 30
Forbes, W. Cameron, 92
Foreign Policy Deliberative Committee, 80
Formosa: acquired by Japan, 90; in Japanese fortifications proposals, 94; in fortifications agreement, 98; Uchida approves in fortifications agreement, 101; covered in Four-Power Treaty, 141
Fortifications: omitted from "stop-now" proposal, 57; Uchida orders on, 84; Kato ties to 10:6 ratio, 86; negotiations on, 90–103; General Board opinion on, 92; Forbes-Wood recommendations on, 92; War Department proposals on, 92; MacMurray supports, 92; Japanese proposal on, 93; preliminary agreement on, 97; Japanese draft on, 98; Balfour proposes a parallelogram, 99; Kato argues for preliminary statement on, 99; dispute over "Japan proper," 97–102; Japanese name specific islands, 101; in Samoa, 101; in Okinawa, 101, 102; American position on, 102; Uchida's instructions, 102; in Aleutians, 102; in Kuriles, 102. *See also* various Pacific islands
Four-Power Treaty: linked to Five-Power Treaty, 95; Hughes refuses alliance, 128; Anderson to make treaty draft, 130; draft by Anderson, 131, 131n; negotiations, 131–35; Hughes and Balfour agree to early announcement, 135; linked to mandate question, 135; Hughes broadens scope, 136; question of Japanese main islands, 136; Lodge presentation of, 137; Senate criticism of, 137–38; un-

Four-Power Treaty (*cont.*)
happiness of American legal advisers over, 138; Borah opposes, 138; dispute over main islands, 139–41; Harding's misunderstanding of, 139; Netherlands note on, 141; Italy's request, 141; Siam's request, 141; supplementary treaty, 141; connection to Japanese mandates, 141–43; advantages of treaty, 143–44; Japanese unwilling to jeopardize, 150; linked to Shantung, 154; pledge by Harding on, 177; Brandegee reservation added, 178; Harding's opposition to reservation, 178; La Follette speaks against treaty, 178; Senate debates, 179–83; Watson attack on Root, 180–81; Cravath controversy, 181; Hughes letter to Lodge on treaty, 181; Underwood promises Democratic votes for, 182; Senate votes on, 182–83; supplementary treaty vote, 183

Fourteen Points, 21

France: in British proposed naval alliance, 21; invited to arms conference, 32; accepts invitation, 36; novel agencies of warfare query, 40; in General Board modified proposal, 52; left out of "stop-now" proposal, 56; Hughes wants inclusion in fortifications agreement, 95; plans for naval conference, 104; on land armaments, 104, 105; fear of Germany, 104, 105; Briand's speech, 105; left out of opening negotiations, 107; asks equality with Japan, 107; General Board proposals, 107–108; dispute over tonnage, 107–13; American proposal on capital ships, 108, 109; advantages of American proposal, 110; rejects American proposal, 110–11; French position analyzed, 111; appeal to Briand, 111; accepts American proposal, 112; submarines, 113–18; attacked by Lee, 115; final position on submarines, 116; final position on auxiliaries, 116; on airplanes, 121; Hughes wants in Four-Power conference, 133, 134

France, Joseph P.: opposes and votes against Five-Power Treaty, 183–84

French-British antagonisms, 107

Friends of Irish Freedom: oppose treaties, 173; attacked by Senator Williams, 173–74

Fries, Amos, 124

Fullam, William F., 50

Geddes, Auckland: advises possibility of naval arrangement, 25–26; on Borah resolution, 26; supports tripartite agreement, 31; discussion with Hughes on Anglo-Japanese Alliance, 31; accepts preliminary conference, 36; drops Pacific conference, 37; on Panama Canal tolls, 41; description of Lodge, 45; British delegate to conference, 66; at table of honor, 70; tripartite pact proposal, 128; on possible treaty, 128

Geddes, Eric: mission to U. S. in 1918, 21; brother of Auckland, 66

General Board: membership, 49; fear of Japanese intentions, 49; recommends accord with Great Britain, 49; sends out questionnaires, 49; asked to make preliminary investigations, 49; initial discussions of, 49; replies to questionnaires, 50; on principles of American foreign policy, 50; wants two-to-one edge over Japan, 50; wants parity with Great Britain, 50; believes Anglo-Japanese Alliance a threat, 50; submits first naval proposal, 51; modifies naval proposal, 52; on "60 per cent" suggestion, 54; opposes "stop-now" proposal, 54–55; predicts disorder, 56; supplies cost estimates, 56; estimates Japanese naval expenditures, 59; on Pacific islands, 92; submarine proposals, 113; rules for submarines, 113; recommendations for aircraft carriers, 119; recommendations for airplanes, 121; advises prohibition of poison gas, 123

General Committee on the Limitation of Armaments, 175

Genrō, 80

Germany: disarming of, 7; submarine campaign of 1919, 21; reason for Anglo-Japanese Alliance, 26; no longer a threat, 28; German islands,

Germany (*cont.*)
38; threat to France, 104–105; acquisition of Shantung, 157
Golovin, Nikolai Nikolaevich, 77
Gompers, Samuel L.: on Advisory Committee, 47; favors treaties, 175; organizes General Committee, 175; shocked at layoffs in navy yards, 175
Great Britain: U. S. wants to limit navy of, 7–8; naval arrangement with U.S., 8; in Borah resolution, 11; battleship investigation, 13; eagerness to attend conference, 16; British-American relations to 1920, 20; proposes naval alliance, 21; against Fourteen Points, 21; willingness to accept League reservations, 22; possible war with U. S., 22; naval parity with U. S., 22, 26, 60; "imperial preference" of, 22; suspicion of, 22; German naval competition, 23; protection of interests, 23; naval tonnages in 1921, 23; naval building program in 1921, 23; fleet in 1921, 24; naval policy of 1921, 25; naval program recommended by Lee, 25; uneasiness at naval race, 25; Defence Subcommittee meeting, 25; feared by Lodge, 26; on Anglo-Japanese Alliance, 26, 30–31; puzzled by U. S., 26; threat of U. S.-Japanese War, 28; Foreign Office on Anglo-Japanese Alliance, 29, 30; arbitration treaty of 1911 with U. S., 29; Hughes proposes arms conference, 32; proposes Pacific conference to Harvey, 32; proposes Pacific conference to China, 32; proposes Pacific conference to Japan, 32; no reply from U. S., 33; purpose of conference proposal, 33; nonacceptance of arms conference proposal, 36; appalled by agenda, 40; feared by American naval officers, 50; navy in General Board first proposal, 51; navy in General Board modified proposal, 52; navy in Special Naval Advisory Board proposals, 53; navy in "stop-now" proposal, 55; preconference naval proposal, 60–62; Lloyd George on naval plans, 61; Admiralty plan, 61; delegation, 66; supports 10:6 ratio, 84; wants to increase tonnage of battle-

Great Britain (*cont.*)
ships, 88; opinion of Five-Power Treaty, 87–88; wanted as signatory to fortifications agreement, 95; base at Singapore, 99; French opposition to, 104; Admiralty on French and Italian fleets, 108; gesture to France, 111; submarine quota, 113–118; prefers to abolish submarines, 114; on auxiliary ship tonnages, 118; wants more aircraft carriers, 119; desires airplane restrictions, 121; French antagonism to, 126; on tripartite pact, 128; drafts tripartite pact, 129; on problems of China, 149; on Open Door policy, 149; on Shantung, 160; offers Weihaiwei, 164–65. *See also* Anglo-Japanese Alliance; Capital ships; Tripartite pact; Five-Power Treaty; Four-Power Treaty; Nine-Power Treaty; Shantung
Grey, Edward: mission to U. S., 23; on arbitration treaty, 29
Guam: naval base location dispute, 81; threat to Japan, 90; acquired by U. S., 90; Mahan on, 90–91; cut off by Japanese, 91; Naval Advisory Committee on, 91; War Department calls indefensible, 92; in Japanese proposal on fortifications, 93; Japan prefers abolition of fortifications on, 94
Guarantee treaties: Versailles, 61, 104; no support for, 106

Hague Peace Conferences: failures of, 4; in Hughes's speech, 71; on bombing unfortified cities, 122
Hale, Frederick: reveals Harding's views on disarmament resolution, 16–17
Hanihara Masanao: Japanese delegate, 65, 67; talk with Root on Shantung, 163
Hankey, Maurice, 130
Hara Takashi: assassinated, 65; approved of conference, 81
Harding, Warren G.: on League issue in 1920 election, 10; on disarmament in election, 10–11; loses disarmament leadership, 11; on Root letter against Borah resolution, 13; inaugural address, 14; opposition to League, 15;

Harding, Warren G. (*cont.*)
supports conference idea, 15; special address to Congress, 15; ideas on diplomacy, 15–16; against Borah resolution, 16; strategy to defeat Borah resolution, 17; supports Porter resolution, 17; letter to Mondell, 18; Geddes advises approach to, 26; issues invitation to conference, 33; statement on purpose of conference, 35; on Panama Canal tolls, 41–42; urged to appoint Borah delegate, 45; choice of Democratic delegate, 46; approves "stop-now" proposal, 54; Lloyd George preference, 65; speech on Unknown Soldier, 68; opening speech at conference, 70; Hughes report on 10:6 ratio, 87; Lodge confers with on Four-Power Treaty, 139; press conference mistake by, 139; admits mistake, 139; pressures Sze on Shantung, 163; closing speech at conference, 172; disapproves of a reservation to Four-Power Treaty, 178; asserts conference was open diplomacy, 176–77; refuses to give records, 177; defines Four-Power obligations, 177; defends treaties, 184
Harrison, Pat, 44
Harvey, George: error on Anglo-Japanese Alliance, 31; difficulties with Hughes, 32–33; held up conference proposal, 33–34; approves preliminary conference, 36; Hughes criticism of, 37; as Ambassador, 37; on Panama Canal tolls, 41–42; notice of Briand approval, 112
Hawaii: acquired by U. S., 90; War Department on fortifications, 92; Japanese proposals in fortifications, 93, 94; Hughes excludes from fortifications agreement, 95; Uchida approves exclusion, 95
Hay, John: Open Door policy notes, 38, 145–46
Hayden, James L.: prepares Hensley resolution of 1916, 6
Hays, Will, 69
Hearst press, 172
Hensley, Walter: offers resolution, 5; resolution passes House, 6
Herrick, Myron, 112

Hilles, Charles D.: opposes selection of Borah as delegate, 44; supports selection of Lodge as delegate, 45
Holmes, Oliver W., 69, 74
Hong Kong: in British plans, 60; status in Japanese proposals on fortifications, 93–94
Hoods: possible construction by Great Britain, 51; in naval proposals of special advisory committee, 53; under "stop-now" proposal, 55; possible conversion to aircraft carriers, 121
Hoover, Herbert: on Advisory Committee, 47; favors loan to China, 147
Hornbeck, Stanley K.: on perversion of Open Door policy, 147; on Shantung Railroad as key to settlement, 160; advises tougher stance against Japan, 163
House, Edward M.: naval agreement with Robert Cecil, 8, 22; Lloyd George threatens naval construction, 21; proposes sale of British ships, 21
Hughes, Charles Evans: opposes renewal of Anglo-Japanese Alliance, 32; proposes arms conference, 32; difficulties with Harvey, 32–33; makes formal proposal, 33; combines two conference proposals, 33; opposes preliminary conference, 35–37; gives press release on invitations, 38; Chinese apprehensions, 39; Panama Canal tolls, 41–42; decision to concentrate on naval limitation, 48; mobilizes government departments, 48–49; request for naval yardstick, 50; "stop-now" proposal, 53–54; request to Denby, 55; opening speech at conference, 70–73; reaction to speech, 73; newspaper reaction, 82; rankles French and Italian delegates, 82; temporarily willing to accept 80 per cent ratio, 83; *Mutsu* controversy 86; 10:7 ratio and fortifications, 86; against greater British tonnage, 88; military opposition to fortifications agreement, 92; proposal on fortifications, 94; discussion with Balfour on fortifications, 94; on no prospect of making Guam a strong base, 95; Harding on fortifications, 95; links Four-Power and Five-Power treaties, 95; wants others

Hughes, Charles Evans (*cont.*)
in fortifications agreement, 95; fortifications negotiations with Kato and Balfour, 96; preliminary agreement on fortifications, 97; opposes Kato on fortifications, 99; accepts British parallelogram, 99; Japanese inform on rejection, 101; includes Alaska, 101; Briand's opinion of, 105; quizzed by Jusserand, 108; presents American naval proposals to French, 109; promise to British, 109; sends cable to Briand, 111; considers proposal to leave France out of Five-Power Treaty, 112; recommends increase in submarine tonnage, 113; presents submarine report, 115–16; makes submarine proposal, 116; auxiliary ship proposals, 118; on aircraft carriers, 119–20; on conversion of cruisers to aircraft carriers, 120; on airplanes, 122; poison gas report, 125; talk with Geddes on tripartite pact, 128; with Balfour on Anglo-Japanese Alliance, 129; rejects Balfour tripartite pact, 129–30; wants to replace Root-Takahira, 130; rejects Anderson's Four-Power Treaty draft, 131; on inclusion of France in Four-Power Treaty, 133; Four-Power Treaty draft, 133–34; ties Four-Power Treaty to Japanese mandates, 135; broadens scope of treaty, 136; includes Japanese main islands, 136; does not consult legal advisers, 138; explains Four-Power Treaty to Harding, 139; Harding press conference mistake, 139; negotiations on Japanese main islands, 140; rejects Root draft, 141; proposals on Yap, 143; adds Lansing-Ishii clause to Nine-Power Treaty, 152; resolutions on monopolies in Ching, 154; opposes Shantung on agenda, 160; further Shantung talks, 162; overrules advisers on Shantung, 163; takes Sze to Harding, 163; announces Shantung settlement, 164; optimism on Five-Power Treaty, 172; drafts Harding refusal on conference minutes, 177; argues in support of Four-Power Treaty, 179–80; letter of support to Underwood, 180

Hughes, William, 31
Huse, Harry P.: on General Board, 49; calls for preparedness in the Pacific, 50

Imperial Conference: to discuss Anglo-Japanese Alliance, 27; discusses Anglo-Japanese Alliance, 31, 32; calls for Pacific conference, 32
Ishii Kikujiro, 11, 146
Italy: in British proposed alliance, 21; accepts conference proposal, 36; naval tonnage in General Board modified plan, 52; left out of "stop-now" proposal, 56; delegation to conference, 68; capital ships, 107–13; General Board tonnage proposals, 107–108; parity with France, 108; American tonnage proposal, 109; wants another aircraft carrier, 119; not admitted to Four-Power pact, 141

Jackson, Robert M., 49
Japan: in Borah proposal, 11; possible conference participant, 16; in British naval alliance, 12; building program in 1921, 23; naval tonnage and fleet in 1921, 23–24; feared by Lodge, 26; gains from Russo-Japanese War, 26; American war threat to British interests, 28; Hughes asked to conference, 32; British propose Pacific conference, 32; revenue spent on military forces, 37; hesitant on Pacific conference, 37–38; accepts invitation to conference, 38; opinions on agenda, 39; questions agenda, 41; accepts agenda, 41; feared by General Board, 49; navy in General Board first proposal, 51; navy in General Board modified plan, 52; navy in Special Naval Advisory Board proposal, 53; navy in "stop-now" proposal, 55; Ministry of Foreign Affairs preconference suggestions, 58; preconference naval plan, 58, 62; on Pacific islands, 58–59; economic difficulties, 59–60; delegation, 67; response to Hughes proposal, 72; Japanese-American tensions, 75–76; "National Defense Policy," 79–81; naval plans,

Japan (*cont.*)
1905–14, 79–80; desires 10:7 ratio, 80; informs Tokyo will have to accept 10:6 ratio, 84; becomes more cooperative, 89; acquisition of Pacific islands, 90; mandates of strategic significance, 91; first fortifications proposal, 93; second fortifications proposal, 94; mainland excluded by Uchida, 95; definition of "Japan proper," 97–102; submarine quotas, 113; wants more aircraft carriers, 119; unpredictable future, 127; tripartite pact draft, 131–32; Shidehara draft of tripartite pact, 132; Four-Power Treaty draft, 135; Open Door policy applied to Pacific, 135; dispute over main islands, 139–41; Privy Council might refuse ratification, 140; mandates, 141–43; Yap, 142–43; mandates agreement with U. S., 143; conflict over China with U. S., 145–48; tactics on China problems, 148–49; emphasis on Root-Takahira agreement, 149; Nine-Power Treaty negotiations, 150–54; possible recognition of interests in Manchuria, 151–53; acquisition of Shantung, 158–59; Shantung negotiations, 159–64; delegates report failure on Shantung, 164; Siberian withdrawal promise, 165–66; opposition to tariff raise by Chinese, 168; on post offices in China, 169; on Japanese troops in China, 169–70. *See also* Anglo-Japanese Alliance; Capital ships; China; Five-Power Treaty; Four-Power Treaty; Fortifications; Nine-Power Treaty; Shantung
Johnson, Hiram, 179
Jones, Hilary P., 175
Jordan, John: tripartite pact proposal, 128; advice on China, 149–50
Jusserand, Jules: delegate to conference, 66; quizzes Hughes on French tonnage, 108; presents French naval demands, 110; informed of Hughes's cable to Briand, 111; delivers Briand's reply to Hughes, 112

Kaga, 53
Kato Hiroharu (Admiral): asks for 70 per cent ratio, 83

Kato Tomasaburo (Baron): as Japanese head delegate, 64, 67; response to American proposal, 82; in charge of details, 83; supports 10:7 ratio, 84; discusses 10:7 ratio with Balfour, 85; reports to Tokyo on 10:7 ratio, 86; defends *Mutsu*, 86; opposes British demand for more tonnage, 88; proposes fortifications arrangement, 90, 94, 97; asks Tokyo for instructions on fortifications, 95; negotiates with Hughes and Balfour on fortifications, 96; preliminary agreement on fortifications, 97; "Japan proper" controversy, 97; talks with Roosevelt on fortifications, 98; British parallelogram proposal, 99; argues for return to preliminary agreement, 99; advises Uchida to accept parallelogram, 100; informs Hughes of Japanese rejection of parallelogram, 101; draft on fortifications, 101; asks for more aircraft carriers, 119; tripartite pact discussion, 130; private talk with Root, 132–33; agrees to France in Four-Power conference, 134; approached by Hughes and Balfour on Shantung, 161
Kent, Fred: meets with Japanese, 85; to make speech on Four-Power Treaty, 179–80
King, William H., 184
Knapp, Harry S.: on General Board, 49; on preparedness in Pacific, 50
Knox, Dudley, 91–92
Knox, Philander, 46
Koo, V. K. Wellington: on Japanese sphere, 27; Chinese delegate, 67; Shantung negotiations, 161
Korea, 76
Kurile Islands: acquired by Japan, 90; fortifications, 102

La Follette, Robert M., 178, 182
Lampson, Miles: on British Shantung error, 160; attends Shantung conversations, 161
Land armaments: on agenda, 40; French proposal to limit, 104, 105; American position, 106; buried at conference, 106
Lansing, Robert: comments on agenda,

Lansing, Robert (*cont.*)
41; not selected as a delegate, 46; scoffs at Washington, D. C., preparations, 63; approves American naval proposal, 74; judges Four-Power Treaty like Article X, 138; on Lansing-Ishii agreement, 146; believes China gained at conference, 176

Lansing-Ishii agreement: Americans recognize Japanese predominance in, 27; Japanese approve of, 76; Hughes wants to terminate, 130; partial text of, 146; used as model by Japanese, 149; secret protocol of added to Nine-Power Treaty, 152; termination of, 154

League of Nations: Wilson's support of, 7; British support of, 8; American entrance looks impossible, 8; supported by Cox, 8; disarmament commission asks U. S. participation, 9; pro-League Republicans support Harding in 1920 election, 10; Harding's statements on in election of 1920, 10; rejected in Harding's inaugural and special address, 14; covenant, 22; Grey's mission to United States, 23

Lee, Arthur: recommends naval program, 25; British Admiralty delegate, 64; response to American proposal, 72; on exclusion of Bonins and Ryukyus, 98; attacks French submarine proposal, 115; defines armed merchant ship, 117; wants more aircraft carriers, 119

Lewis, John L., 47

Lexington: cruiser conversion to aircraft carriers, 120–21

Literary Digest, 173

Lloyd George, David: threatens to build superior British navy, 21; naval spheres of influence, 25; disagreement with Canada, 27; opens Imperial Conference, 31; on conference rumors, 32; supports American proposal for conference, 33; high opinion of Root, 46; naval plans for conference, 61; not present at conference, 65; supports naval holiday, 87; rejects Balfour-Beatty appeal on holiday, 88; sees French militarism, 105; instruc-

Lloyd George, David (*cont.*)
tions on auxiliary ships, 118; on Anglo-Japanese Alliance, 128

Lodge, Henry Cabot: supporter of Mahan's theories, 5; disapproval of Wilson's tactics, 8; objects to Edge resolutions, 14; letter from Harding against League, 15; on British and Japanese naval threats, 26; selected as American delegate, 45; doubtful of success of "stop-now" proposal, 54; approves Hughes's speech, 74; opinion that Congress would not vote naval funds, 95; approves cable to Briand, 111; disapproves of Anglo-Japanese Alliance, 129; instructs Anderson to draft treaty, 130; approves Anderson draft, 131; ties Shantung to tripartite pact, 132; approves Hughes's Four-Power Treaty draft, 133; presents Four-Power Treaty to conference, 137; calms Harding on press conference mistake, 139; on Japanese main islands, 140; finds Chinese difficult on Shantung, 163; in charge of treaty fight, 176; supports Four-Power Treaty, 179; letter from Hughes on Four-Power Treaty, 181; repeats denial from Cravath, 181; Four-Power supplementary treaty vote, 183; success at getting treaties through, 183, 184

Lovett, Robert M., 44

Lowell, A. Lawrence, 174

McKinley, William, 10, 44

MacMurray, John Van Antwerp: supports neutralization of Pacific islands, 92, 93; prepares Root resolutions on China, 151; aids on Hughes's resolution on monopolies, 154; on Shantung Railroad as key to settlement, 160; attends Shantung conversations

Madden, Martin B., 16

Mahan, Alfred Thayer: theories on sea power, 5; on threat of Guam to Japan, 90

Manchuria: Japanese possible sphere, 26; Japanese penetration into, 76; Ashlon-Gwatkin on Japanese role in, 149; possible American recognition of Japanese interests in, 152–54

Mandates: Japanese acquisition of, 28; topic on agenda, 40; Japan receives, 76, 91; British mandates, 134; covered in Four-Power Treaty arrangements, 141; Japanese agreement with U. S., 142–43

Manila, 81

Mariana Islands, 90, 91, 142

Marion, Ohio, 10

Marshall, Thomas, 46

Marshall Islands, 90, 91, 142

Massey, William F., 31

Meighen, Arthur: opposes renewal of Anglo-Japanese Alliance, 31

Millard, Thomas, 78–79

Millard's Review, 78

Mitchell, William: American delegate, 64; proposes abolishment of airplanes, 121–22; court-martialed for views, 123

Mondell, Frank W.: testifies on Borah resolution, 12; withdraws Porter resolution, 18; letter from Harding to support Borah resolution, 18

Monroe Doctrine, 22

Mutsu: Japan could complete, 53; Japanese wanted to retain, 83; Kato calls for retention, 86; Hughes calls for scrapping of, 86–87; escalator effect, 88; retained, 88

Narcotics, 38

National Council for the Limitation of Armaments, 174–75

Naval Act of 1916: supported by Daniels and Borah, 6; Hensley resolution added to, 6; changed by war demands, 7; uncertain fate of ships at end of war, 7; in Naval Acts of 1917 and 1918, 7; support for completion in 1921, 13; Harding wishes to complete construction program, 16; appeared as threat to British, 21, 24; cost differences to complete construction under, 56

Naval Act of 1917, 7

Naval Act of 1921: fails to pass, 14, 16; passes Senate with Borah resolution, 17; passes House without Borah resolution, 17; passes House and Senate, 18

Naval Advisory Committee: sees

Naval Advisory Committee (*cont.*) Guam and Philippines as strategic problems, 91

Naval construction programs: in 1921, 23–24. *See also* various naval acts

Naval disarmament. *See* Borah resolution

Naval holiday: called for in Hensley resolution, 5; Daniels supports, 6; affected by nonappropriation of funds, 17; British internal disputes over, 87; not actually secured, 89

Naval officers: opposed treaty, 3, 21; muted opposition, 175

Naval parity: Great Britain willing to accept, 26; not actually secured, 89

Naval Program of 1918: proposed by Daniels, 7; used by Wilson in naval negotiations, 8; raised again by Daniels, 8

Naval race: between U. S., Great Britain, and Japan, 22; status in 1921, 23; British fears of, 25; journalistic speculation on, 77–79

Naval tonnages: in 1921, 23; projected, 23

Navy Department: preparations for possible conference, 49; naval proposal, 49

Navy League, 5

Neilsen, F. K., 138

Netherlands: invited to conference, 42; Hughes wants in fortifications agreement, 95; Root drafts treaty to include in new version of Four-Power Treaty, 141; Hughes rejects Root draft, 141; identical notes sent to, 141

New York *Times:* exposes French demands, 107

Nine-Power Treaty: Root connects to Four-Power Treaty, 141; Open Door policy background, 145–48; Japanese preparations for, 148–49; British position on, 149–50; lack of American proposal, 150; Geddes suggests treaty on China, 151; Chinese present ten principles, 151; Lansing-Ishii clause added, 152; Sadao Asada thesis on American recognition of Japanese interests, 152–54; criticism of Root resolutions, 154; make-up of treaty, 154–55; passes conference, 155; weak-

Nine-Power Treaty (*cont.*)
ness of, 155–56; vote on in Senate, 184. *See also* Open Door policy

Ogasawara, 94
Okinawa, 101. *See also* Ryukyus
Okuma Shigenobu, 80
Oliver, James, 50
Open Door policy: British threat to, 27; U. S. wants on agenda, 38; agenda discussions of, 39; notes of 1899 and 1900, 145–46; in Lansing-Ishii agreement, 146; in opinion of Admiral Rodgers, 147; Hoover's proposal, 147; pessimism of Hornbeck, 147; seen as dream by Pershing, 147; definition by Clark, 148; American public support sought for, 150; written into Nine-Power Treaty, 150–56. *See also* Nine-Power Treaty
Orange Plan, 81
Osborne, Sidney, 78

Pacific Conference: called for by Imperial Conference, 32; proposed by Curzon, 32; British primary interest, 33; suggested by Curzon, 35; misunderstanding, 35–37; proposal withdrawn by British, 37
Panama Canal: tolls possible agenda item, 41–42; bill passes Senate, 42; bill dies in House, 42; excluded from fortifications restriction, 101
Parker, John, 47
Peace Commission Treaty of 1911, 29
Pearce, George F.: Australian delegate, 66; supports naval holiday, 87
Pearl Harbor, 3
Pershing, John J.: testifies on Borah resolution, 12–13; on Advisory Committee, 47; as American delegate, 64; approved Hughes's speech, 74; poison gas report, 123; pessimism on Open Door policy, 147; misrepresented in Hearst newspaper, 173
Pescadores Islands: acquired by Japan, 90; seen as threat to Philippines, 92; in British and Japanese records, 94; included in fortifications agreement, 98; Uchida approves inclusion, 99; covered in Four-Power Treaty, 141
Philippine Islands: Japanese threaten routes to, 76, 91; naval base dispute,

Philippine Islands (*cont.*)
81; threat to Japan, 90; degree of importance, 91; threatened by Japanese in Pescadores, 92; coveted by Japan, 92; in Japanese preconference proposal on fortifications, 93, 94; Congress would not vote funds to fortify, 95; Kato got inclusion of in fortifications agreement, 100; American lack of recognition of importance, 102
Phipps, Lawrence, 176
Pitkin, Walter B., 79
Pittman, Key, 183
Poindexter, Miles: presents Harding's views on Borah resolution, 16–17; withdraws opposition to Borah resolution, 17
Poison gas: placed on agenda, 40; American Advisory Committee against, 123; General Board against, 123; subcommittee report, 124–25; War Department supports, 124; part of report left out, 125; Root resolution on, 125
Pomerene, Atlee, 176
Porter, Stephen G., 47
Porter resolution: offered, 17; debate on, 18; withdrawn, 18
Portugal, 42
Pratt, William V.: member of General Board, 49; on Special Naval Advisory Board, 52, 52n; suggests conversion of cruisers to aircraft carriers, 120
Preliminary Conference. *See* Pacific Conference
Public opinion: support of disarmament, 5; support of Borah resolution, 12, 19; support for Hughes's speech, 74; support for conference treaties, 173

Quakers, 174

Ratification of treaties. *See* United States Senate
Ratios: in 1921, 23; projected, 23–24; 10:6 in General Board first proposal, 51; 10:5 in General Board modified plan, 52; 10:6 Special Naval Advisory Board proposals, 53; 10:6 basis

Ratios (*cont.*)
of Hughes's proposal, 54; 10:5 not in "stop-now" proposal, 56; General Board predicts disaster for 10:5, 56; 10:6 in "stop-now" proposal, 56, 73; 10:8 temporarily accepted by Hughes, 83; Japanese ask for 10:7, 83; dispute over 10:7, 84–87; 10:6 preserved in treaty, 88; advantage to France, 110

Reed, James A.: against Four-Power Treaty, 137–38, 179; speech against Five-Power Treaty, 183

Referendum diplomacy, 116

Robinson, Joseph T.: offers reservation to Four-Power Treaty, 180

Rodgers, William L.: member of General Board, 49; asks for 2:1 ratio over Japanese navy, 49; submits submarine report, 115; pessimism on Open Door policy, 147

Rodman, Hugh, 50

Rolandi-Ricci, Vittorio, 68

Roosevelt, Theodore, 5

Roosevelt, Theodore, Jr.: member of Advisory Committee, 47; asks General Board to prepare plan, 49; remarks on General Board first proposal, 51; member of Special Naval Advisory Board, 52; pessimistic about acceptance of "stop-now" proposal, 54; supports Hughes's proposal, 74; argues for existing strength basis, 84; *Mutsu-Settsu* deal, 87; shocked at Root proposal, 88; talks with Kato on fortifications, 98; attempts to discover French naval plans, 107; opposes French demands, 108; proposal on submarine tonnage, 114–15; supports cruiser conversion to aircraft carriers, 120; low opinion of Root resolutions on China, 152; favorable to Shantung settlement, 164; skeptical of Shidehara promise to leave Siberia, 166

Root, Elihu: fashions Republican 1920 platform, 10; open letter against Borah resolution, 13; selected as delegate, 45-46; puts indirect pressure on Japanese to accept 10:6, 85; willing to accept greater British tonnage, 88; Congress will not vote funds, 95; on

Root, Elihu (*cont.*)
Hughes's cable to Briand, 111; supports submarine rules, 117; opposes cruiser conversion, 120; instructions to Anderson on Four-Power Treaty draft, 130; indiscretion with Kato, 132; ties Shantung to tripartite pact, 132; approves Hughes's Four-Power Treaty draft, 133; assures Kato of U. S. support, 133; resolutions on China, 134; Anderson protests to, 138; would not change Four-Power Treaty, 139; drafts Netherlands treaty, 141; would never go to war over China, 150; encouragement of Japanese peace group, 150; with Hanihara on Shantung, 163; attacked on Four-Power Treaty, 180

Root resolution on poison gas, 125

Root resolution on submarines, 117

Root resolutions on China: text of, 152; Sadao Asada thesis, 152-54; criticism of, 154

Root-Takahira agreement: preferred by Japanese, 76, 128, 149; Hughes desires to end, 130

Roskill, Stephen, 91

Russia: in British proposed naval alliance, 21; entente of 1908, 26; U. S. wants on agenda, 38; desires invitation, 42-43; not invited, 43; fear of, 105

Ryukyus: acquired by Japan, 90; in Japanese proposals on fortifications, 94; Lee wants in fortifications agreement, 98; Japanese delegates willing to include, 99; in final agreement, 101–102

Saburi Sadao: discusses tripartite pact with Hankey, 130

Sakhalin: (Southern) acquired by Japan, 90; (Southern) covered in Four-Power Treaty, 141; (Northern) withdrawal promised by Japanese, 166

Samoa: acquired by U. S., 90; Hughes attempts to exclude from fortifications agreement, 101; British prevent exclusion of, 101

Saratoga, 120–21

Sarraut, Albert: French delegate, 66;

Sarraut, Albert (*cont.*)
demands capital ships, 110; rejects American proposal, 111; announces French position on submarines, 116
Sato Kojiro, 79
Schanzer, Carlo: Italian delegate, 64, 68; response to American proposal, 82; proposal on armed merchant ships, 117; airplane restriction, 122
Schofield, Frank H., 49
Schwab, Charles M., 174
Scrapping of ships: proposed in General Board modified proposal, 52; in Special Naval Advisory Board plans, 53; in Navy Department plan, 53; Hughes's proposal, 54; number in "stop-now" proposal, 55; misleading totals in proposal, 57; numbers in Hughes's proposal, 72–73; less than proposed, 89
Seiyūka, 81
Settsu, 87
Shantung: Japanese possession of, 28; agenda discussions of, 39; Uchida wants to exclude, 39; Chinese want on agenda, 40; Japanese take over, 76; Lodge-Root link to tripartite pact, 132; important to success of conference, 157; German acquisition of, 157; position in Twenty-One Demands, 158; item in secret treaties, 158; clause in Versailles Treaty, 158; in 1918 Sino-Japanese agreement, 158; Japanese willing to negotiate over, 159; embarrassing problem to U. S., 159; China wants U. S. as mediator, 159; Hughes against putting on agenda, 160; negotiations at conference, 161–64; British-American observers on, 161, 162; agreement reached on all but railroad, 161; talks break off, 162; Chinese and Japanese proposals on railroad, 162; four American proposals on, 162–63; Harding pressures Sze on, 163; talks resume on, 164; settlement of, 164. *See also* China; Japan
Shidehara Kijuro: preconference thoughts, 41; Japanese delegate, 64; presents tripartite pact draft, 131; presents second Four-Power Treaty

Shidehara Kijuro (*cont.*)
draft, 135; wants Japanese main islands excluded, 136; withdraws exclusion, 136; ordered to reopen main islands clause, 139; worries about Senate opposition, 139–40; discusses Yap, 142; presents draft on Yap, 143; indicates Japanese willingness to negotiate on Shantung, 159; presents Japanese proposals on Shantung, 161; makes second offer on Shantung, 162; promises Japanese will leave Siberia, 165
Siam, 141
Siberia: Uchida wants to exclude from agenda, 39; on agenda, 40; Japanese occupation of, 76, 165; Japanese promise to leave, 165–66; Japanese leave, 166
Sims, William S., 81
Singapore: British plans for, 60; Japanese proposal on fortifications, 93; outside British parallelogram, 99; excluded from fortifications agreement, 102
Smith, Edgar F., 124
Smuts, Jan Christiaan, 3
South America, 22
Spanish-American War, 5
Special Naval Advisory Board: personnel, 52; three proposals, 52–53
Spheres of influence, 27
Stevens, John F., 170
Stoddard, Lothrop, 78
"Stop-now" naval proposal: origin, 53; Roosevelt predicts nonacceptance, 54; supported by Harding, 54; supported by Lodge, 55; final polishing of, 55; inconsistencies of, 56. *See also* Capital ships
Submarine rules: Root resolutions on, 117; treaty of, 117–18; French refuse to ratify, 118
Submarines: outmode battleships, 13; on agenda, 40; in General Board's first proposal, 51; discussion of quotas, 113–18; American proposition, 116; French final position, 116; controversy over American Advisory Committee report, 116
Sutherland, George, 47

Sze, Sao-ke Alfred: Chinese delegates, 67; presents China's ten principles, 151; wanted U.S. as mediator, 159; talks to Hughes and Balfour on Shantung, 161; pressured by Harding, 163

Taft, William H., 176
Taft-Katsura agreement, 76
Tanaka Kunishige: Japanese general delegate, 67; opposed French addition to fortifications agreement, 95; defines Japan proper, 97; fortifications proposal, 100; unhappy with Four-Power Treaty, 140; on U.S. goals in Manchuria, 153; report to regent on China, 153
Thomas, Norman, 44
Tokugawa Ieyesato, 64
Tripartite pact: suggested as solution to British problem, 30; supported by Geddes, 31; proposed by Geddes, 128; Balfour draft of, 129; Jordan proposal of, 129; British-Japanese talks on, 130; Shidehara draft of, 132. *See also* Anglo-Japanese Alliance; Four-Power Treaty
Tsingtao-Tsinanfu Railroad, 161
Tumulty, Joseph P., 73
Twenty-One Demands, 76, 158

Uchida Yasuya: sends Japan's acceptance to conference, 38; excludes Shantung from agenda, 39; excludes Siberia from agenda, 39; orders acceptance of 10:6 ratio, 86; accepts Hawaii exclusion, 95; agrees to adhesion of France and Netherlands, 95; excludes Japanese mainland from fortifications clause, 96; asks for definition of Japan proper, 97; defines Japan proper, 99; orders rejection of British parallelogram, 100; orders rejection of treaties, 100; approves inclusion of Bonins, 101; approves inclusion of Amami-Oshima, 101; delegates appeal to, 101; final instructions on fortifications, 102; sends Four-Power Treaty draft to Shidehara, 135; excludes Japanese main islands, 136; orders Shidehara to reopen negotiations, 139; warns delegates of domestic pressures, 140; orders Shidehara to exclude main islands, 140

Uchida Yasuya (*cont.*)
gates of domestic pressures, 140; orders Shidehara to exclude main islands, 140
Underwood, Oscar W.: selected as American delegate, 46–47; advises Congress will not vote funds, 95; approves Hughes's cable to Briand, 111; opposes cruiser conversion to aircraft carriers, 120; on airplanes, 122; would change Four-Power Treaty, 139; states American position on tariff, 169; receives letter from Hughes on Four-Power Treaty, 180; promises Democratic votes on Four-Power Treaty, 182
Unitarian Layman's League, 174
United States: in proposed British naval alliance, 21; failure to join League, 22; possible war with Great Britain, 22; naval tonnages in 1921, 23; building program in 1921, 23, 24; fleet in 1921, 24; no reply to British proposals, 26; British threat to Open Door policy, 27; only check to Japanese expansion, 28; proposed disarmament conference, 32; primary interest in arms conference, 33; decision to stress naval limitation, 48; status in General Board plans, 51, 52; presents "stop-now" proposal, 55; proposes naval limitation, 71–73; Orange Plan, 81; acquisition of Pacific islands, 90; proposal on French tonnage, 108; submarine proposals, 113; would not present proposal on China, 150; China wants as mediator, 159
United States Army: no threat to disarmament, 5; at conference, 106
United States Congress: resolution to attend League talks, 9; would not vote funds for bases, 95
United States delegation: selection of, 44–47; first meetings, 48; argues for 10:6 ratio, 83–85; position on submarine quotas, 114
United States Department of State, 59
United States House of Representatives: hearings, 12
United States Navy: growth, 1880–

United States Navy (*cont.*)
1920, 5; naval parity with Great Britain, 26, 89
United States Senate: rejects League, 9; Hughes bows to, 133; reported opposition of, 139–40; used Shantung
United States Senate (*cont.*)
against Wilson, 159; asks for record of Four-Power Treaty negotiations, 177; Four-Power Treaty debate, 179–83; Four-Power Treaty vote, 182–83; supplementary treaty vote, 183; vote on Five-Power Treaty, 184; vote on Nine-Power Treaty, 184; vote on Poison Gas and Submarine Treaty, 184; vote on Chinese Customs Treaty, 184
United States Senate Foreign Relations Committee: on Borah resolution, 13; reports Brandegee reservation, 178
United States War Department: reports lack of Guam fortifications, 92; supports use of poison gas, 124
Unknown Soldier, 68

Versailles Treaty: Allied arms reduction under, 7; China refuses to sign, 158
Villard, Oswald Garrison, 44
Viviani, René: French delegate, 66; presents Four-Power Treaty draft, 134

Wake Island: acquired by United States, 90; Tanaka puts outside limits, 100
Walsh, Thomas, 164
Wang, Chung-hui, 67
Warren, Charles B., 83
Washington Conference: criticism by journalists, 3; failure to deal with new weapons, 123; assessment of, 185–90
Washington *Post*, 17
Watson, Thomas E., 180
Weihaiwei, 164–65
Wellesley, Victor: opinion on Anglo-

Wellesley, Victor (*cont.*)
Japanese Alliance, 29–30; talk with J. B. Wright, 30
Wells, H. G., 69
White, Henry, 12
White, William A., 73
Wickersham, George, 174
Willert, Arthur: suggests tripartite pact, 30
Williams, E. T.: prepares Root resolutions on China, 151; on Shantung Railroad as key to settlement, 160; advises tougher stance against Japan, 163
Williams, John S., 173–74
Wilson, George Grafton, 49
Wilson, Woodrow: American Peace Society member, 5; on Bryan "cooling-off" treaties, 6; supports 1916 naval program, 6; supports international police force, 7; approves 1918 naval program, 7; uses fleet as diplomatic weapon, 8; stops 1918 program, 8; policies supported by Cox, 9; Harding warns of dangers of League, 10; instructed by Senate, 13; Harding approves his ideas, 16; Fourteen Points used, 21; rejects British naval alliance, 21; urged to build more destroyers, 21; Geddes advises not to approach, 26; had not chosen senators for delegation, 44; not selected as delegate, 46; on Underwood as delegate, 47; at burial of Unknown Soldier, 68; surrender to Japanese on mandates, 91; hurt on Shantung, 159; Lodge compared to, 183
Women: influence on disarmament movement, 12
Wood, Leonard, 92
World War I; belief caused by arms race, 4
Wright, Butler, 30

Yap: negotiations, 142–43; vote in Senate, 178
Yen, W. W., 39